KU-489-354

THE MEMOIRS OF
SERGEANT BOURGOGNE
1812-1813

The Memoirs of Sergeant BOURGOGNE 1812-1813

Translated from the French and edited by
Paul Cottin and Maurice Hénault
With a Foreword and Historical Introduction
by David G. Chandler

ARMS AND ARMOUR PRESS
London—Melbourne

HIPPOCRENE BOOKS, INC
New York

Published in Great Britain, 1979,
by Arms and Armour Press,
Lionel Leventhal Limited,
2-6 Hampstead High Street,
London NW3 1QQ,
and at
4-12 Tattersalls Lane,
Melbourne, Victoria 3000.

Published in the U.S.A., 1979,
by Hippocrene Books, Inc.,
171 Madison Avenue, New York,
N.Y. 10016

Memoirs of Sergeant Bourgogne, 1812-1813
Edited by Paul Cottin and Maurice Hénault
was published in 1899 by
William Heinemann, London

This edition © Lionel Leventhal Limited, 1979
Foreword and Historical Introduction © David G. Chandler, 1979

British Library Cataloguing in Publication data
Bourgogne, A F B F
The memoirs of Sergeant Bourgogne, 1812-1813.
1. Napoleon I, *Emperor of the French*—Invasion of
Russia, 1812
I. Cottin, Paul II. Hénault, Maurice
940. 2'7'0924   DC235
ISBN 0-85368-143-0

The maps that accompany the Foreword and Historical
Introduction to this edition are excerpted from the atlas
to *Alison's History of Europe*, constructed and arranged
under the direction of Sir Archibald Alison by Alex. Keith
Johnston, FRSE, FRGS, FGS, published by Wm. Blackwood &
Sons, Edinburgh and London, 1875. Note that the spelling
of place-names does not always correspond to the spelling
adopted in the text to Bourgogne's *Memoirs*.

Printed and bound in Great Britain by
Billing and Sons Limited, Guildford,
London and Worcester .

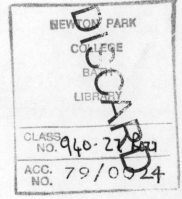
NEWTON PARK
COLLEGE
BATH
LIBRARY
CLASS NO. 940-27 Bou
ACC. NO. 79/0924
DISCARD

CONTENTS

v

CONTENTS

CHAPTER VI.

CHAPTER VII.

CHAPTER VIII.

CHAPTER IX.

CHAPTER X.

CHAPTER XI.

FOREWORD

BY DAVID G. CHANDLER
MA (Oxon), FRHistS, FRGS

Significant battles apart, history contains a number of epic military marches that have caught the imagination of posterity. The famous 'March of the Ten Thousand'—Greek mercenaries hired by Cyrus the Younger at the turn of the fourth century BC, who travelled by foot all the way from Sardis in Asia Minor to the approaches to Babylon, and then retreated homewards by way of Nineveh, Trepezus and the Black Sea to Byzantium—was in every sense a classical example of human endurance and determination. In modern times, Mao Tse Tung's 5,000-mile 'Long March' from Kiangsi to Yenan—which in the full year it took to complete, from October 1934 to the same month in 1935, reduced the original half million participants to a mere 45,000 survivors—is a justly celebrated feat. Russia, too, has been the scene of epic advances and retreats; we need only mention the sweeping advances of the Khans from the heartlands of Eurasia at the head of their Mongol and Tartar hordes in the thirteenth century, Charles XII's doomed advance to Pultava in 1708-1709, or the German Wehrmacht's frightful attritional struggle which took them to the very gates of Moscow and then all the way back to the fuhrer-bunker in Berlin between June 1941 and May 1945. But no military epic can rival the gripping fascination of Napoleon's ill-fated invasion of Russia in June 1812: a military adventure that took the greatest soldier of modern history, at the head of an army that eventually totalled over 600,000 men, to the Kremlin. An achievement that only proved to be the precursor of possibly the most terrible retreat ever recorded. Barely 93,000 woe-begone, exhausted, tattered and verminous soldiery survived to re-cross the River Niemen in mid-December 1812, just five months after the launching of the French offensive.

One of those survivors was the author of this book, Sergent-vélite Bourgogne of the Fusiliers-Grenadiers of la Garde Impérial. Many, many books have been written on the subject of the Russian campaign of 1812—both by contemporaries who took part and by subsequent authors. Of the former, the Comte de Ségur's celebrated two volume study, *History of the Expedition to Russia* (English version published in 1825) is of special importance. Of later writers attracted to this daunting subject, none surpassed the great novelist, Count Tolstoi, whose *War and Peace* is a literary masterpiece as well as a magnificent monument to the memory of those who perished, Russians and French alike, between 1805 and 1812: But the former wrote as a staff-officer, the latter as a novelist imparting a message, indeed a series of messages, to mankind concerning the ultimate futility of martial pomp and, indeed, of war itself. No one would claim that Sergeant Bourgogne's recollections can stand against de Ségur's moving and skilfully-written history or Tolstoi's gripping narrative skills, but as a testimony to the ability of the human spirit to withstand, and ultimately triumph over, the most appalling circumstances of personal suffering and deprivation, it has few peers. It is as a human document that this book demands attention, and it is to the credit of Arms and Armour Press that they have seen fit to republish a book that first appeared in English in 1899. As Bourgogne himself described his intention in 1835: "I have not written my memoirs either out of vanity or from a desire to talk about myself. I have merely wished to recall the memory of this gigantic campaign, so fatal to us and those fellow-soldiers who went through it with me. Their ranks, alas! are thinning day by day." A little further on he writes: "Those that went through this lamentable but glorious campaign proved, as the Emperor said, that they must have been made of iron to bear so many privations and so much misery; this was surely the very greatest test to which men were ever exposed." Some may question the veracity of Bourgogne's last observation; but no reader of this compelling book, however inaccurate some of its historical detail, however incomplete its coverage of this immense campaign (indeed, it effectively begins with the French already in Moscow), will criticise its value as a document about human survival—of the triumph of one man's will over the very-real threat of personal disaster and death.

Adrien Jean Baptiste François Bourgogne was born on 12 November 1785, the son of a cloth-merchant. He grew up in Condé-sur-Escaut, and in 1805, aged 20, he was recruited into the Vélites of la Garde Impériale, his father guaranteeing the necessary payment of 200 francs a year. The corps of vélites, as the *Anatomy of Glory* reveals*, was created by the First Consul in January 1804 to serve as a source of future officers —supplementing the Special Military School (later St. Cyr) founded two years earlier. In some ways it reflected the practice under Louis XIV of making aspirants for commissions serve in the ranks of the Régiment du Roi, but under the Consulate and Empire the clientele came from the cream of the annual conscription classes drawn from the well-to-do bourgeoisie rather than the remaining nobility or labouring classes—hence the requirement for a qualifying payment each year to the authorities. A vélite was paid at Guard rates, but was usually posted elsewhere on commissioning. His training included further education as well as purely military instruction, much of which was carried out at Fontainebleau. A formation of vélites was attached to each major formation of the Old Guard, and the members wore the uniform of the adoptive unit. Thus, there were vélite Grenadiers, Chasseurs, Horse Grenadiers, Horse Chasseurs, and Artillery (called the vélite canoniers), raised on various

---

*The Anatomy of Glory, by H. Lachouque and Anne S. K. Brown, republished by Arms and Armour Press, 1978. Vélites are described on pp. 35-7 and 506-7.

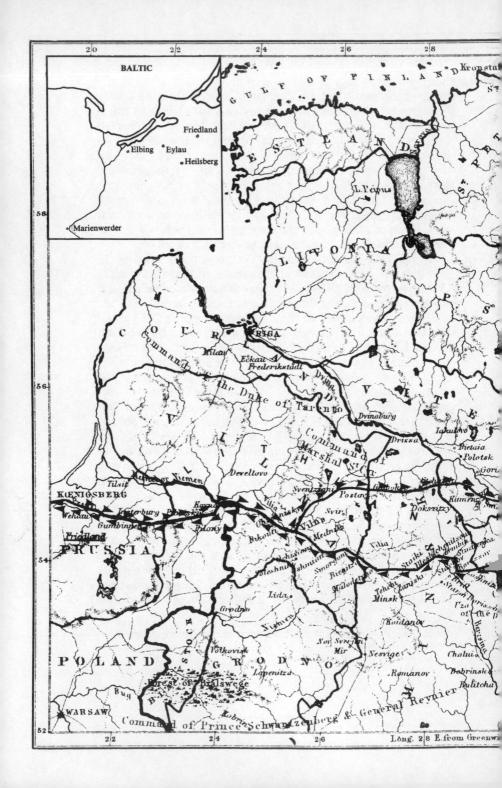

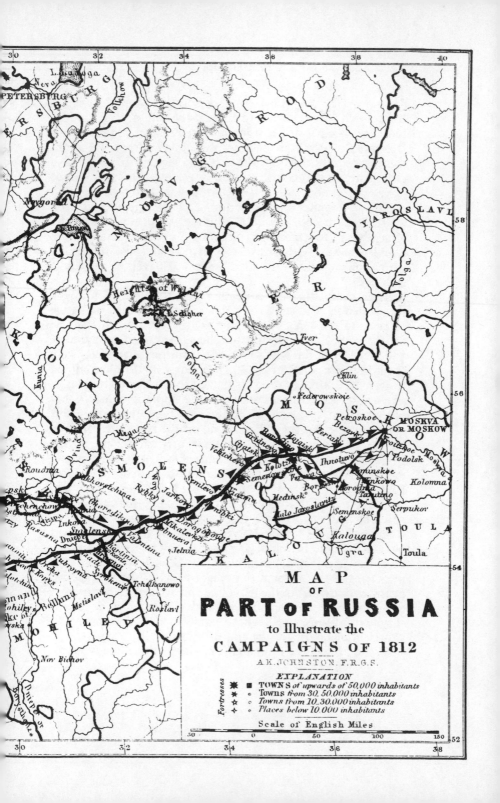

MAP
OF
PART OF RUSSIA
to Illustrate the
CAMPAIGNS OF 1812
A.K. JOHNSTON. F.R.G.S.

EXPLANATION

Fortresses

* ✹ ▨ TOWNS of upwards of 50,000 inhabitants
* ✶ ○ Towns from 30.50,000 inhabitants
* ☆ ○ Towns from 10.30,000 inhabitants
* ○ Places below 10,000 inhabitants

Scale of English Miles

dates from 29 July 1804 to 15 April 1806, and in 1809 a further two formations were raised—the vélites of Turin and Florence. As befitted a nominally republican régime (until December 1804), their name was taken from the light skirmishers attached to the Roman legions of antiquity. Originally, one squadron of vélites was attached to a Guard Cavalry Regiment, and a two-company battalion to a Guard Infantry Regiment, numbering 250 troopers and 300 guardsmen respectively; but in time of outright war the attachments to infantry formations of the Guard were doubled in size. Originally 1,600 strong in 1804, this élitist formation eventually totalled some 4,000 vélites (all units included).

After completing his education and training, Bourgogne was posted to Prussia in late 1806, and commenced his active service. In 1807 he was promoted to caporal; in 1809 he fought in the Danube campaign, being wounded on the neck and in the leg at the Battle of Essling; the next two years were spent in Spain and Portugal. Then, early in 1812, promoted to sergent, Bourgogne and his unit were transferred to Prussia as part of the concentration of the Imperial Guard that preceded the invasion of Russia in June that year. His experiences in Russia will be found on the pages that follow, but by the New Year of 1813 his original regiment, the Fusiliers-Grenadiers, had been reduced to just 26 officers and men. By March he had made his way back from Elbing to France, where he was soon promoted sous-lieutenant and posted to the 145th Regiment of the Line. He accompanied his new unit back to Prussia and fought through much of the Campaign of 1813, including the Battle of Bautzen, but was wounded at the action at Dessau on 12 October and taken prisoner. During his captivity he began to record his memories of the Russian campaign, to which he later added passages drawn from the letters he had written to his mother and from the recollections of old comrades and fellow-survivors of the retreat whose names and appointments he conscientiously lists at the end of his book.

A veteran of nine campaigns, credited with three wounds,

FOREWORD

15* major battles and 20 lesser engagements, he refused to take service under the Bourbons after his release, but resigned his commission. In later years he changed from the trade of draper to dabble in industrial experiments, which cost him most of his money. He married twice, having two daughters by his first wife. In 1830 he was recommended for both the Légion d'Honneur and the post of Major de Place de Condé, but in the end became Lieutenant-Adjutant of Brest. On 21 March 1832 he at last gained the coveted Cross. From 1832 he became Major de Place at Valenciennes, where he remained for a number of years. He died on 15 April 1867. Bourgogne's writings only cover the retreat from Moscow, with a brief introductory chapter on the invasion of Russia and, given his wide-ranging experience, it is disappointing that he did not chart his full military career. Nevertheless, his account of the retreat is one of the classic sources of this terrible yet inspiring episode in French and Russian military history.

His writings—in an edited and 'improved' form—first appeared in 1857 in a publication called *L'Echo de la Frontière*; the first full and unadulterated version, edited by Paul Cottin and M. Hénault, was published as part of the *Nouvelle Revue Rétrospective* (1896), and the first English version came out three years later.

What can we say was his contribution to our knowledge of the events he describes so graphically? In the first place, he provides a series of eye-witness accounts of great value. His description of the burning of Moscow (and of the Imperial Guard's share in the looting of the Russian capital), as seen from an NCO's point of view, is almost unique. The ambivalent attitude of the French soldiers towards the Russians in Moscow is notable: on the one hand he claims that Russian wounded received the same treatment as the French, but at the same time it is clear he saw nothing wrong

---

*His major battles were Jena (1806), Pultusk (1806); Eylau, Heilsberg, Friedland (all 1807); Somosierra and Benavente (both 1808); Essling and Wagram (both 1809); Smolensk, Borodino, Krasnoë, the Beresina (all 1812); and Lutzen and Bautzen (both 1813). Smaller engagements included Malo-Yaroslavets in 1812.

BATTLE
OF
BORODINO
7th September 1812.

in meting out rough justice to any citizens suspected of being arsonists. When some prisoners who were pulling waggons of loot and rations through the blazing streets were killed, he rather callously remarks that ". . . we did not much regret them but the loss of our provisions distressed us very much, especially the eggs." In later pages he shows more than a trace of anti-Semitism in his description of encounters with Russian and Polish Jews, and tells some appalling stories which do little for the reputation of the ghetto communities who seemingly battened upon the distressed Frenchmen. In return, many received short shrift from the desperate soldiery—not always deservedly to all appearances. But these incidents, however unedifying, remain part of the story—as do the instances of cannibalism by Croats and others that Bourgogne records.

The Sergeant has also provided us with a number of valuable vignettes of notable moments of the retreat. His description of the rescue of Napoleon from Cossacks at Malo-Yaroslavets is very vivid; so is his account of the Emperor approaching the Beresina on foot at the head of his staff, surrounded by the wreck of his army, dressed in his "large cloak lined with fur, a dark-red velvet cap with black fox fur on his head", and "a baton" in his hand. His participation in some of the last engagements as the rear guard crossed the Niemen includes some interesting glimpses of the indomitable Ney, "the bravest of the brave."

Above all, however, it is the mass of little incidents—small in themselves but often a matter of life and death to Bourgogne and his comrades—that lend so much vividness and value to his recollections. The varied response of human nature to the very real circumstances of personal disaster and impending death as recorded by his pen provides many insights. The terrible sufferings involved for both men and women alike—these will be found on almost every page. Possession of nine frozen potatoes constituted a veritable treasure, for which men would murder one another without pity. On the other hand, there are many stories of men who, despite their own problems and misery, were still prepared to offer what help they could to even less-fortunate comrades fallen by the roadside. The reader will long remember Bourgogne's adventures in Smolensk, when, lost on a bitter night, he and others follow the sound of ghostly music—and find themselves in a church where some drunken soldiers are extemporising on the organ. Similarly, his escapades at the hands of human scavengers will remain in the mind. It is possible that his touching account of Sergeant Dauberton's efforts to save the unofficial regimental mascot—the mongrel 'Mouton' who had accompanied the formation all the way from Spain and who was carried across a pack when his paws became frost-bitten—inspired Tolstoi to include a similar pet, Platon's dog, in *War and Peace*. Time after time we wonder at the resilience of Bourgogne and others like him, at their sheer determination to stay alive and crawl on in the hope of surviving. On one occasion it was the discovery of some snow impregnated with brandy from broken bottles that enabled him to stagger on; on another, the discovery of a little sugar. The attentions of those perpetual "camp-followers of war"—body lice, and the fevers and debilitation men suffered, go a long way to justify his comment that ". . . it (Russia) is the devil's own country for it is hell all through". So, indeed, it must have seemed. And on top of everything else, there were the remorseless attentions of the pitiless bands of marauding and harassing Cossacks to be faced and beaten off.

Somehow, Bourgogne's remarkably tough constitution and indomitable spirit brought him through. The last stages of the retreat to the relative haven of Elbing contained some amazing incidents. The comrade (last seen in Moscow) who hands over a parcel he had agreed to carry containing an overcoat of fine cloth and an ink-stand from Count Rostopchin's palace, and, in the pocket, a silk handkerchief containing a little box or valuable rings, is barely credible, but then strange things happen in war. The comfort found in Elbing at the hospitable home of the Frenchwoman, Madame Gentil was clearly Bourgogne's salvation. After all he had gone through she must indeed have appeared as a ministering angel. Very often, however, it is the smallest things that our narrator recalled that prove of special value. The nickname 'Ville-au-Schnapps' bestowed on Vilna by the troops on the outward journey, on account of the profusion of brandy they had found (and evidently enjoyed) there, is just one instance which reminds one of British soldiers of a later generation referring to 'Wipers'. And the use of the soldier's expression 'monter à la rue', to denote the looting of the army's treasure waggons on the hill of Ponari, is another. And his sudden discovery of a regiment of negroes, with black officers, opposite Murat's quarters in Elbing, is only one of many strange sights and happenings that he so graphically and yet modestly describes.

All in all, therefore, we have reason to be grateful to vélite-sergent Bourgogne and his urge to record his terrible and yet often inspiring adventures and experiences for the benefit of later generations. Here is the reality of soldiering under the grim realities of defeat and starvation in an alien and hostile country amidst terrifying natural conditions of deep winter. But through it all shines the virtues of human fortitude in adversity. And the amazing fact is that at no point in the narrative does any Imperial Guardsman express criticism of the man who they might have blamed for getting them into such a spot—the Emperor Napoleon. One old soldier, hearing a rumour that Napoleon had been captured, insisted on presenting arms as a salute to le tondu. What further proof do we require of the high state of morale prevalent in la Garde Impériale, in bad times as well as good—or of the bond of almost mystical affection that linked the leader and the led? It is also as a memorial to that relationship that this book deserves to be preserved for posterity.

R. M. A. Sandhurst, 1979

HISTORICAL INTRODUCTION

BY DAVID G. CHANDLER
MA (Oxon), FRHistS, FRGS

As Sergeant Bourgogne's recollections are essentially a personal account of his own adventures during the retreat from Moscow, the following short account of the whole campaign has been produced for the convenience of those readers who may not be fully acquainted with the development of events.

The alliance between Russia and France drawn up at Tilsit in July 1807 to all appearances brought Tsar Alexander I and the Emperor Napoleon into a close personal relationship. This entente, however, rapidly cooled over succeeding years. In 1809, Napoleon felt, with some justification, that the Tsar had not honoured his undertakings vis-à-vis Austria made at the Conference of Erfurt the previous year. For his part, the Tsar rapidly came to resent the economic complications and restrictions involved in Russia's adherence to the Continental System, and friction soon developed over France's attitude towards Russia's ambitions in the Balkans and concerning Constantinople. Another bone of contention was the Grand Duchy of Warsaw—a French-inspired creation which in part vitiated Russia's interests in Poland. Personal issues were added to these complaints: the Tsar publicly resented the snub implied by Napoleon's sudden marriage to Marie-Louise of Austria whilst negotiations for the hand of a Russian princess were still in progress; and then the seizure of the lands of the Duke of Oldenburg (brother-in-law of the Tsar) added further fuel to the ill-feeling. Both sides, therefore, felt they had genuine grievances against the other.

Determined to bring the Tsar into a more compliant attitude, in late 1811 Napoleon began to transfer more and more troops to the western frontiers of Russia's Polish possessions. It is quite possible that he hoped this demonstration of force would suffice to secure Russia's return to the Continental System. However, with British financial aid and political encouragement, Russia managed to settle outstanding issues over Finland and with the Turks, and thus freed her hands and resources to call Napoleon's bluff, if such it should prove to be. The Emperor was not the man to back down in such a situation. So after holding a meeting with a glittering array of Kings and Princes at Dresden (the rulers of both Austria and Prussia attended) and, for propaganda purposes, launching one last appeal to the Tsar in the hope of avoiding recourse to war, he ordered his troops to cross the River Niemen on 24 June, 1812—and 449,000 men (less than half of them native Frenchmen) in three armies and two flanking corps invaded Russian Poland. Napoleon expected a quick decision to the war; one major battle in Poland and the Tsar would come to terms—or so Napoleon hoped. But he had misjudged the Tsar's determination—bolstered by British aid and the pressures applied by powerful court factions in St. Petersburg. Russia could immediately field only some 220,000 troops to defend her western frontiers, in two armies commanded by Generals Barclay de Tolly and Bagration, respectively. A third army, under Tormassov, was in process of formation far to the south. Under these circumstances, the Russian strategy would appear to have envisaged a withdrawal towards the fortified river-lines formed by the Dvina and the Dnieper, about 170 miles to the east of the Niemen, and there turn to hold the gap between the two rivers to the west of Smolensk.

Napoleon had decided to attack near Kovno to the north of the Pripet marshes—close to his bases at Danzig and Königsberg. Three main armies were drawn up in echelon for the invasion, commanded by Eugène Beauharnais, King

Jérome Bonaparte and the Emperor himself. He hoped that Jérome would lure Bagration and the Second Army of the West toward Warsaw, aided by General Schwarzenberg's Austrian corps to the south, leaving Napoleon and Eugène free to come to conclusions with Barclay de Tolly's First Army. Farther north, Marshal Macdonald, at the head of a Franco-Prussian force, was to press up the Baltic coast towards Riga. Aware that Poland and west Russia would prove inhospitable, unprecedented steps were taken to provide La Grande Armée de Russie with waggon-trains of supplies and a depot system. But Napoleon never for one moment envisaged a march all the way to Moscow—or the possibility of a winter campaign. Behind the 449,000 men of the front-line forces, a further 200,000 reserves prepared to follow into Russia to hold the lines of communication and support the offensive by the forward army group.

The crossing of the Niemen bridges began on 24 June, but from the first the advance was hampered by their unaccustomed reliance on slow-moving transport and ration columns made unavoidable by the barren nature of much of west Russia. Consequently, a succession of attempts to trap the First Army of the West into a decisive battle failed. By 8 July Murat had captured Vilna, but Eugène's army could not move up from the south as intended to cover Napoleon's right flank; and Jérome was proving even less successful in pinning Bagration who was able to break contact and head north-east in the hope of joining his colleague. Stung by his brother's bitter criticisms, after Davout had swept south from Vilna in the hope of trapping the Russians only to strike empty air, Jérome threw up his command and returned to Westphalia.

Pausing to reorder his forces and organise the rear areas, Napoleon next launched a second offensive northwards in the hope of pinning Barclay on the Dvina near the fortified positions of Drissa or Dunaburg, whilst Davout (newly appointed to command in Jérome Bonaparte's place) was ordered to pursue the elusive Bagration and prevent any link-up. Once again, however, the operations conducted between 16 and 26 July failed to produce the desired battle,

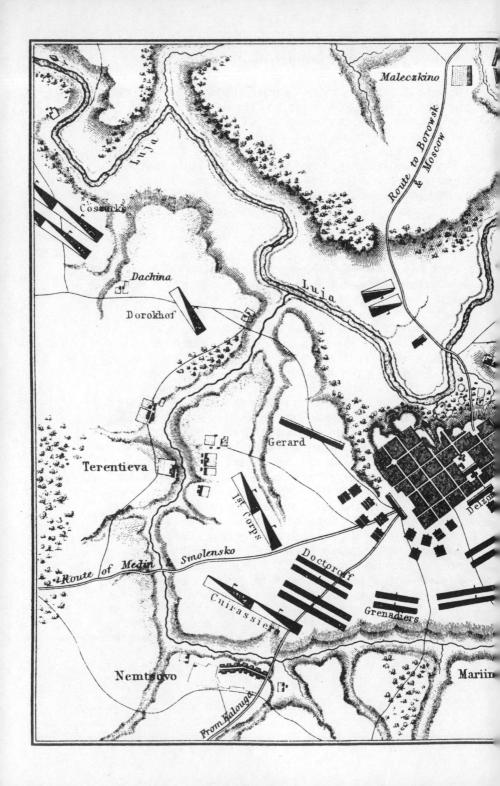

BATTLE OF
MALO-JAROSLAWITZ
24ᵗʰ October 1812.
A.K. JOHNSTON. F.R.G.S.

French   Russians
Cavalry   Infantry   Artillery

SCALES
Military Steps 2½ feet each
1000   500   0   1000   2000
English Miles
½   ¼   0   ½   1

but the Russians were forced to abandon the Dvina river-line. Up to this point the Russian retreat was probably deliberate, but now Barclay had no alternative but to continue the retreat with his 110,000 troops in the hope of a junction with Bagration's 44,000 men. The two Russian armies were now fast converging—and Napoleon was already deeper into Russia than he had ever anticipated.

After a second pause to rest his men and reorganise his communications, again the Emperor launched his men towards Smolensk. The blazing heat of the Russian summer was now taking a heavy toll of both men and horses. Far away to the south, meanwhile, the Russian Third Army of the West was in action against the French right wing, but the focus of attention was in the North. Oudinot fought a bitter action around Pulotsk—and the French front already measured all of 500 miles, causing ever-growing problems of supply and control. Worse still, on 4 August Barclay at last linked up with Bagration west of Smolensk—but they were soon in violent disagreement over future policy.

Determined to retrieve the situation, Napoleon rushed his men into the river gap. Whilst Murat lured the Russians west-wards towards Inkovo on 8 August, the bulk of the army crossed the broad Dnieper in a surprise move hoping to capture Smolensk by a coup de main and thus sever the Russian line of retreat. However, the staunch fighting with-drawal by a single Russian corps south of the Dnieper slowed the French advance, and this provided Barclay and Bagration with time to appreciate their peril and to order a precipitate retreat. The result was a three-day battle around Smolensk (17-19 August), but the result was inconclusive as the Russians were able to continue their eastwards retreat owing to General Junot's failure to block their path at Lubino. So, Napoleon had still not found his decisive action, and his battle-power was rapidly shrinking the farther he had to advance. Even worse, the rear areas were already being subjected to Cossack and partisan attacks.

Napoleon now faced the critical decision of the campaign. He could either halt around Smolensk, and resume the campaign the following spring, or press on immediately. He opted for the latter course although his fighting power was now only 156,000 men—and all of 280 miles still lay between his army and Moscow. The advance was accordingly resumed on 28 August.

Important decisions were also being taken at St. Petersburg. The Tsar decided to replace Barclay de Tolly as supreme commander with the 67-year-old General Golenischev-Kutusov. His orders were on all accounts to fight for the Holy City of Moscow. On 5 September, as the leading French formations approached from the west, Kutusov occupied a position around Borodino, and prepared to make his stand. Field-works were constructed, and the wily general played upon the religious susceptibilities of his moujik-soldiery to wring the utmost response from them in the hard battle that lay ahead.

The great Battle of Borodino (or of the Moscova as it is often referred to, after the local river) was fought on 7 September. The Emperor was unwell, and insisted upon an unsubtle frontal battle of attrition. As a result, after a ferocious day's fighting against Kutusov's 120,800 men and 680 cannon, the 133,000 French and Allies (with 585 guns) failed to win a decisive victory. They inflicted 44,000 casualties for a cost of 30,000, but Kutusov was able to draw off in good order. A week later, Napoleon entered an abandoned Moscow.

The Emperor was surprised to receive so cold a welcome, but next day other matters came to the fore, as incendiaries set fire to large areas of the city—on the order of the Civil Governor, Count Rostopchin. What then befell is graphically described by Sgt. Bourgogne. Fully two-thirds of the Russian Holy City lay in smoking ruins, but there was shelter a-plenty for the French forces, and many luxuries as well as basic supplies to be found in the cellars. But although Kutusov's outposts spoke of an approaching offer of terms, any such hopes proved illusory. The Tsar, who was at St. Petersburg, refused to treat with Napoleon. And so the weeks dragged by with little activity of any kind. Then, abruptly, on

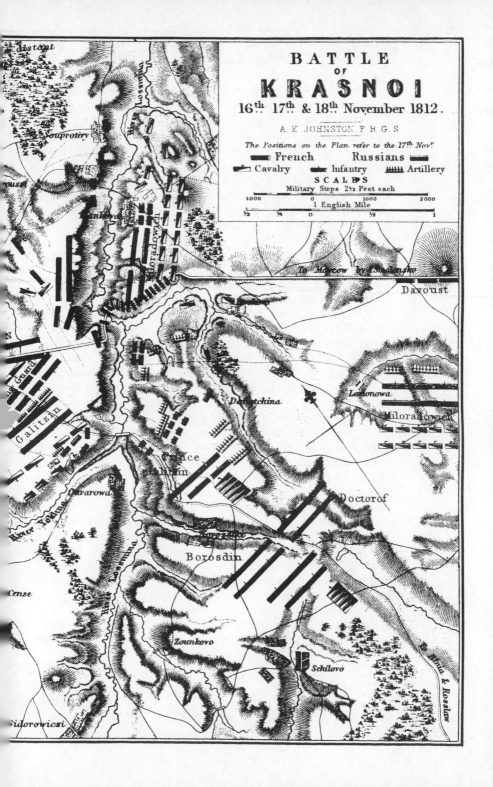

BATTLE
OF
KRASNOI
16th. 17th. & 18th. November 1812.

A. K. JOHNSTON, F.R.G.S

The Positions on the Plan refer to the 17th. Nov.

French   **Russians**

Cavalry   Infantry   Artillery

SCALES
Military Steps 2½ Feet each

| 1000 | 0 | 1000 | 2000 |

1 English Mile

½   ¼   0   ½   1

To Moscow by ye Smolensko

Davoust

Souprotiry

Uwarowo

Gard

Galitzin

Uwarowa

River Vokina

River Losmina

Cense

Sidorowicsi

Zoumkovo

Borosdin

Schilovo

Dobrotchina

Uwance militim

Doctorof

Larionowa

Miloradowitch

Tula & Rosslaw

18 October, the Russians surprised the drowsy French cavalry to the south-east of the city, and inflicted a sharp reverse on Prince Murat's command. In fact, the Emperor had already determined to retreat—the Tsar had effectively called his bluff—and on the 120th day of the campaign the exodus from Moscow began.

The army, burdened with many luxuries as our Sergent-vélite reveals, set out southwards, planning to break through to Kaluga and the neighbouring fertile areas of unravaged country. However, a sharp action at Malo-Jaroslavets between the 23 and 25 October, in which the Emperor was only narrowly saved from Cossacks—as Bourgogne relates—altered the aspect of affairs; and aware that the army of Finland was approaching from the north, and another force under Admiral Tshitsagov was marching up from Moldavia, Napoleon decided to fall back towards Smolensk along the ravaged line of advance. The 50-mile-long convoy painfully wound its way westwards over the grisly site of the battlefield of Borodino, and the weather fast began to deteriorate. Hounded by Cossacks, and with a wary Kutusov keeping only one step behind, the cohesion and morale of the French began to crack.

The advance guard reached Smolensk on 9 November, but the considerable supplies of food were looted and wantonly destroyed by the famished first-comers as order broke down in the ranks. (Bourgogne's vivid relation of his adventures in the city and of the condition of the army at this time will be found below.) The army soon staggered onwards, under perpetual harassment and amidst increasing blizzards of snow and far below zero temperatures. However, when the Russians closed in for the kill on the 17th they received a sharp lesson from the Imperial Guard and other units at Krasnoe—an action in which Bourgogne participated. Kutusov decided against a direct confrontation and continued to shadow the weakening army, which was now heading for the food depots at Minsk. However, on the 18th Napoleon learnt that these supplies had fallen into Tshitsagov's hands, and morale sank to a new low when it was discovered that

Marshal Ney and the rearguard had become detached from the main column. Then the near-miraculous reappearance of "the bravest of the brave" and his survivors, after an astounding series of feats of arms, gave morale a brief filip, and the 40,000 men still under arms (followed by perhaps twice as many stragglers) moved on toward Borisov, the site of bridges over the River Beresina, the last natural obstacle between the French and Poland.

Once again, the Russians arrived there first, and on the 22nd Napoleon learnt that the bridges had been destroyed. Fearing the worst, the Emperor ordered the burning of his state papers and the eagles and other colours of the army; and to still further lighten his column and provide a few more starving horses for the artillery-teams he also had the bridging train burnt at Orsha. He was relying on the continuation of the present spell of severe frosts to keep the river solid with ice—but now a snap-thaw intervened to turn the river into a fast-flowing torrent. With Wittgenstein closing in from the north with 30,000 men, Tshitsagov and 34,000 more to the west, and Kutusov at the head of 64,000 troops moving up from the east and south, the position of the French seemed hopeless. It was at about this time that Bourgogne saw the Emperor on foot at the head of his staff, escorted by the "sacred legion" consisting of officers ranging from generals to colonels who had no men to command.

When all seemed lost, a near miracle took place. By chance, an unguarded ford was discovered near Studienka and, thanks to Baron Elbé of the pontoon train having saved a few cart-loads of vital tools from the conflagration at Orsha and after fooling Tshitsagov about the intended point of passage, it proved possible to construct two rickety bridges. From 25 November the French began to cross the river amidst appalling scenes of alternate panic and total passivity on the part of the mass of non-combattants accompanying what was left of the army. For four days the crossing continued, amidst bitter fighting as Tshitsagov attempted to close the avenue of escape from the south and Wittgenstein closed in on the rearguard from the north-east. But the French could still fight,

PASSAGE
OF THE
BERESINA
26th 27th & 28th Novr. 1812.

A.K. JOHNSTON, F.R.G.S.

French   Russians

Cavalry   Infantry   Artillery

SCALES

Military Steps 2½ Feet each

1000   0   1000   2000   3000   4000   5000   6000

English Miles

1   ½   0   2

First positions coloured light.

and the bulk of the horde passed over the river before the bridges were set on fire (after several breakdowns) early on the 29th. Perhaps 40,000 French survived this battle, but fully 50,000 of their comrades died or froze to death on the banks of the Beresina.

The road to Vilna and Poland now lay open before the French, but grave news of the Malet conspiracy in Paris had now reached the Emperor (Bourgogne had seen the courier), and on 5 December he set out almost alone for his capital, leaving first Murat, and ultimately Eugène, to bring the sorry remnants of the former Grande Armée de Russie to relative safety. Despite the constantly cruel weather and the incessant attentions of Cossacks and other human marauders, whom Bourgogne graphically describes, the survivors at last reached a measure of safety and comfort at Elbing and other fortresses in East Prussia in the New Year of 1813.

It is estimated that out of over 600,000 French and Allied troops that had entered Russia during the summer of 1812, only 94,000 came out (to include 69,000 of the flank forces). A further 20,000 Prussians under General Yorck had defected to the Russians at Taurrogen on 3 December. Of course the Russians had also suffered severely in both the military and civilian sectors, but at least Kutusov could declare to his master the Tsar that the enemy had been driven from the soil of Holy Russia. The price had been perhaps a million civilians and 125,000 Russian troops. But in no small measure the legend of Napoleonic invincibility had been shattered, and soon the scene of war would be switched to Germany as the Campaign of Liberation opened. But Napoleon would still have some surprises to spring over the next 18 months. As Bourgogne reveals, his hold over the loyalty and affections of his men remained as strong in times of disaster as they had in the heady days of triumph and conquest.

CHAPTER I.

IT was in the month of March, 1812, while we were engaged against the English army commanded by Wellington, at Almeida in Portugal, that we received orders to march for Russia.

We crossed Spain, each day being marked by an engagement, sometimes by two, and in this way reached Bayonne, the first town over the frontier in France.

On leaving this place, we travelled by the stage as far as Paris, where we expected to stay and rest; but after a halt of forty-eight hours, the Emperor reviewed us, and, deciding that we were not in need of rest, marched us all along the boulevards. Then we turned to the left in the Rue St. Martin, crossed La Villette, and found several hundred coaches and other vehicles waiting for us; we halted, but were ordered to mount four into every carriage —and, crack! we were off to Meaux. From there onwards to the Rhine in waggons, travelling day and night.

We stayed at Mayence, and then crossed the Rhine, afterwards passing on foot through the grand-duchy of Frankfort,* Franconia, Saxony, Prussia, and Poland. We crossed the Vistula at Marienwerder, entered Pomerania,

* Frankfort had been raised to a grand-duchy by Napoleon in 1806, in favour of the Elector of Mayence.

I

and on the morning of June 25, a beautiful day (not, as M. de Ségur said, in bad weather), we passed over the Niemen by our pontoons, and entered Lithuania, the first province in Russia.

On the next day we left our first position, and marched until the 29th, without anything noteworthy happening; but during the night of the 29th and 30th we heard a rumbling noise—it was thunder accompanied by a furious wind. Masses of clouds gathered over our heads, and broke. The thunder and the wind lasted for more than two hours, and in a few minutes our fires were put out, our shelter torn away, our piled arms thrown down. We were lost, and did not know which way to turn. I ran to take shelter in the direction of the village where the General was lodged, but I had only the lightning to guide me—suddenly, in one of the flashes, I thought I saw a road (it was unfortunately a canal, swollen by the rain to the level of the ground). Expecting to find solid earth under my feet, I plunged in and sank. On rising to the surface I swam to the other bank, and at last reached the village. I walked into the first house I saw, and entered a room filled by about twenty men, officers, and servants, all asleep. I took possession of a bench placed near a large warm stove, and, undressing, wrung the water out of my shirt and other clothes, huddling myself up on the bench till they were dry; when daylight came, I dressed as well as I could, and left the house to look for my weapons and knapsack, which I found scattered in the mud.

On the 30th, a beautiful sun dried everything, and the same day we reached Wilna, the capital of Lithuania, where the Emperor had arrived the day before, with some of the Guard.

While we were there, I received a letter from my mother, enclosing another addressed to M. Constant, the

Emperor's chief valet, who came from Peruwelz* in Belgium. This letter was from his mother, an acquaintance of my mother's. I went to the Emperor's lodging to deliver the letter, but only saw Roustan, the Emperor's mameluke, who told me that M. Constant had gone out with His Majesty. He invited me to wait till he returned, but, as I was on duty, I could not do so. I gave him the letter, and decided to come back and see M. Constant another time. But the next day, July 16, we left the town, at ten o'clock in the evening, going towards Borisow, and on the 27th we reached Witebsk, where we encountered Russians. We took up our position on a height above the town. The enemy occupied hills to right and left.

The cavalry, commanded by Murat, had already made several charges. Just as we arrived we saw 200 Voltigeurs of the 9th Regiment, who had ventured too far, met by a portion of the Russian cavalry, which had just been repulsed. Unless help arrived speedily to our men, they were lost, as the river and some deep gullies made access to them very difficult. But they were commanded by gallant officers, who swore, as did also the men, to kill themselves rather than not come honourably out of it. Fighting as they went, they reached a piece of favourable ground. They formed a square, and having been under fire before, their nerves were not shaken by the number of the enemy. They were quite surrounded, however, by a regiment of Lancers and other horse trying in vain to cut through them, and soon they had a rampart of killed and wounded all round them, both of men and horses. This formed another obstacle for the Russians, who, terrified, fled in disorder, amid cries of joy from the whole army.

* A large Belgian town, seven kilometres from Condé ; a favourite excursion, on account of the pilgrimage of Bonsecours.

Our men came back again quietly, as conquerors, every now and then stopping to face the enemy. The Emperor at once sent for the most distinguished, and decorated them with the order of the Legion of Honour. From a height opposite to ours, the Russians had, like us, seen the engagement and flight of their cavalry.

After this brush we made our bivouacs, and directly afterwards I had a visit from twelve young men from my own country (Condé); ten of them were drummers, one a drum-major, and the twelfth was a corporal of Voltigeurs. They all wore side-arms. I told them how much pleasure it gave me to see them, and said I was sorry I had nothing to offer them. The drum-major said :

'*Mon pays*, we did not come for that, but to beg you to come with us and share what we have, wine, gin, and other things very good for you. We took them yesterday evening from the Russian General. There was a little cart holding his kitchen and everything belonging to it. We have put it all into the canteen cart, with Florencia our *cantinière*—she is a pretty Spaniard. She might be taken for my wife : I protect her—honourably, I can tell you !' As he said this, he struck the hilt of his long rapier. 'She is a good woman : ask the others—no one dares say anything else. She had a fancy for a sergeant, who was to have married her ; but he was murdered by a Spaniard from Bilbao, and until she has chosen someone else she must be taken care of. Well, then, *mon pays*, it is settled : you—you'll come with us. If there's enough for three, there's enough for four. Come, right about ! march !" And we set off towards their army corps, which formed the advance guard.

Well, we got to the camp of the natives of Condé. There were four guests—two dragoons, Mellé, who was from Condé, Flament from Peruwelz, and Grangier, a non-commissioned officer in the same regiment as myself. We sat down near the *cantinière's* cart. She really was a very pretty Spaniard, and she was overjoyed to see us, as we had just come from her own country, and could speak her language pretty well—the dragoon Flament best of all—so we spent the night in drinking the Russian General's wine and talking of our country.

Day was just breaking, when a sound of artillery put a stop to our talking. We went back to our own quarters, hoping to meet again.

The poor fellows little thought that in a few days eleven of them would not be alive.

This was the 28th. We expected to fight, but the Russian army retreated, and the same day we got to Witebsk, where we stayed a fortnight. Our regiment occupied one of the faubourgs of the town.

I was quartered with a Jew, who had a pretty wife and two charming daughters with lovely oval faces. In this house I found a little vat for making beer, some barley, and a hand-mill for grinding, but no hops. I gave the Jew twelve francs to get some, and for fear he might not return we kept Rachel his wife and his two daughters as hostages. However twenty-four hours after his departure Jacob the Jew returned with the hops. In our company was a brewer, a Fleming, who made us five barrels of excellent beer.

On August 13, when we left the town, we still had two barrels of beer left; we put them under the care of Mother Dubois, our *cantinière*. The happy idea then occurred to her of staying behind and of selling the beer for her own profit to the men who were following us, while we, in the sweltering heat, were nearly dead of thirst.

Early on the morning of the 16th we arrived before Smolensk. The enemy had just retired there, and we took up our position on the Champ Sacré, so called by the natives of the place. This town is surrounded by very strong walls, and old towers, half made of wood. The Boristhène (Dnieper) runs on one side of the town. The siege was begun at once and a breach made, and on the morning of the 17th, when we were preparing to make an assault, to our surprise we found the town evacuated. The Russians were retreating, but they had demolished the bridge, and from a height which commanded the town they rained down bombs and shot on us.

During that day of the siege I, with one of my friends, was stationed at the outposts whence batteries were playing on the town. Marshal Davoust commanded this position. Recognising us as belonging to the Guard, he came to us and asked where the Imperial Guard was. Directly afterwards he was told that the Russians had left the town, and were advancing in our direction. He immediately ordered a battalion of Light Infantry to take the advanced position, saying to the officer in command, ' If the enemy advances you will drive them back.' I remember an old officer of this battalion, as he went forward, singing Roland's song :

> ' Combien sont-ils ? Combien sont-ils ?
> C'est le cri du soldat sans gloire !'*

Five minutes afterwards they advanced with the bayonet on the Russian column, and forced it to re-enter the town.

As we returned to our own camp, we were very nearly killed by a shell; another fell on a barn inhabited by Marshal Mortier, and set it on fire. I recognised among

---

* ' Combien sont-ils ? Combien sont-ils ?
  Quel homme ennemi de sa gloire
  Peut demander ! Combien sont-ils ?
  Eh ! demande ou sont les perils,
  C'est la qu'est aussi la victoire !'

These are the exact words of the third verse of ' Roland à Roncevaux,' a song (words and music) by Rouget de L'Isle.

the men who brought water to extinguish the fire a young soldier from my own country; he was in a regiment of the Young Guard.*

While we stayed outside the town, I visited the cathedral, where a large number of the inhabitants had taken refuge, their houses having been destroyed.

On the 21st we left, and the same day we crossed the Valoutina plain, where two days before a terrible encounter had taken place, and the brave General Gudin had been killed.

We continued to advance, and by forced marches arrived at a town called Dorogoboui. We left on the 24th, following up the Russians as far as Viazma, which was already in flames, and found there some brandy and a little food. We went on to Ghjal, which we reached on September 1st; there we stayed until the 4th, when we went forward again, and on the 5th met the Russian army in position. The 61st captured their first redoubt.

We got ready on the 6th for the great battle on the next day; some cleaned muskets and other weapons, others made bandages for the wounded, some made their wills, and others, again, sang or slept in perfect indifference. The whole of the Imperial Guard received orders to appear in full uniform.

At five o'clock on the morning of the next day we were under arms. The Emperor passed near us while he reviewed the whole line; he had been mounted for more than half an hour.

The battle began at seven o'clock. I cannot describe it in detail, but the whole army was overjoyed to hear the roar of the artillery, feeling certain that this time the Russians had not decamped, and that we should come face to face with them. The evening before, and for part

* Dumoulin, died of fever at Moscow.—*Author's Note.*

of the night, a fine cold rain had fallen, but on this great day the weather was magnificent. This, like all our great battles, was won by the artillery, which fired 120,000 rounds. The Russians lost at least 50,000 men, either killed or wounded. Our loss was 17,000 men; forty-three Generals disabled, eight of whom, to my knowledge, were killed on the spot. These were: Montbrun, Huard, Caulaincourt (the brother of the Emperor's equerry), Compère Maison, Plauzonne, Lepel, and Anabert. This last was Colonel of a regiment of foot chasseurs. Each moment a message was sent to the Emperor, 'Sire, such and such a General is killed or wounded,' and his place had to be filled on the spot. This was how Colonel Anabert was made General. I remember it very well, for I was close to the Emperor at the time. His words were:

'Colonel, I appoint you General; lead the division which is in front of the great redoubt, and take it.'

The General galloped off, with his adjutant-major following him as his aide-de-camp. A quarter of an hour afterwards the aide-de-camp returned, and announced to the Emperor that the redoubt was taken, but that the General was wounded. Eight days afterwards he died, along with several others. I heard that the Russians lost fifty Generals, either killed or wounded. While the fighting lasted, we were placed in reserve, behind General Miaut's division; balls fell all amongst our ranks, and round the Emperor.

The battle ended with the day, and we remained on the field all night, and all the next day (the 8th). I spent that day in walking over the field—a sad and terrible spectacle. Grangier was with me, and we went as far as the ravine, the position so hotly disputed during the battle. Murat had ordered his tents to be pitched there. Just as we arrived we saw him superintend the amputation by his own surgeon of the legs of two gunners of the Imperial Russian Guard. When the operation was over, he gave them each a glass of wine. Afterwards he walked on the edge of the ravine, examining the plain which lies on the other side, fringed by a wood. There, on the preceding day, he had made more than one Muscovite bite the dust while he and his cavalry charged the retreating enemy. He was splendid to look at—so distinguished by his gallantry, his cool courage, and his handsome appearance—giving his orders to those under his command, and raining blows on his enemies. He was easily picked out by his cap, his white aigrette, and his floating cloak.

On the morning of the 9th we left the battlefield, and during the day reached Mojaisk. The Russian rear-guard was on a height the opposite side of the town from that occupied by us. A company of Voltigeurs and Grenadiers, with more than a hundred men of the 33rd, making part of the advance-guard, ascended the hill without troubling themselves about the number of the enemy waiting for them. A part of the army, still in the town, watched them astonished, as several squadrons of Cuirassiers and Cossacks advanced and surrounded the Voltigeurs and Grenadiers. But, as if they had foreseen all that, they quietly reunited, formed into platoons, then in a square, and fired from all four sides on the Russians surrounding them.

We gave them up for lost, knowing the distance separating us from them, and no help being possible. A Russian superior officer went up to them, telling them to surrender; the officer in command of the French answered him by killing him. Upon this the cavalry, terrified, ran away and left our men masters of the field.*

* One of my friends, a Vélite Captain Sabatier, commanded the Voltigeurs.—*Author's Note.*

On the 10th we followed the enemy until the evening; and when we stopped I was put in command of a guard near a château where the Emperor lodged. I had just placed my men on a road leading to the château, when a Polish servant, whose master was on the Emperor's staff, passed near us, leading a horse laden with baggage. The horse was worn out, sank down, and refused to get up again. The servant took the baggage and went off. He had hardly left us when the men, who were hungry, killed the horse, so that all night we were busy eating it and cooking for the next day.

Soon afterwards the Emperor passed on foot, accompanied by Murat and a member of the Conseil d'Etat, on their way to the highroad. I made my sentries present arms. The Emperor stopped in front of us, and near the horse, which filled up the road. He asked me if we were eating it.

I replied, 'Yes.'

He smiled and said, 'Patience! In four days we shall be at Moscow, where you will have rest and proper food—however good that horse may be.'

His prediction was fulfilled, for four days afterwards we arrived at that city.

The next day (the 11th) and following days we marched in beautiful weather. On the 13th we slept at a place near a beautiful abbey, and several other fine buildings. We could see that we were approaching a great capital.

On the 14th we set out very early; we passed near a ravine where the Russians had begun to make redoubts for defence, and directly afterwards we entered a great forest of pines and birches, where we found a beautiful road. Now we were quite near Moscow.

On that day I was with an advance guard of fifteen men. After marching for an hour, the Imperial column halted, and just then I saw a linesman with his left arm in a sling. He was leaning on his musket, and seemed to be waiting for someone. I recognised him at once as one of the Condé men who had been to see me at Witebsk. He was there hoping to meet me. I went up to him, and asked him after his friends.

'They are well,' he answered, striking the ground with the butt-end of his musket. 'They all died on the field of honour, as they say, and were buried in the great redoubt. They were killed by round shot. Ah, sergeant,' he went on, 'never shall I forget that battle—what slaughter!'

'And you,' I said—'what is the matter with you?'

'Ah, bah! nothing. A ball between the elbow and shoulder. Sit down for a minute, and let us talk of our poor comrades and the young Spaniard, our *cantinière.*'

This is what he told me:

'We had been fighting since seven in the morning, when General Campans, who commanded us, was wounded. The officer who took his place was wounded also, and then the third. A fourth came. This one from the Guard. Directly he took command, he ordered the drums to sound the charge. That was how our regiment (the 61st) was destroyed by grapeshot—that was how our friends were killed, the redoubt taken, and the General wounded. It was General Anabert. During the action I got a ball in the arm, without knowing it at the time.

'Soon afterwards my wound began to pain me, and I went to the ambulance to have the ball extracted. I had not gone many steps before I met the young Spaniard, our *cantinière;* she was in tears. Some men had told her that nearly all the drummers of the regiment were killed or wounded. She said she wanted to see them, to help them if she could; so, in spite of the pain I suffered from my wound, I determined to accompany her. We walked in the midst of wounded men; some moved painfully and with difficulty, and others were carried on litters.

'When we got near the great redoubt and that field of carnage, she uttered heart-rending cries. But when she caught sight of all the broken drums of the regiment strewing the ground, she became like a madwoman. " Here, my friend, here !" she cried; "they are here !" And so they were, lying with broken limbs, their bodies torn by shot. Mad with grief, she went from one to the other, speaking softly to them; but none of them heard. Some, however, still gave signs of life, one of them being the drum-major, whom she called her father. She stopped by him, and, falling on her knees, she raised his head and poured a few drops of brandy between his lips. Just at that moment the Russians made an effort to retake the redoubt, and the firing and cannonade began again. Suddenly the Spaniard cried with pain; she had been struck by a ball in her left hand, which crushed her thumb and entered the shoulder of the dying man she held. She fell unconscious. Seeing her danger, I tried to raise her, and take her to the baggage and ambulance waggons. But with only one arm I had not strength enough. Happily, a Cuirassier passed on foot close to us. He did not need asking; he only said, " Quick! we must hurry; this is not a pleasant place." In fact, the bullets were whistling round us. Without more ado he lifted the young Spaniard and carried her like a child. She still remained unconscious. After walking for ten minutes, we got to a little wood where there was an ambulance of the Guard Artillery. Here Florencia came to her senses.

'M. Larrey, the Emperor's surgeon, amputated her thumb, and extracted the ball from my arm very cleverly, and now I feel all right again.'

This is what I heard from Dumont, the man from Condé, corporal of the Voltigeurs of the 61st. I made him promise to come to see me at Moscow, if we stayed there; but I never heard of him again.

Thus perished twelve young men from Condé in the famous Battle of Moskowa, September 7th, 1812.

End of the abstract of our march from Portugal to Moscow.

BOURGOGNE,*

Ex-Grenadier of the Imperial Guard, Chevalier of the Légion d'Honneur.

* Bourgogne's signature at the end of this chapter shows that he considered it as a kind of introduction.

CHAPTER II.

THE FIRE AT MOSCOW.

AT one o'clock in the afternoon of September 14th, after passing through a great forest, we saw a hill some way off, and half an hour afterwards part of the army reached the highest point, signalling to us who were behind, and shouting 'Moscow! Moscow!' It was indeed the great city; there we should rest after all our labours, for we of the Imperial Guard had marched more than twelve hundred leagues without resting.

It was a beautiful summer's day; the sun was reflected on all the domes, spires, and gilded palaces. Many capitals I have seen—such as Paris, Berlin, Warsaw, Vienna, and Madrid—had only produced an ordinary impression on me. But this was quite different; the effect was to me—in fact, to everyone—magical.

At that sight troubles, dangers, fatigues, privations were all forgotten, and the pleasure of entering Moscow absorbed all our minds. To take up good quarters for the winter, and to make conquests of another nature—such is the French soldier's character: from war to love, and from love to war! While we were gazing at the city, the order was given to appear in full uniform.

On that day I was in the advance-guard with fifteen

men, and I had under my charge several officers taken prisoner in the great battle of the Moskowa, some of whom spoke French. Amongst them was a pope (a priest of the Greek Church), probably chaplain of a regiment. He, too, spoke French very well, but he seemed much sadder and more preoccupied than his companions in misfortune. I noticed that, when they arrived at the hill where we were stationed, all the prisoners bowed and crossed themselves several times. I went to the priest and asked him the reason.

'Monsieur,' he said, 'this hill is called the Mont du Salut, and every good Muscovite on seeing the holy city must bow and cross himself.'

Soon afterwards we descended the Mont du Salut, and after a quarter of an hour's march we found ourselves at the gate of the town.

The Emperor was there already with his staff. We halted, and I noticed to our left an immense cemetery. After waiting a moment, Marshal Duroc came out of the town, which he had just entered, and, addressing the Emperor, presented to him several of the inhabitants who could speak French. The Emperor questioned them; then the Marshal told His Majesty that in the Kremlin there were a great number of persons under arms, the greater part of whom were criminals released from the prisons; they had been firing at Murat's cavalry, who formed the advance-guard. In spite of several orders, they persisted in keeping their doors closed.

'These wretches,' said the Marshal, 'are all drunk, and cannot listen to reason.'

'Open the doors with cannon,' replied the Emperor, 'and drive out all you find behind them.'

The thing was done already—Murat had undertaken it himself: two cannon-shots, and all the riff-raff was dispersed through the town. Then Murat continued his progress, pressing hard on the Russian rear-guard.

The order ' Garde-à-vous !' was now given, preceded by a rolling of drums from the Guard, the signal for entering the town. It was three o'clock in the afternoon, and we made our entrance marching in close columns, the bands playing in front. I was in the advance guard of thirty men, commanded by M. Césarisse, the Lieutenant of our company.

We had hardly entered the outskirts of the town, when we met several of the miserable creatures expelled from the Kremlin ; they had all horrible faces, and were armed with muskets, staves, and pitchforks. In passing over the bridge leading from the suburbs to the town itself, a man crept from underneath the bridge, and placed himself in front of the regiment. He was muffled up in a sheepskin cape, long gray hair fell on his shoulders, and a thick white beard came down to his waist. He carried a three-pronged fork, and looked like Neptune rising from the sea. In these accoutrements he walked proudly up to the drum-major, moving as if to strike him, no doubt taking him for the General with his smart uniform and gold lace. He aimed a blow at him with his pitchfork, which luckily the drum-major managed to avoid, and, snatching the miserable creature's weapon from him, he seized him by the shoulders ; then, kicking him behind, he launched him over the bridge and into the water he had just left. He did not get out again, however ; swept away by the current, we only saw him come up at intervals. Finally he disappeared altogether.

We met several others of the same kind, who fired at us with loaded arms. There were even some of them who had nothing but wooden flint-locks to their muskets ; as they wounded no one, we contented ourselves with taking

16

their arms from them and breaking them, and if the creatures returned we got rid of them by blows in the back with the butt-end of our muskets. Some of these weapons had been taken from the arsenal at the Kremlin; the muskets with the wooden flint-locks certainly came from that place.

We knew that these wretches had tried to stab an officer of Murat's staff.

After passing over the bridge, we marched along a large and beautiful street. We were astonished not to see anyone come out—not even a lady—to listen to our band playing 'La victoire est à nous.' We could not understand this total silence, and we imagined that the inhabitants, not daring to show themselves, were peeping at us from behind their shutters. Here and there we saw a few servants in livery, and some Russian soldiers.

After marching for about an hour, we got to the first enclosure of the Kremlin. Turning sharp to the left, we entered a larger and finer street than the one we had left, leading to the Place du Gouvernement. Just as we stopped, we saw three ladies at a ground-floor window. I happened to be on the pavement, and near one of the ladies, who gave me a piece of bread as black as a coal, and full of long pieces of straw. I thanked her, and in return gave her a bit of white bread, which I had just got from Mother Dubois, our *cantinière*. The lady blushed, and I laughed; then she touched my arm—I cannot tell why—and I went on my way.

At last we arrived on the Place du Gouvernement. We massed ourselves together opposite the palace of Rostopchin, the Governor of the town, who ordered it to be fired. We were told that the regiment was to camp, and that no one on any pretence whatever was to absent himself. An hour afterwards, however, the whole place was filled with everything we could want—wines of all kinds, liqueurs, preserved fruits, and an enormous quantity of sweet cakes and flour, but no bread. We went into the houses on the Place asking for food and drink, but as we found no one in them we helped ourselves.

We had placed one guard under the principal entrance to the palace. On the right was a room large enough to hold all the men of the guard, and a few Russian officers—prisoners who had been found in the town. We had left the others by order at the gates of the town.

The Governor's palace is large, and its construction quite European. Opposite the entrance are two beautiful staircases, which unite on the first floor. On this story is a large drawing-room, containing an oval table and a very large painting of Alexander, Emperor of Russia, on horseback. Behind the palace is a large courtyard surrounded by servants' offices.

The fire began an hour after our arrival. On our right we saw a thick smoke, then a whirl of flames, not knowing from whence it came. We were told the fire was in the bazaar, the merchants' quarter.

'They are probably freebooters,' we were told, 'who have carelessly set fire to the shops in searching for provisions.'

Many people who were not in the campaign have said that it was the fire at Moscow that ruined the army. I, and many others with me, think just the contrary. The Russians need not have set fire to the town; they might have thrown all the provisions into the Moskowa, and wasted the country for ten leagues round—an easy thing to do, as part of the country is a desert already. Had this been done, we should have had to leave in a fortnight. After the fire there were still houses enough left to shelter the army, and, even supposing all the houses had been burnt, there were the cellars remaining. At seven o'clock the fire reached the back of the Governor's palace. The Colonel gave orders that a patrol of fifteen men should leave at once. I was among them. M. Césarisse came with us, and took command. We went in the direction of the fire, but we had hardly gone three hundred steps before we heard some firing on our right. We did not pay much attention, thinking it was only a few drunken soldiers; but fifty steps further we heard it again. It came from a sort of blind alley, and was directed at us. At the same moment I heard the cry of a wounded man close to me. He had a ball in the leg; but the wound was not dangerous, as he could still walk. We had orders to go back at once to our regiment; but we had hardly turned round, when more firing from the same quarter changed our direction again. We advanced to the house where the firing came from; we beat in the door, and came face to face with nine great rogues, armed with lances and muskets to prevent an entrance.

Then we fought in the yard, the numbers unequal. We were nineteen against nine; but, believing there were more of them, we had started by knocking down the three first. A corporal was wounded between his shoulder-belts and his coat; feeling nothing, he seized his adversary's lance, which placed him at a disadvantage, as he had only one hand free, having to hold his musket with the other. He was thrown violently back against the cellar door, still holding the lance fast. At that moment the Russian fell wounded by a bayonet. The officer had just wounded another in the wrist with his sword to make him drop his lance; but, as he still held firm, he was struck by a ball in the side, sending him to the shades. While this was going on, I with five men held the remaining four (for three had run away) so closely against a wall that they could not use their lances. At the first movement they made, we could run them through with our bayonets held against their breasts. They kept striking their weapons with their fists out of bravado. These unfortunate fellows were drunk with the brandy they had found in quantities, so that they were like madmen. We were obliged at last to finish them off.

We hurried into the house, and in one room we found two or three of the men who had made off. They were so frightened when they saw us that they had no time to seize their firearms, upon which we fell at once; while we were doing so, they jumped from the balcony.

As we had only found two men, and there were three muskets, we searched for the third, who was under the bed, and came out without being told, crying, 'Bojo! Bojo!' which means, 'My God! my God!' We did nothing to him, but kept him by us as a guide. Like the others, he was frightful and loathsome—like them, a convict clothed in a sheepskin, with a leather belt round his middle. We left the house, and found in the street the two convicts who had jumped from the window—one was dead, his head being smashed on the pavement; the other had both his legs broken.

We left them as we found them, and set out to return to the Place du Gouvernement; but what was our surprise to find this impossible, the fire having spread to such an enormous extent! To right and left was one wreath of flames, the wind was blowing hard, and the roofs were falling in. We were forced to take another course. Unfortunately, we could not make our prisoner understand us; he seemed more like a bear than a man.

After walking two hundred paces, we found a street on our right; but before entering it, we wished out of curiosity to see the house from which they had fired on us. We made our prisoner go in, following close behind ; but we had scarcely taken the precaution, when we heard a cry of alarm, and saw several men flying off with lighted torches in their hands. After crossing a large courtyard, we saw that the house we had taken for an ordinary one was a magnificent palace. We left two men as sentinels at the first entrance to warn us, should we be surprised. As we had candles with us, we lit several and entered. Never in my life have I seen such costly and beautiful furniture as met our eyes, and, above all, such a collection of paintings of the Flemish and Italian schools. Amongst all these grandeurs, a chest filled with firearms of great beauty attracted our attention first. I took possession of a brace of horse-pistols, inlaid with pearls and precious stones. I also took a small machine for gauging the force of powder.

We had been wandering about in these vast and beautiful rooms for more than an hour, when we heard a terrible explosion overhead. The shock was so great that we felt certain of being crushed under the ruins of the palace. We ran downstairs cautiously, but were horror-struck on discovering that the two men we had placed below as sentries were gone. We looked a long while for them, and at last found them in the street. They told us that on hearing the explosion they had taken to their heels as fast as possible, thinking that the whole palace was falling on them. Before leaving we tried to discover the cause of our terror. In the great dining-hall the ceiling had fallen, and a large glass chandelier was broken in a thousand pieces. A bomb had been concealed in an earthenware stove. The Russians evidently considered that any means were good enough to destroy us.

While we were still in the palace we heard the cry ' Fire !' from our two sentinels, who saw that the palace was burning. The smoke was now bursting out in several places thick and black, then it became red, and finally the whole building was in flames. At the end of a quarter of an hour the roof, made of coloured and varnished iron, fell in with a frightful noise, bringing with it three-quarters of the entire building.

After a great many windings in and out, we entered a wide, long street with splendid palaces on each side, which ought to have led us in the direction from which we had come, but our convict guide could tell us nothing. He was only useful in occasionally carrying our wounded man, who walked with great difficulty. We met several men with long beards and sinister faces looking still more terrible by the lurid light of the torches they carried; we let them pass us quietly.

We then met a number of Chasseurs of the Guard, who told us that the Russians themselves had set fire to the town, and that the men we had just met did the business. Soon afterwards we surprised three of these wretches setting fire to a Greek church. On seeing us, two of them threw away their torches and fled. We went up to the third, who kept his torch, and in spite of us tried to go on with his work ; a stroke with the butt-end of a musket on the head soon punished him for his obstinacy.

Just then we met a patrol of Fusilier-Chasseurs, who like us had lost their way. The sergeant in command told me that he had met convicts setting fire to a great many houses, that he had found one whose wrist he had to cut with his sword to force him to drop the torch, but that he had picked up the torch with his left hand to continue his piece of work, and they were obliged to kill im.

Further on we heard cries from some women calling in

22

French for help; we went into the house from whence the cries came, believing that the women must be *cantinières* taken by the Russians. But on entering we saw spread about here and there several costumes of different kinds, all very costly, and two ladies of very dishevelled appearance came running up to us. They had with them a boy of twelve or fifteen. They begged our protection against the soldiers of the Russian police, who were going to burn their house without giving them time to take away their possessions. Amongst their things were Cæsar's mantle, Brutus's helmet, and Joan of Arc's cuirass : for the ladies told us that they were actresses and Frenchwomen, but that their husbands had been forced to serve in the Russian army. For the time we were able to stop the burning of the house, and we took the Russian police (four of them) to our regiment, which was still in the Place du Gouvernement. After all these troubles we got there at two o'clock in the morning, from the opposite side to that by which we had left. When the Colonel heard that we had come back, he came to tell us how displeased he was with us, and to ask us what we had been doing since seven o'clock yesterday evening. But when he saw our prisoners and our wounded man, and we had told him of all the dangers we had been through, he said he was pleased to see us again, as he had been very uneasy about us.

On glancing at the Place where the men bivouacked, it seemed to be an assembly from all parts of the world, for our soldiers were clothed as Kalmucks, Chinese, Cossacks, Tartars, Persians, and Turks, and many of them covered with splendid furs. There were even some dressed in French Court dress, wearing swords with steel hilts shining like diamonds. Add to this that the space was covered with all kinds of dainties to eat, abundance of wines and liqueurs, a little fresh meat, a quantity of hams and fish, a little flour, but no bread.

On that day (the 15th), the day after our arrival, the regiment left the Place du Gouvernement at nine in the morning for the neighbourhood of the Kremlin, where the Emperor had taken up his quarters. I was left at the Governor's palace with fifteen men.

About ten o'clock I saw a General on horseback riding up, looking like General Pernetty.* He was leading a young man dressed in a sheepskin cape, fastened by a red woollen belt. The General asked me if I was in charge of the guard, and on my saying 'Yes,' he continued :

' Very good. You will see that this man is put to death with the bayonet. I have just caught him with a torch setting fire to the palace where I am staying.'

I told off four men, therefore, to carry out the General's orders. But French soldiers are not made for this kind of work—in cold blood. Our blows did not pierce through his sheepskin, and we should have spared his life on account of his youth (moreover, he had not the appearance of a criminal), but that the General remained looking on till he saw the poor wretch fall from a shot in the side. We left him lying where he was.

Soon after another man came, an inhabitant of the place, but a Frenchman and Parisian by origin. He said he was proprietor of the baths, and asked me for a safe-conduct, as they were setting fire to his establishment. I gave him four men, who came back almost directly, however, saying that the place was in flames already.

A few hours after our dreadful execution, the men came to tell me that a woman walking through the Place had thrown herself on the unfortunate young man's body. I

* I learned since that it was General Pernetty, commander of the gunners of the Imperial Guard.—*Author's Note.*

went to see her, and she tried to make us understand that it was her husband, or at any rate a relation. She was sitting on the ground, holding the dead man's head on her lap, stroking his face, and from time to time kissing him, but without shedding a tear. At last, not able to bear such a heart-rending scene, I brought her into the guard-room and gave her a glass of liqueur, which she eagerly drank, then a second, and a third, in fact, as much as she could drink. She gave us to understand that she would stay for three days where she was, waiting for the dead man to come to life again, believing, like all the Russian peasants, that the dead revive in three days. She fell asleep at last on the sofa.

At five o'clock our company came back, and was again put on picket duty, so I was there for another twenty-four hours. The rest of the regiment was busy trying to extinguish the fire round the Kremlin; they were successful for the time, but the fire broke out again afterwards more fiercely than ever.

After the company had returned, the Captain sent patrols in different directions. One was sent to the baths, but came back directly, telling us that the moment they arrived the whole place fell in with a terrible noise, and that the sparks, carried far by a west wind, had caused fires in many places.

During all that evening and for part of the night, our patrols were bringing in Russian soldiers from all quarters of the town, driven out by the fire from the houses where they were hidden. Amongst them were two officers—one of the regular army, the other of the militia; the first allowed himself to be disarmed of his sword, only asking that he might keep a gold medal hanging at his side; but the other, a young man, having a cartridge-belt besides a sword, objected to my taking them, and, speaking in

25

French, told us he was in the militia. However, after he had given us his reasons, we made ours pretty clear to him.

At midnight the fire broke out again near the Kremlin; there were fresh efforts made to extinguish it. But on the 16th, at three o'clock in the morning, it recommenced more violently than ever; this time it spread.

During the night of the 15th and 16th, I and two of my friends, non-commissioned officers like myself, decided to explore the city and the Kremlin we had heard so much of—so we set out. There was no need of a torch to light us; but, as we intended to pay visits to the houses and cellars of the Muscovite gentlemen, we each took a man with us armed with candles.

My comrades knew their way a little, but as at every instant fresh houses fell in, the streets lost their character, and we were soon hopelessly lost. After walking aimlessly for some time, we fortunately met a Jew tearing his beard and hair at seeing the synagogue of which he was rabbi burning away. As he spoke German, he told us his troubles, saying that he and others of his religion had put everything valuable they possessed into the synagogue for safety, but that now all was lost. We tried to comfort this child of Israel, took him by the arm, and asked him to lead us to the Kremlin. I can hardly help laughing now when I remember that, in the midst of such a disaster, the Jew asked us if we had anything to sell or exchange. I really think he asked the question from force of habit, as just then no trading was possible.

After going through several districts of the town, the greater part of them on fire, and admiring the fine streets still standing, we reached a little open place on a slight hill not far from the Moskowa. Here the Jew pointed out to us the towers of the Kremlin, as clear as day by the light of the fires. We stayed here to visit a cellar which some Lancers of the Guard were just leaving. We took some wine and sugar and a quantity of preserved fruits, and gave them all to the Jew to carry, under our protection. It was daylight when we reached the first enclosure of the Kremlin. We passed under a door built of gray stone, surmounted by a belfry and a bell in honour of St. Nicholas, whose statue stood in a niche over the door. This saint, at least six feet high, richly dressed, was worshipped by every Russian who passed by, even the convicts. He is the patron saint of Russia.

When we had passed through the first enclosure we turned to the right, and after crossing a street with much difficulty, on account of the disorder caused by a fire which had just burst out in some houses where the *cantinières* of the Guard were lodged, we reached a high wall topped by great towers with golden eagles on them. Passing through a large gateway, we found ourselves in a courtyard and opposite the palace. The Emperor had been there since the day before; the 14th and 15th he had slept in the suburbs.

As soon as we arrived we found some friends in the 1st Chasseurs picketing there, who invited us to breakfast. We ate some good meat, a treat we had not enjoyed for a long time, and we had also some excellent wine to drink. The Jew, who was still with us, was forced to eat with us, in spite of his repugnance to the ham. I ought to say, however, that the Chasseurs, who had some silver bullion taken from the Mint, had promised to do business with him. The ingots were of the size and shape of a brick. It was getting on to mid-day while we sat at breakfast with our friends, our backs against the enormous guns which guard each side of the arsenal, when we heard the cry ' Tò arms !' The fire had attacked the Kremlin, and

firebrands began to fall into the courtyard where the
Artillery of the Guard were stationed with all their *caissons*.
There was besides a great quantity of tow, left by the
Russians, part of which was already in flames. The fear
of an explosion disordered everything, and the confusion
was increased by the presence of the Emperor, who was
obliged to leave the Kremlin.

We parted from our friends while this was going on,
and set out to rejoin the regiment. We had explained to
our guide where it was, and he tried to take us there by a
short-cut which we found to be impossible, as the flames
drove us back. We had to wait till the passage was free,
for now the fire had spread all round the Kremlin, and the
violence of the wind blew bits of red-hot wood against our
legs, forcing us to shelter in a cellar where several men
had taken refuge already. We stayed there for some time,
and when we came out, we met the Guards going to the
Peterskoë Palace, whither the Emperor had now to betake
himself. Only the first battalion of the 2nd Chasseurs
remained at the Kremlin. It kept back the fire from the
palace, for the Emperor returned there on the 18th. I
forgot to say that the Prince of Neufchâtel, wishing to see
the extent of the fire round the Kremlin, had mounted
with an officer on one of the battlements of the palace,
and had been nearly blown over by the fearful wind.

The fire and the wind continued to rage, but there was
now a free passage by which the Emperor had just gone
out. We followed it, and found ourselves almost directly
on the banks of the Moskowa. We walked along the
quay, following it till we found a street free from flames,
or one altogether burnt out. By the road the Emperor
had taken, several houses had fallen in ruins, and passage
that way was impossible. We found ourselves at last in a district all burnt to

cinders, and the Jew tried with much difficulty to find a street leading to the Place du Gouvernement. As we walked, the wind blew hot ashes into our eyes, so that we could not see. We plunged through the streets with no worse mishap than getting our feet scorched, for we had to walk over the iron sheeting from the roofs and on the burning cinders which covered the streets.

We had already gone a long distance, when suddenly we found a clear empty space to our right. This was the Jews' quarter; the houses, being all of wood, had been burnt to the ground. On seeing this, our guide uttered a cry of despair, and fell down unconscious. We hastened to take off the burdens he carried, and, unpacking a bottle of liqueur, we made him swallow a few drops, then poured a little over his face. He soon opened his eyes, and when we asked him why he had fainted, he told us that his house had been burnt, and that probably his family had perished. On saying this, he again fell unconscious, so that we were obliged to leave him in spite of not knowing which way to turn without a guide. In such a labyrinth we had to make a decision, however, and we gave the package to one of the men to carry, and continued our way, but we were stopped directly by obstacles across our road.

The distance round to the next street was about 300 yards, but we dared not traverse it on account of the blinding hot ashes. While we were deciding what to do, one of my friends proposed making an excursion to reconnoitre. I advised him to wait, and the others agreed with me, when, seeing our irresolution, he cried, 'Who loves me follows me!' and set off. The other followed with two of our men, and I remained with the man bearing the package, which consisted of three bottles of wine, five of liqueurs, and some preserved fruits.

They had hardly gone thirty yards, however, when the leader disappeared; he fell all his length, and the second picked him up. The two last had to cover their faces with their hands, nearly blinded by the ashes like the first, who could not see at all, enveloped as they were by a whirling cloud of this dust. The first one, not being able to see, cried and swore like the devil. The others were obliged to leave him, as they could not bring him back to where I was. I was afraid to join them, the path becoming more and more dangerous. We had to wait for an hour before I could get to them, and we provisionally emptied one of the bottles.

When at last we were reunited, we saw the impossibility of advancing without danger. We decided to retrace our steps, and the idea struck us of each taking a sheet of iron to cover our heads, holding it to the windy and dusty side. After bending the iron into the shape of shields, we set out, one of the men in front; then I came leading the half-blinded man by the hand, the others following. We succeeded after an infinite deal of trouble, stumbling time after time.

We now found ourselves in a new street, where several Jewish families and some Chinese were huddled up in corners, keeping guard over the few possessions they had saved or had taken from others. They seemed surprised to see us; they had, perhaps, not seen any other Frenchmen in that quarter. We went up to a Jew, and made him understand that he was to lead us to the Place du Gouvernement. A father came with his son, and as the streets were blocked by ruined houses, or by others in flames, it was only after many windings and great difficulties, and many halts for rest, that at eleven o'clock at night we at last reached the place we had left the evening before. I had had no rest since we came to Moscow, so I lay down on some beautiful furs our soldiers had taken, and slept till seven the next morning.

The company was not yet off duty, as for thirty-six hours all the regiments, the Fusiliers, and even the Young Guard, had been occupied in suppressing the fire under the direction of Marshal Mortier, who had been appointed Governor of the town. As soon as it was extinguished on one side it broke out again on another. However, sufficient houses were preserved for lodgings, but with infinite difficulty, as Rostopchin had removed all the hand-pumps. A few were found, but they were quite useless.

During the 16th orders had been given to shoot everyone found setting fire to houses. This order was executed at once. A little open space near the Place du Gouvernement was called by us the Place des Pendus, as here a number of incendiaries were shot and hung on the trees.

The Emperor, on the day of our entry, had commanded, through Marshal Mortier, that no pillage was to be allowed. The order had been given in every regiment; but as soon as it was known that the Russians themselves had fired the town, it was impossible to restrain the men. Everyone took what he needed, and even things that were not needed. On the night of the 17th the Captain allowed me to take ten men on special duty and hunt for provisions. He sent twenty in a different direction, as pillage* was to be allowed, but enjoining as much order as possible. So I set out on my third night's expedition. We crossed a wide street leading from our Place, which had been preserved from the fire, and here many superior officers and a large number of army employés had quartered themselves. We walked through several other streets, where nothing was left but piles of sheet-iron off the roofs;

* Our soldiers called the pillage of the town the *foire de Moscou.*— *Author's Note.*

the wind of the day before had swept them clean of cinders.

The quarter of the town we reached was still standing, but we saw nothing except a few hackney coaches without horses. Absolute silence reigned. We looked at the carriages, and found nothing; but we had hardly got away, when we heard a ferocious cry behind us. This was twice repeated, and in two different directions. We listened for some time, and heard nothing more; so we decided to enter two of the houses—I into the first with five men, and a corporal into another with five others. We lighted the lanterns we had with us, and, sword in hand, we made ready to force our way wherever we could find what we wanted.

The house I tried was shut up, and the door fastened by large plates of iron. This was annoying, as we wanted to effect our entrance quietly; but, noticing that the cellar door was open, two of our men went down, and there they discovered a trap-door communicating with the house, and in this way they opened the door for us. When we had entered, we saw that we were in a grocer's shop. Everything was left in order, except in a dining-room, where some cooked meat was left on the table, and several bags of small change on a chest.

After exploring the house, we collected provisions. We found flour, butter, quantities of sugar and coffee, and a large barrel full of eggs arranged in layers and packed in hay. We made our choice without disputing about price, for we considered we might as well help ourselves, as the house had been deserted, and at any moment it might take fire. While we were engaged this way, the corporal sent to tell me that the house he had entered belonged to a coach-builder, and contained more than thirty of the pretty little carriages the Russians call *drouschkys;* and that he had found a lot of Russian soldiers lying on rush beds, who, seeing the Frenchmen, had fallen on their knees, their hands crossed on their breasts, their foreheads to the ground, imploring mercy. Seeing, however, that they were wounded, the corporal tried to relieve them, as they were in no state to help themselves, nor could they hurt us.

I went immediately to the coach-builder's, and chose two pretty convenient little carriages to transport all our provisions.

I also saw the wounded men; five of them were gunners with broken legs. There were seventeen altogether amongst them, some Asiatics, recognisable by their manner of saluting.

As I was going out with my carriages, I caught sight of three men, one of whom had a lance, the second a sword, and the third a lighted torch, setting the grocer's house on fire. The men I had left there were so busy choosing and packing up all the good things that they were quite unaware of what was going on. We shouted out to frighten the rascals, but they never budged, and looked quietly at us. The man with the lance even put himself in a position of defence, should we attack them. This was difficult, as we had no swords. The corporal came up, however, with two loaded pistols taken from the room where he found the wounded men; he gave one to me, and made as if to fire with the other at the man with the lance. I prevented him at the moment, fearing that the noise might bring out · a greater number upon us.

On seeing this, one of our men, a Breton, seized the pole of one of the little carriages, and, using it as a quarter-staff, attacked the man, who was not used to this sort of fighting, and broke both his legs. He uttered a terrible cry as he fell; but the Breton, in his rage, gave him no time to cry again, and struck him a violent blow on the head. No cannon-ball could have done the work better. He would have served the two others in the same way, had not we prevented him. The fellow with the lighted torch ran into the grocer's house with two of our men after him, and only after two blows with the sword would he listen to reason. He then submitted with a good grace, and was harnessed to one of the carriages, together with a man just seized in the street.

We now got ready for our departure. Our two carriages were packed with everything in the shop—on the first, drawn by the two Russians, we had placed the barrel of eggs, and had taken the precaution to tie the men round the middle by a stout rope with a double knot ; the second carriage was drawn by four of our own men, until we could find a team like the first.

But just as we were setting off, we saw fire coming from the coachmaker's house. We could not leave the wounded men to perish in agony, so we carried them into a stable separated from the house. That was all we could do, and, after performing this action of common humanity, we departed as quickly as possible to get out of reach of the flames, which were bursting out in several directions. Hardly, however, had we gone twenty-five yards, when we heard the poor wounded wretches shrieking frightfully. We stopped again, and the corporal went back with four men to find out the cause. The fire had caught some straw in the yard, and was fast gaining on their place of shelter.

The corporal and his men did all in their power to save them, and then rejoined us ; but it is more than probable that the wounded men perished.

We went on our way, and for fear of being overtaken by the fire we forced our first team to trot, urging them on by blows from our swords. However, there were no means of avoiding the fire, for when we got near the Place du Gouvernement we saw that the principal street where many of our superior officers were quartered was in flames. This was the third time it had been set on fire, but it was also the last.

We now saw that the fire was only burning here and there, and that by running one could get through the clear spaces. When we reached the first of the burning houses we stopped, considering whether it was possible to get across them. Several had fallen already, and those nearest to us threatened to crush us under the flames. However, we could not remain where we were, for we saw that the houses behind us had also caught fire.

Thus, not only were the flames in front of and behind us, but also on each side, and we were compelled to pass through a great vault of fire. We sent the carriage on first, but the Russians objected to be in front, in spite of several blows from the flat of our swords. Our own men, therefore, went first, and, encouraging each other, got over the worst place triumphantly. We therefore redoubled our blows on the Russians, who, fearing there was worse to follow, rushed forward crying 'Houra!'* in great danger from the different articles of furniture which continually fell into the street. As soon as the last carriage had got over, we followed them, running, and found ourselves in a place where four streets met, all on fire, and although the rain was now pouring down, the fire still raged, and at every moment houses, and even entire streets, disappeared in the smoke and ruins.

It was necessary to rejoin the rest of the regiment as quickly as possible, but we saw how impracticable this was, and that we should have to wait till the whole street was reduced to ashes. So we decided to turn back, and

* _Houra !_ means 'En avant !'— _Author's Note._

immediately acted on this. The Russians this time went first without hesitation, but just as they had traversed the dangerous passage, and we were about to follow, we heard a terrible noise—the rending of beams, and the fall of burning wood and iron roofs crashing on to our carriage. Instantly everything was annihilated, even the Russians. We did not much regret them, but the loss of our provisions distressed us very much, especially the eggs. Our situation was now dreadful; we were blocked in by the fire without any means of retreat. Happily for us, just where the four streets met, there was a place where we could shelter from the flames, and wait until the entire demolition of a street should afford us a passage. While sheltering thus, we noticed that one of the houses was an Italian confectioner's shop, and although it was on the point of burning, we thought we had better try to save a few good things if we could. The door was locked, but a window was open on the first floor, and chance provided us with a ladder, which, placed on a barrel found against the house, was long enough for the men to reach the window.

Although part of the house was already on fire, nothing stopped them. They opened the door to us, and we discovered, greatly to our satisfaction and delight, that everything was left in the house. We found all kinds of preserved fruits and liqueurs and a quantity of sugar, but what astonished us most of all was the finding of three large sacks of flour. Our surprise was greater still on seeing some pots of mustard from the street of St. André des Arts, Paris.

We hastily emptied the shop, and made a store of everything in the middle of the street we occupied, until we could transport it all to our company. As the rain still poured down, we made a shelter with the doors of the houses, and bivouacking there, we stayed for more than four hours, waiting for an opening through the fire.

To pass the time we made jam-fritters, and when we departed we took away all we could possibly carry. The remaining carriage and our sacks of flour we left under the care of five men, meaning to come back with others to fetch them. It was quite impossible to make use of the carriage, as the middle of the street was filled up with a quantity of furniture, broken and half burnt up, pianos, glass chandeliers, and an infinity of other very expensive things.

At last, after crossing the Place des Pendus, we reached the rest of the company at ten in the morning; we had parted from them at ten the preceding evening. We lost no time in sending back for what we had left behind, and ten men set out at once. They returned an hour afterwards, each carrying something, and, in spite of difficulties, bringing the carriage also. They told us they had been obliged to clear out the place where the Russians had been crushed, and that they had found the bodies quite burnt and withered up.

On the same day (the 18th) we were taken off duty, and we took possession of our quarters in a fine street hitherto preserved from fire, not far from the first enclosure of the Kremlin. Our company had a large café assigned to it; one of the rooms contained two billiard-tables. The non-commissioned officers were quartered in a boyar's house, which occupied the first floor. Our men took the billiard-tables to pieces to make room, and some of them made capes for themselves of the cloth.

We found a great quantity of wine in the cellars, and some Jamaica rum, also a large cellar filled with barrels of excellent beer, packed in ice to keep it fresh during the summer. We found at our boyar's house fifteen large cases of wine and sparkling champagne. The same day our men discovered a large sugar store, of which we took a quantity to make punch with. This lasted all the time we were at Moscow, and we never missed a day without drinking some. Every evening we made enough for three or four times, in a large silver bowl which the Russian boyar had forgotten to take away. This bowl held six bottles at the least. Add to all this a fine collection of pipes and some excellent tobacco.

On the 19th the Emperor inspected us at the Kremlin opposite the palace, and on the same day I had orders to join a detachment of Fusilier-Chasseurs and Grenadiers and a squadron of Polish Lancers—200 men in all. Our object was to keep the Empress's summer palace, at the farther end of Moscow, free from fire. This detachment was commanded by a General whom I took to be General Kellerman.

We left at eight in the evening, and it was half-past nine before we arrived at a spacious building looking about the size of the Tuileries, built of wood, and covered with stucco to represent marble. Guards were immediately posted outside, and patrols were sent out for greater safety. I was sent with several men to inspect the interior, to see if anyone were hidden there.

I was fortunate in having this opportunity of seeing this immense building, furnished with all the combined splendour and brilliance of Europe and Asia. It seemed as if everything had been lavished on its decoration, and yet within an hour it was entirely consumed. A quarter of an hour after we had used all the precautions possible against fire, it broke out behind us, in front of us, to right, to left, and we were unable to see who set it going. There it was in a dozen places at once, and flaring from every attic window.

38

The General immediately called for the sappers to try to cut the fire off, but it was impossible. We had no pumps, and not even any water. Directly afterwards we saw several men, some of them with torches still burning, come out from under the great staircase, by some subterranean way, and try to go quietly off. We ran after them and stopped them ; there were twenty-one of them, and eleven others were arrested on the other side. These were not seen coming out of the palace, and nothing about them showed that they were incendiaries. More than half of them, however, were evidently convicts.

The utmost we could do was to save some pictures and a few other valuables, amongst which were Imperial ornaments, velvet mantles lined with ermine, besides many other precious things which we afterwards had to leave behind. About half an hour after the fire broke out, a furious wind got up, and in less than ten minutes we were hemmed in by the fire, and could neither advance nor retreat. Several men were hurt by falling pieces of burning timber. It was two o'clock in the morning before we could get out of this hell, and we then found that the fire had spread for more than half a league all round—for the whole of this quarter was built of wood, and was very beautiful.

We set out again to return towards the Kremlin, taking with us our prisoners, thirty-two in number. I was put in command of the rear-guard, and the escort of the prisoners, with orders to bayonet those who tried to run away or refused to follow.

Two-thirds of these wretches were convicts, with sinister faces ; the others were middle-class citizens and Russian police, recognised by their uniform.

As we went along, I noticed amongst the prisoners one who was muffled up in a fairly clean green cloak, crying like a child, and saying repeatedly in good French:

'Mon Dieu! I have lost my wife and my son in the fire!'

He seemed very unhappy, so I asked him who he was. He told me that he was Swiss, and came from near Zurich, and that for seventeen years he had been at Moscow teaching German and French. He then began again to cry out in despair, always repeating:

'My dear son! my poor son!'

I was very sorry for the poor fellow. I tried to comfort him, telling him that very likely he would find them; and, as I knew that he would be condemned to die with the others, I determined to save him. Two men walked near him arm-in-arm, one young, and the other middle-aged. I asked the Swiss who they were; he told me they were tailors, a father and son.

'But,' he said, 'the father is happier than I; he is not separated from his son, and they can die together.'

He knew the fate that awaited him; he had heard the order given in French. While he was speaking to me, he stopped suddenly, and gazed wildly in front of him. I asked him what was the matter, but he did not answer. Soon afterwards he sighed heavily and began to weep again, saying that he was looking for the place where his house had stood, and that it must be there, as he recognised the large stove still standing. I must here say that we could see as plainly as in broad daylight, not only the town itself, but far beyond.

Just then the head of the column, which was detached from the Polish Lancers, stopped still, not knowing where to turn, as the narrow street was completely blocked up. I took advantage of this delay to let the unhappy man satisfy himself whether the bodies of his wife and son

were among the ashes of his house, and I offered to
accompany him. We went to the site of the house, and
at first saw nothing to confirm his suspicions. I was
beginning to comfort him, saying that no doubt they were
saved, when, at the entrance to the cellar, I saw something blackened and without form, all twisted up. I
examined it, and found it to be a dead body, but whether
man or woman it was impossible to see. I had hardly
time, either, for the Swiss, who had come up behind me,
uttered a frightful cry and fell to the ground. I raised
him with the help of a man who stood near, but when he
came to himself, he rushed in despair all over the ruins of
his house, and with another terrible cry he called for his
son, and flung himself into the cellar, where I heard him
fall heavily like an inert mass.

I did not wish to follow him; I hastened to rejoin the
detachment, reflecting sadly on what I had just seen.
One of my friends asked me what I had done with the
man who spoke French, and I told him of the tragic
scene I had just witnessed. As we were still halted, I
asked him to come and see the place. We went to the
cellar door, and heard groaning. My comrade proposed
to go down and help him, but, knowing that to save him
from the cellar was to lead him to certain death, as all
the prisoners were to be shot, I said that it would be
very foolhardy to descend into such a place without a
light.

Luckily the order 'To arms!' was given at that
moment. We waited while the left column started, and
as we were preparing to follow, we heard steps behind us.
I turned round, and was astounded to see the poor Swiss,
looking like a ghost, and with his arms laden with furs to
cover the bodies of his wife and son. He had found his
son dead in the cellar, but not burnt; the body at the

door was his wife's. I advised him to return to the cellar, and hide himself till we had left, when he could perform his painful duty. I do not know if he understood me, but we left him.

We reached the Kremlin at five o'clock in the morning, and put the prisoners in a place of safety; but I took the precaution to keep back the two tailors, father and son, on my own account. As will be seen, they were very useful to us during our stay in Moscow.

On the 20th the fire had slackened a little. The Governor of the town, Marshal Mortier, and General Milhaud, who was appointed Commandant of the Place, were both very active in organizing a body of police. This was formed from the Italians, Germans, and Frenchmen living in Moscow who had escaped Rostopchin's rigorous orders to leave the city by hiding themselves.

While I was looking out of the window of our quarters at mid-day, I saw the shooting of a convict. He refused to kneel down, but met his death bravely, and, striking his breast, he seemed to defy his executioners. A few hours afterwards our prisoners met with the same fate.

I spent the day quietly enough, but at seven o'clock the Adjutant-Major, Delaitre, ordered me to surrender myself at a place he named to me for having allowed three prisoners entrusted to me to escape. I made what excuses I could, and went to the place indicated; other non-commissioned officers were there already. I reflected that my conscience was quite clear for having saved the lives of these men, convinced as I was of their innocence.

The room I was in opened on to a long, narrow gallery connecting the house with another wing of the building.

A part of this wing had been burnt, so that no one inhabited it, and I noticed that the portion still standing
had not been examined.   I was naturally curious to see it,
and having nothing to do, I went to the end of the gallery.
I fancied I heard a noise coming from a room with a
closed door.   I listened, and thought I distinguished the
words of a language I did not understand.   I knocked at
the door, but no one answered, and profound silence
followed.   I then looked through the keyhole, and saw a
man lying on a sofa, and two women standing, who
appeared to be keeping him from talking.   I knew a few
words of Polish, which is much like Russian, so I knocked
again, and begged for some water.   No answer came; but
at my second request, which I made more forcible by a
kick on the door, they came and opened it.   When I
entered the room, the two women rushed out into another.
I closed the door, but the man on the sofa never moved.
At once I recognised him for a criminal of the lowest
type, dirty all over from his beard to his boots.   His
clothes consisted of a sheepskin cloak and a leather belt;
near him were a lance and two torches, besides two pistols
at his belt.   These last I took from him, and seizing one
of the torches, I hit him on the side with it, and made him
open his eyes.   On seeing me, he jumped up as if to spring
upon me, but fell flat down again.   I aimed one of his
pistols at him, but he only gazed at me stupidly, and,
trying to rise, fell again.   After some time, he at last
succeeded in keeping on his feet.   Seeing how drunk he
was, I took hold of his arm, and leading him from the
room, I took him to the end of the gallery.   When we
reached the top of the staircase, which descended straight
down like a ladder, I gave him a push; he rolled down
like a barrel, and fell almost against the guard-room door
opposite the stairs.   The men dragged him to a room

where they locked up all of his description, and I did not hear him speak again.

This expedition over, I returned to the room where I had found the man, and shut myself in. I looked well round to see that there was no one about, then opened the second door, and saw the two Dulcineas sitting on a sofa. They did not seem surprised to see me, but both started talking at once, I not understanding a word. I tried to ask them if they had anything to eat; they understood me perfectly, and gave me cucumber, onions, a large piece of salt fish, and a little beer, but no bread. Afterwards the younger of the two brought me a bottle of something she called *kosalki;* when I tasted it, I knew it was Dantzig gin. In less than half an hour we had emptied the bottle, my two Muscovites doing more service than I.

I stayed for some time with these two sisters, and then I returned to my room. I found there a non-commissioned officer of my company, who had been waiting for me a long time. When I related my adventures, he seemed delighted, as he could find no one to wash clothes. He seemed to think the two Muscovite ladies would be only too much honoured by being asked to wash and mend for French soldiers. We waited till ten o'clock, when everyone was asleep, as we wished to keep our secret; then the non-commissioned officer returned with the sergeant-major, and we went to look for our beauties. They made a lot of difficulties at first, not quite knowing where we were taking them, but making me understand I was to go with them. I went as far as our quarters, where they followed us willingly, laughing as they went. We found a small room at liberty, which we made over to them, furnishing it with whatever we could find — all kinds of pretty things which the noble Muscovite ladies had not been able to carry away. Although our friends had had

the appearance of common servants, they were thus trans-
formed into elegant ladies—ladies, however, who had to
wash and mend for us.

On the next morning, the 21st, I heard a loud report of
firearms, and was told that several convicts and members
of the police force had just been shot; they had been
caught setting fire to the Foundling Hospital, and to the
hospital containing our wounded men. The sergeant-
major came to tell me directly afterwards that I was free.

When I got back to our quarters, I saw that the two
tailors I had saved were already at work making some
capes out of the cloth off the billiard-tables we had taken
to pieces. I went into the room where we had left our
women, and found them at the wash-tub, and making
but poor work of it. This was very natural, however, as
they were wearing some silk dresses belonging to a
Baroness. But for want of anything better one had to
put up with it. During the remainder of the day I was
busy arranging our quarters and getting in provisions, as
we were apparently to stay here for some time. To last
for the winter we had seven large cases of sweet champagne,
a large quantity of port wine, five hundred bottles of
Jamaica rum, and more than a hundred great packets of
sugar. And all this was for six non-commissioned officers,
two women, and a cook.

Meat was difficult to get, but on this evening we had a
cow. I don't know where she came from, but probably
from some forbidden place; so we had to kill her at night
to escape observation. We had a large number of hams,
having found a shop full of them; add to all this a quantity
of salt fish, a few sacks of flour, two large barrels filled
with suet, which we had taken for butter, and as much
beer as we wanted. These constituted our provisions, in
case we had to spend the winter in Moscow. In the

evening orders were given for a roll-call at ten o'clock; eighteen men were missing. The remainder of the company slept luxuriously in the billiard-room, lying on rich furs, sable, lion, fox and bear's skins; many of them had their heads wrapped up turban-fashion in fine cashmeres, looking, in fact, like Sultans instead of Grenadier Guards; only the houris were wanting to complete the picture.

I prolonged my roll-call to eleven o'clock, so that I should not have to report the absent men, and they returned soon afterwards bending beneath their burdens. Amongst other valuable things they brought were several silver plaques in relief; also each had a silver ingot, the size and form of a brick. For the rest there were furs, Indian shawls, silk stuffs brocaded in silver and gold. They asked for leave to make two other journeys to fetch some wine and preserved fruits left behind in a cellar. I gave them permission, and a corporal went with them. We non-commissioned officers had a right to 20 per cent. of all the things saved from the fire.

On the 22nd we rested, added to our stock of provisions, sang, smoked, laughed and drank, and amused ourselves. I paid a visit the same day to an Italian print-seller, whose house had escaped the fire. On the morning of the 23rd a convict was shot in the courtyard. That same day we had orders to be ready the next morning for inspection by the Emperor. At eight o'clock on the morning of the 24th we set out for the Kremlin. Many other regiments were collected there for the same reason, and that day many medals were given and many promotions made. Those who were rewarded deserved well of their country, having shed their blood many times on the field of battle.

I took advantage of this occasion to look at all the wonderful things in the Kremlin, and while several other regiments were being inspected, I went to see the Church of St. Michael, the tomb of the Russian Emperors. Some soldiers of the Guard (the 1st Chasseurs) picketed at the Kremlin had come here the first day of our arrival, hoping to find the treasure said to be concealed. They searched through the enormous crypt, but found instead of treasures nothing but tombs in stone, covered over with velvet, having inscriptions on silver plates. They found also several people from the town who had fled there for refuge, thinking that the presence of the dead would protect them. Amongst them was a pretty young woman, said to belong to one of the best Moscow families, who had foolishly become infatuated with one of the superior officers. She behaved more foolishly still by following him in the retreat. Like so many others, she died of cold, hunger, and want.

After the crypt of St. Michael, I went to see the famous bell. It is nineteen feet high, and a great part of it is embedded in the earth, probably by its own weight, as it has lain on the ground ever since the fire burned down the tower in which it hung. Near it, and opposite to the palace, is the arsenal, with an enormous cannon on each side of the door. On the right, farther off, is the cathedral, its nine bell-towers covered with gilded copper. The cross of Ivan the Great is on the highest tower, and dominates them all. It is made of wood, thirty feet high, covered with silver-gilt plates, and is held in its place by gilded chains.

Some days after this, the men on extra duty, carpenters and others, were ordered to take down this cross, to be conveyed as a trophy to Paris; but, on their attempting to remove it, it fell by its great weight, nearly killing the men, who were dragged down by the chains they held. The same thing happened with the great eagles on the towers round the Kremlin walls.

It was mid-day by the time we had been inspected. We went out by the arched gateway containing the great

St. Nicholas. Several Russian slaves were praying there, bowing and crossing themselves before the saint ; they were no doubt making intercession against us.

On the 25th I and several friends explored the ruins of the town. We saw much that we had not seen before. Everywhere we met Russian peasants—women dirty and repulsive, some of them Jews, mixing helter-skelter with soldiers, and searching in cellars for things which might have escaped the fire. Besides wine and sugar, they were loaded with shawls, cashmeres, magnificent Siberian furs, stuffs brocaded with silk, gold and silver, and several with silver plate and other precious objects. There were Jews there, too, with their wives and daughters, making all kinds of offers to our men for the possession of our things.

On the evening of the same day a Greek church opposite to us was set on fire, close to the place where Marshal Mortier was quartered. We could not extinguish the fire, in spite of all our efforts, and this church, which was in beautiful preservation, was reduced in an incredibly short time to ashes. Many unfortunate people had taken refuge there with the few things remaining to them. This made the circumstance much worse.

On the 26th I was on guard over the Emperor's carriages in a coach-house at the farther end of the town. Opposite were some large barracks saved from the fire, where part of our army was quartered. To get there I had to traverse more than a league of ruins on the left bank of the Moskowa, only seeing here and there a few rafters of the churches left. Everything else was reduced to ashes. On the right bank a few pretty country-houses were still left, only partially burnt. Close to where I placed my guard there was a house which had quite escaped the flames, and out of curiosity I went to see it. I met by chance there a man who spoke French very well, who told me he came from Strasbourg, and had been led by fate to Moscow only a few days before us. He also said that he was a wine-merchant dealing in Rhine wines and sweet champagne, and that by strokes of bad luck he had lost more than a million—partly on account of wine destroyed in shops by the fire, and partly by all we had drunk and were still drinking. He had not even a piece of bread to eat, so I asked him to come and share my rice soup ; he accepted gratefully.

The Emperor issued orders for a thorough organization in Moscow, in preparation for remaining there for the winter while waiting for peace. The first steps taken were for hospitals for the wounded, the Russians being treated like ourselves. The stores of provisions scattered through the town were concentrated as much as possible. Several churches which had escaped the fire were re-opened for worship. Near our quarters was a Catholic church, where an emigrant French priest said Mass. A theatre was even opened, where French and Italian actors played comedies—at least, so I was told ; but whether this was true or not, I know they were paid in advance for six months, in order to convince the Russians that we were going to remain for the winter.

On the 27th I was agreeably surprised to meet two of my fellow-townsmen coming to see me. These were Flament, from Peruwelz, vélite in the Dragoon Guards, and Mellé, a dragoon from the same regiment, from Condé. They were very welcome, for that day we felt merry, so we invited them to dine and spend the evening with us. In the men's various foraging expeditions, they found a quantity of men's and women's costumes of all nations, even French dresses of the time of Louis XVI., all of most beautiful materials. So this evening, after dinner, we decided to have a ball and wear all these dresses.

But I must not forget to say that Flament had told

us a sad piece of news — the loss of the brave
Lieutenant-Colonel Martod, who commanded the regiment. On reconnoitring in the outskirts of Moscow two
days before the 25th, they had fallen into an ambus-
cade, and were attacked by 3,000 men, both cavalry
and infantry. Colonel Martod was mortally wounded; a
Captain and the Adjutant-Major were made prisoners
after fighting desperately. Two days after we heard that
the Colonel was dead.

Now I must return to our ball—a real carnival, as we
were all disguised. First of all we dressed up the Russian
women as French Marquises; as they knew nothing of
the business, Flament and I superintended their toilette.
Our two Russian tailors were dressed as Chinese, I as a
Russian boyar, Flament as a Marquis—each of us in
different costume, even our *cantinière*, Mother Dubois,
who wore a beautiful Russian national dress. As we had
no wigs for our Marquises, the regimental perruquier
dressed their hair. For grease he used suet, and flour for
powder. They looked splendid, and when everyone was
ready we began to dance. I forgot to say that during all
this time we drank a great deal of punch dealt out to us by
Mellé, the old dragoon. Our Marquises and the *cantinière*,
although they could stand a good deal, were beginning to
feel their heads swim in consequence of the large quantity
they had swallowed.

For music, we had a flute played by a sergeant-major,
accompanied by the drum to keep time. We began with
the air :

> ' On va leur percer les flancs
> Ram, ram, ram, tam plan ;
> Tire-lire, ram plan.'

Just as the music struck up, however, and Mother
Dubois advanced with our Quarter-master, our Marquises,

excited no doubt by the music, began to jump like Tartars, flying from right to left, swinging their arms and legs, falling backwards, getting up, only to fall again. They seemed to be possessed by the devil. There would have been nothing so very extraordinary had they worn their Russian clothes, but to see two French Marquises jump about like lunatics made us nearly die with laughing, and the flute-player was obliged to stop playing, the drum filling up the pauses by sounding the attack. The Marquises began again with redoubled energy, until, exhausted, they sank on the floor. We lifted them up and applauded them, and then we went on drinking and dancing until four o'clock in the morning.

Mother Dubois, true to her trade, and knowing the full value of the clothes she wore (silk brocade in gold and silver), went off without a word. As she left, however, the sergeant of the guard on police duty, seeing a strange lady in the street so early, and thinking he had found a prize, went to her, and tried to take her by the arm and lead her to his room. But Mother Dubois, who had a husband, and, moreover, had drunk a good deal of punch, dealt the sergeant such a vigorous blow on the face that she knocked him completely over. He shouted out, and, as we had not gone to bed yet, we ran down to help him. The sergeant was so furious that we had a great piece of work to din into his head that he must not arrest a woman like Mother Dubois.

The 28th and 29th we spent in looking after our provisions. We went out in reconnoitring-parties during the day, and at night we went back to take the things away.

On the 30th we were inspected in the street opposite our quarters ; when it was over it occurred to the Colonel to show the inspector how the troops were quartered. When the turn of our company came, the Colonel took the Captain and the sergeant of the week with him; and the Adjutant-Major, Roustan, who knew our quarters, walked in front and opened all the doors. After seeing nearly everything, the Colonel said:

' And what about the non-commissioned officers ?'

' Oh, they are very comfortable,' said the Adjutant-Major Roustan. And he began to open the doors of our rooms.*

But, unfortunately, we had not removed the key from the door of our Dulcineas' little room (which everyone had taken for a cupboard). This the Adjutant-Major opened, and, surprised at seeing a space within, he looked and saw our birds. He said nothing, locked the door, and put the key in his pocket. When he was in the street, he held up the key on seeing me, and coming up to me he laughed.

' Ah !' he said, ' you have some caged birds, and you keep them all to yourselves. What in the devil's name do you do with those queer customers, and where did you find them ? There are not many about.'

I told him then how I had found them, and how we kept them to wash our clothes.

' Well, then,' he said to the sergeant-major and me, ' you might lend them to me for a few days to wash my shirts, as they are horribly dirty. I hope you will be friendly, and not refuse me this.'

He took the women away the same evening, and no doubt they washed all the officers' shirts, as they did not come back for seven days.

A strong detachment of the regiment was sent on

* It is necessary here to say that we had opened a door of communication between our quarters and those of the company.— *Author's Note.*

52

October 1st to plunder a large country-house some leagues from Moscow. We found very little—only a cart loaded with hay. As we returned, we met some Russian cavalry, who began caracoling round us without meaning to attack us seriously. We marched, however, in such a way as to show them that the advantage would not be theirs, for, although far fewer in numbers than they were, we had disabled several of them. They followed us to within a quarter of a league of Moscow.

On the 2nd we heard that the Emperor had given orders to arm the Kremlin; thirty pieces of cannon and howitzers of various calibre were to be placed on all the towers round the outside wall. The men on extra duty of every regiment of the Guard were commanded on the 3rd to dig and carry away all the materials coming from the old walls round the Kremlin, which the sapper-engineers had demolished, and all foundations which had been undermined.

On the 4th I went in my turn with the extra-duty men of our company; the next day the Colonel of the Engineers was killed close to me, by a brick from a mine just exploded. On the same day I saw near a church several dead bodies with the legs or arms eaten away, probably by wolves or dogs.

On the days off duty we drank, smoked, and laughed, talking of France and the distance separating it from us, and the possibility of being sent still farther off. When evening came, we invited our Muscovite slaves to join us (or, rather, our two Marquises, as we called them since the night of the ball), and we sat drinking Jamaica rum-punch.

The remainder of our stay in the town was passed in reviews and parades, up to the day when a courier came to inform the Emperor, in the middle of a review, that the Russians had broken the armistice, and had taken Murat's cavalry by surprise. The order to leave was therefore given, and the whole army was in instant movement; but our regiment only knew in the evening that we had orders to leave the next day. We gave the Muscovite women and the two tailors their share of the booty which we could not carry away. They threw themselves on the ground to kiss our feet twenty times—never had they imagined such riches.

CHAPTER III.

DURING the evening of October 18th, when, according to
our daily custom, several non-commissioned officers were
assembled together, stretched at full length like pashas
on ermine, sable, lion and bear skins, smoking costly
tobacco in magnificent pipes, an enormous silver bowl
filled with punch before us, above which a huge loaf of
sugar was melting, held in its place by two Russian
bayonets—just as we were talking of France and of the
glory of returning there as conquerors after so long an absence, just as we were composing farewells and promises of
fidelity to our female Mongol, Chinese, and Indian friends—
we heard a tremendous noise in the large room where the
soldiers of our company slept.   And who should enter but
the Quarter-master with the announcement that we must
hold ourselves in readiness to leave. The next day (the 19th)
the town was filled with Jews and Russian peasants—the
first-named to buy of the soldiers what they could not
carry away, the last to pick up what we threw into the
streets. We heard that Marshal Mortier was to remain
at the Kremlin with 10,000 men to defend it if necessary.

We set out in the afternoon, packing some liquor from

our stores on Mother Dubois's cart, as well as our large silver bowl ; it was almost dark when we got outside the town. We found ourselves amongst a great number of carts and waggons, driven by men of every nationality, three or four in a line, and stretching for the length of a league. We heard all round us French, German, Spanish, Italian, Portuguese, and other languages also, for there were Muscovite peasants among them, and a great number of Jews. This crowd of people, with their varied costumes and languages, the canteen masters with their wives and crying children, hurried forward in the most unheard of noise, tumult and disorder. Some had got their carts all smashed, and in consequence yelled and swore enough to drive one mad. This was the convoy of the whole army, and we had a great deal of trouble in getting past it. We marched by the Kalonga road (we were then in Asia) ; soon we stopped to bivouac in a wood for the rest of the night. As the hour was already far advanced, we had not long to rest.

We resumed our march at dawn, but before we had gone a league we again met a large part of the fatal convoy, which had passed us while we were asleep. Most of the carts were already shattered, and others could not move, the wheels sinking deep in the sandy road. We could hear screams in French, oaths in German, entreaties to the Almighty in Italian, and to the Holy Virgin in Spanish and Portuguese.

After getting past this babel we were forced to wait for the left of the column. I spent the time in making an examination of my knapsack, which seemed too heavy. I found several pounds of sugar, some rice, some biscuit, half a bottle of liqueur, a woman's Chinese silk dress, embroidered in gold and silver, several gold and silver ornaments, amongst them a little bit of the cross of Ivan the Great*—at least, a piece of the outer covering of silver gilt, given me by a man in the company who had helped in taking it down. Besides these, I had my uniform, a woman's large riding-cloak (hazel colour, lined with green velvet ; as I could not guess how it was worn, I imagined its late owner to be more than six feet high) : then two silver pictures in relief, a foot long and eight inches high ; one of them represented the Judgment of Paris on Mount Ida, the other showed Neptune on a chariot formed by a shell and drawn by sea-horses, all in the finest workman-ship. I had, besides, several lockets and a Russian Prince's spittoon set with brilliants. These things were intended for presents, and had been found in cellars where the houses were burnt down.

No wonder the knapsack was so weighty ! to lighten it, therefore, I left out my white trousers, feeling pretty certain I should not want them again just yet. I wore over my shirt a yellow silk waistcoat, wadded inside, which I had made myself out of a woman's skirt ; above that a large cape lined with ermine, and a large pouch hung at my side, underneath the cape, by a silver cord. This was full of various things—amongst them, a crucifix in gold and silver, and a little Chinese porcelain vase. These objects seemed to have escaped the general ruin by a sort of miracle, and I still keep them as relics. Then there were my powder-flask, my fire-arms, and sixteen cartridges in my cartridge-case. Add to all this a fair amount of health, good spirits, and the hope of presenting my respects to the Mongol, Chinese and Indian ladies I hoped to meet, and you will have a very good idea of the Vélite sergeant of the Imperial Guard.

* I forgot to say that in the middle of the large cross of Ivan the Great was a small one in solid gold about a foot long.—*Author's Note.*

I had scarcely finished reviewing my treasures*, when in front of us we heard a report of fire-arms : we were ordered to set off in double-quick time. We arrived half an hour afterwards at the place where part of the convoy, escorted by a detachment of red Lancers of the Guard, had been attacked by partisans. Several of the lancers were killed, also some Russians and many horses. Near a cart was a pretty woman, stretched on her back on the ground, killed by the shock. We marched on by a fairly good road, and stopped in the evening to bivouac in a wood.

Early the next morning we resumed our march, and met at noon a party of Cossacks of the regular army. The artillery made short work of them. We marched for most of this day over fields, and at night encamped on the banks of a stream.

There was rain on the 22nd, and it was slow and difficult walking all day. In the evening we posted ourselves near a wood. During the night we heard a loud explosion. Afterwards we discovered that Marshal Mortier had blown up the Kremlin, putting a great quantity of powder in the cellars. He left Moscow three days after we did with his 10,000 men. Two of the regiments were the Young Guard, which we met on the road to Mojaisk a few days afterwards. For the rest of the day we got on very slowly, although we were marching all the time.

On the 24th we found we were near Kalonga, and that same day, at Malo-Jaroslawetz, the army of Italy, commanded by Prince Eugene, engaged the Russian army, which was endeavouring to prevent our passage. In this bloody struggle 16,000 of our men met 70,000 Russians. The Russians lost 8,000 men, and we 3,000. Many of

* On account of the Continental blockade, a rumour ran through the army that we were to penetrate into Mongolia and China, and seize the English possessions there.—*Author's Note.*

our superior officers were killed and wounded—amongst them General Delzous, struck on the forehead by a ball. His brother, a Colonel, in trying to save him, was himself shot, and both died together on the same spot.

On the 25th I had been on guard since the previous evening near a little house where the Emperor had spent the night. There was a thick fog, as there often is in October. All at once, without informing anyone, the Emperor mounted his horse, merely followed by some orderly officers. He had scarcely gone, when we heard a great noise. Just at first we supposed it to be cries of ' Vive l'Empereur !' but then we heard the order 'Aux armes !'—' To arms !' Six thousand Cossacks, commanded by Platoff, had come to surprise us, favoured by the fog and the deep ravines. The squadrons of the Guard on duty flew across the plain. We followed them, crossing a ravine to make a short-cut. We found ourselves directly in front of this host of savages, who howled like wolves as they drew back. Our squadrons came up with them, recaptured what they had taken of our baggage and waggons, and inflicted heavy losses on them.

When we got to the plain, we saw that the Emperor was in the midst of the Cossacks, surrounded by Generals and by his orderly officers, one of whom was dangerously wounded through a fatal mistake. Just as the squadrons arrived on the plain, many of the officers, for their own defence and that of the Emperor, who had nearly been taken in the midst of them, had been obliged to use their swords against the Cossacks. One of the orderly officers dropped his hat and his sword after killing and wounding several of the Cossacks ; so, finding himself defenceless, he threw himself on a Cossack, and took his lance from him. Just at that moment a mounted Grenadier of the Guard caught sight of him, and, thinking from his green cloak and his lance that he was a Cossack, rushed at him, and ran him through the body.

The unhappy Grenadier, on seeing his mistake, endeavoured to get killed. He flung himself amongst the enemy, striking to right and left, but everyone fled before him. After killing several men, without being able to die himself, he returned, alone and covered with blood, to ask after the officer he had wounded. Fortunately he recovered, and was taken back to France in a sledge.

I remember that, just after this incident, the Emperor was talking to Murat, laughing at the narrow escape he had had of being taken. Monfort, the Grenadier-vélite from Valenciennes, again distinguished himself, killing and wounding many Cossacks.

We waited for some time longer in this place, and then resumed our march, leaving Kalonga on the left. We crossed a muddy river by a very bad bridge, and took the direction of Mojaisk. It began to freeze during the night.

On the 28th we started very early, and during the day, after passing over a little river, we arrived at the famous battlefield (the Moskowa), covered all over with the dead, and with débris of all kinds. Legs, arms, and heads lay on the ground. Most of the bodies were Russians, as ours had been buried, as far as possible; but, as everything had been very hastily done, the heavy rain had uncovered many of them. It was a sad spectacle, the dead bodies hardly retaining a human resemblance. The battle had been fought fifty-two days before.

Further on we fixed our bivouac, passing on our way the great redoubt where General Caulaincourt had been killed and buried. We sheltered ourselves as well as we could, and made a fire with broken remains of rifles, carts, gun-carriages. We had no water, however, for the little stream flowing near was full of decaying bodies. We had to go a quarter of a league to find any fit for drinking. When we had everything settled, I went with a friend* to explore the battlefield; we went as far as the ravine where Murat had pitched his tents.

On that same day a report went round that a French Grenadier had been found still living on the battlefield. He had both his legs cut off, and was sheltered by the body of a horse, whose flesh he had eaten to keep himself alive. His drink was the water from the stream full of the dead bodies of his comrades. I heard that he was saved—and no doubt for the time it was true—but afterwards he would be left behind, like so many others. That evening many whose store of provisions had come to an end began to feel hunger. Up till then everyone contributed his share of flour for the soup; but now, seeing that some did not contribute, men began to hide what they had to keep it for themselves. The soup made out of horseflesh—which we had eaten for the last few days—was all we had to eat in common.

On the following day we passed near a convent, used as a hospital for many of our wounded in the great battle. Many of them were still there, and the Emperor gave orders for them to be taken away on any of the carts, beginning with his own; but the canteen men, who had the care of these unfortunate people, left them for one pretext or another on the road, in order to keep all the booty they had brought from Moscow, which filled their carts.

We slept that night in a wood behind Ghjat, where the Emperor stayed. Snow fell for the first time during the night.

The next day (the 30th) the road had become very

* Grangier, a sergeant.—*Author's Note.*

heavy, and many carts laden with booty had the greatest difficulty in getting along. Several were damaged, and others were lightened by throwing away useless parts of the load. I was that day in the rear-guard, and could see from the extreme rear of the column the beginning of the frightful disorder that followed. The road was heaped with valuable things—pictures, candlesticks, and quantities of books. For more than an hour I was picking up volumes, which I glanced through, and then threw down again, to be taken up by others, who in their turn left them on the road—books such as Voltaire, Jean Jacques Rousseau, and Buffon's 'Natural History,' bound in red morocco and gold.

I had the good fortune that day to obtain a bearskin coat found by a man in our company in a broken-up waggon. On the same day our *cantinière* lost her cart containing our provisions, and our beautiful silver punch-bowl of so many pleasant memories.

On the 30th we got to Viasma—called by our men Ville au Schnaps, on account of all the brandy they had found there on going to Moscow. The Emperor stopped here, but our regiment went forward.

I forgot to say that before arriving at this town we made a halt, and while I was resting near a little pine wood I met a sergeant in the Chasseurs of the Guard, whom I knew.* He had taken advantage of a ready-made fire to cook a potful of rice, and invited me to share it. He had with him a *cantinière* of the regiment—a Hungarian. They were the best friends possible. She still had her cart with two horses intact, well filled with provisions, furs, and silver. I stayed for more than an hour with them. While I was there a non-commissioned Portuguese

* This man's name was Guinard; he was a native of Condé.— *Author's Note.*

officer came up to warm himself at our fire. I asked him where his regiment was, and he replied that it was dispersed, but that he, with a detachment, was under orders to escort seven or eight hundred Russian prisoners. They had no food, and were reduced to eating each other. Literally, when one of them died, he was cut up and divided between them, and afterwards eaten. He offered to let me see for myself—this I refused. This took place not a hundred yards from our resting-place. We learnt some days afterwards, that, having no food for the rest, they had been abandoned.

The sergeant and *cantinière* of whom I spoke afterwards lost everything they had at Wilna, and were both taken prisoners.

On November 1st we slept near a wood, as we had done the preceding night. For the last few days we had nothing but horseflesh to eat. The few provisions we had brought from Moscow were all gone, and now, with the cold weather, our real miseries began. I had saved a little rice for myself, which I meant to keep for a great pinch, foreseeing much greater hardship in the future.

I was in the rear-guard again to-day. We were all non-commissioned officers, as many of the men stayed behind to rest and warm themselves at the fires made by those in front. As I walked, I saw to my right several men from different regiments round a large fire. The Adjutant-Major sent me to tell them to follow, and when I got near them I recognised Flament, a Dragoon-vélite. He was cooking a piece of horseflesh on the point of his sword, and invited me to join him. I asked him to follow the column. He said that he would come as soon as he had finished his meal, but that he was unfortunately obliged to walk in his riding-boots, as in an encounter with the Cossacks the day before his horse had strained himself, and he was forced to lead the animal. Luckily, I was able to give Flament a pair of shoes, so that he could walk like a foot soldier, and said good-bye to him, little thinking that I was not to see him again. Two days afterwards he was killed near a wood, just as he and some other stragglers were lighting a fire to rest themselves.

On the 2nd, before getting to Slawkowo, we saw close to the road a *blockhaus*, or military station—a kind of large fortified shed, filled with men from different regiments, and many wounded. All those who could follow us did so, and the slightly wounded were placed, as many as possible, in our carts. Those more seriously wounded were left, with their surgeons and doctors, to the mercy of the enemy.

CHAPTER IV.

DOROGOBOUI—VERMIN—A CANTINIÈRE—HUNGER.

ON the 3rd we stayed at Slawkowo, and saw Russians to the right of us all the day. The other regiments of the Guard, who had remained behind, now joined us. We made a forced march on the 4th to reach Dorogoboui, the 'cabbage town.' We gave it this name on account of the vast number of cabbages we found there on going to Moscow. This was also the place where the Emperor settled the number of artillery and rifle-shots to be fired in the great battle. By seven in the evening we were still two leagues from the town, but the depth of the snow made marching exceedingly difficult. It was with infinite labour we got so far, and for a short time we lost our way.

It was quite eleven o'clock before we made our bivouac. Amongst the débris from the houses (for this town had been almost burned down, like so many others), we found wood enough to make fires and get thoroughly warm. But we had nothing to eat, and we were so horribly tired that we had not the strength to go and look for a horse, so we lay down to rest instead. One of the men in the company brought me some rush matting to make a bed, and with my head on my knapsack, my feet to the fire, I went to sleep.

I had slept for about an hour, when I felt an unbearable tingling over the whole of my body. Mechanically I passed my hand over my chest and other parts of my body, and to my horror discovered that I was covered with vermin! I jumped up, and in less than two minutes was as naked as a new-born babe, having thrown my shirt and trousers into the fire. The crackling they made was like a brisk firing, and my mind was so full of what I was doing that I never noticed the large flakes of snow falling all over me. I shook the rest of my clothes over the fire, and put on my only remaining shirt and pair of trousers; and, feeling miserable almost to the point of tears, I sat on my knapsack, covered with my bearskin, and, my head in my hands, spent the rest of the night as far as possible from the cursed rush matting on which I had slept. The men who took my place caught nothing, so I suppose I monopolized them all.

Early the next morning we set out (November 5th). Before leaving, a distribution of hand-mills was made in every regiment of the Guard, in case of finding any corn to grind; but as we found none, and the mills were very heavy, we got rid of them before twenty-four hours were over. This was a sad day—so many of our sick and wounded died. Up till now they had made superhuman efforts in the hope of reaching Smolensk and finding food and shelter.

In the evening we stopped near a wood, and the order was given to make shelters for the night. Just afterwards our *cantinière*, Madame Dubois, the regimental barber's wife, was taken ill, and in the midst of the falling snow, with twenty degrees of frost, *i.e.*, about ten below zero, she was delivered of a fine boy—a miserable position for the poor woman. Colonel Bodel, who commanded our regiment, did all he possibly could to make her comfortable, lending his cloak to cover the shelter where she lay. Madame Dubois bore her pain and discomfort bravely ; the surgeon did his best, and all ended happily. That same night our men killed a white bear, which was eaten at once. After spending a miserable night, on account of the fearful cold, we set out again. The Colonel lent Madame Dubois his horse. She held her new-born infant wrapped in a sheepskin in her arms, and she herself wore the cloaks of two men who had died during the night.

There was a dense fog that day, November 6th, and more than twenty-two degrees of frost. Our lips were frozen, our brains too ; the whole atmosphere was icy. There was a fearful wind, and the snow fell in enormous flakes. We lost sight not only of the sky, but of the men in front of us. As we approached a wretched village,* a horseman came at full speed, asking for the Emperor. We heard afterwards that it was a General bringing news of Malet's conspiracy in Paris.

We were just then packed very closely together near a wood, and had a long time to wait before we could resume our march, as the road was narrow. As several of us sat together beating with our feet to keep warm, and talking of the fearful hunger we felt, all at once I became aware of the smell of warm bread. I turned round and behind me saw a man wrapped in a great fur cape, from which came the smell I had noticed. I spoke to him at once, saying, 'Sir, you have some bread ; you must sell it to me.' As he moved away, I caught him by the arm, and, seeing that he could not get rid of me, he drew out from under his cloak a cake still warm. With one hand I seized the cake, while with the other I gave him five francs. But hardly had I the cake in my hand, when my companions

---

* The name of the village was Mickalowka.—*Author's Note.*

threw themselves on it like madmen, and tore it from me. I only had the little bit I held between my thumb and two first fingers.

While this was going on, the Surgeon-Major (for it was he) went off, and well for him he did so, as he might have been killed for the sake of the rest of the cake. He had probably found some flour in the village, and had had time to make the cake while waiting for us.

During this half-hour several men had lain down and died; many more had fallen in the column while marching. Our ranks were getting thinned already, and this was only the very beginning of our troubles. Whenever we stopped to eat hastily, the horses left behind were bled. The blood was caught in a saucepan, cooked, and eaten. But often we were forced to eat it before there was time to cook it. Either the order for departure was given, or the Russians were upon us. In the latter case we did not take much notice. I have sometimes seen men eating calmly, while others fired at the Russians to keep them off. But when the order was imperative and we were obliged to go, the saucepan was carried with us, and each man, as he marched, dipped his hands in and took what he wanted; his face in consequence became smeared with blood.

Very often we were obliged to leave the horses, for want of time to cut them up, and men would drop behind and hide themselves for fear of being forced to follow their regiments. Then they would throw themselves on the meat like vultures. These men seldom reappeared; they were either taken by the enemy or they died of cold.

This day's march was not so long as the preceding one; it was still daylight when we stopped. A village had been burnt down, and only a few rafters here and there remained. The officers encamped against these for the night, getting a little shelter this way. Besides the fearful pains we felt all over through our great fatigue, we were by this time quite famishing. Those of us who still had a little rice or oatmeal, hid themselves to eat it in secret. We had no friends left; we looked suspiciously at each other, and even turned against our best comrade. I will not keep back a base act of ingratitude I committed against my truest friends. Like everyone else that day I was devoured by hunger; but besides that, I was also devoured by vermin I had got the previous day. We had not even a bit of horseflesh to eat, and we were waiting for some men of our company to come up who had stayed behind to cut up the. fallen horses. I was standing near one of my friends, Poumot, a sergeant, close to a fire we had made, in quite indescribable torment, and looking round continually to see if no one was coming. Suddenly I seized his hand convulsively, and said :

' Look here : if I met anyone in the wood with a loaf of bread, I should force him to give me half !' And then, correcting myself, ' No,' I said, ' I would kill him to have it all !'

Almost before I had finished I strode off towards the wood, just as if I expected to meet the man and the loaf. When I got there, I roamed about for a quarter of an hour, and then, turning in the opposite direction from our bivouac, close by the borders of the wood, I saw a man seated near a fire. On the fire was a pot in which something was evidently cooking, as the man took a knife and, plunging it into the pot, drew out a potato, which he pinched, and then put back again, as if it were not boiled enough.

I ran towards him as hard as I could, but fearing that he might escape me, I made a little circuit, so as to come up behind him without his seeing me. The brushwood crackled, however, as I came through, and he turned round ; but before he had time to speak, I said :

'Look here, comrade : you must either sell or give me your potatoes, or I shall carry away the pot by force !'

He seemed quite taken by surprise, and as I put out my sword to fish with it in the pot, he said it did not belong to him, but to his master, a Polish General, who was camping close by, and that he had been ordered to hide himself here to cook the potatoes ready for the next day.

Without answering him, I offered him money, and began to take the potatoes. He told me they were not boiled enough yet, and as I seemed not to believe him, he took one out for me to feel. I tore it from him, and devoured it just as it was.

'They are not fit to eat—you can see that for yourself,' he said ; 'hide yourself for a little while, try to be patient, and don't let anyone see you till the potatoes are boiled, and then I will give you some.'

I did as he bade me, hiding behind a bush, but not losing sight of him. After about five or six minutes, thinking no doubt that I was some distance off, he looked stealthily to right and left, and taking the pot, he ran off with it. Not far, however, as I soon stopped him, and threatened to take the whole if he did not give me half. He said again that the potatoes belonged to his General.

'I must have them if they are the Emperor's,' I cried. 'I am dying of hunger.'

Seeing he could not get rid of me, he gave me seven. I paid him fifteen francs, and left him. He then called me back, and gave me two more. They were hardly cooked at all, but that did not matter much to me. I ate one, and put the rest in my bag. I reckoned that, with a little horseflesh, they would last me for three days, allowing two each day.

As I walked on, thinking of my potatoes, I lost my way. I was made aware of this by hearing cries and curses from five men, who were fighting like dogs ; the leg of a horse on the ground was the cause of the disturbance. One of them, on seeing me, told me that he and his companion, both artillery soldiers, had killed a horse behind the wood, and that, on returning with their portion, they had been attacked by three men of another regiment. If I would help them they would give me a share. I feared the same sort of fate for my potatoes, so I replied that I could not wait, but that if they could hold on for a little I would send some people to help them. A little further on I met two men in our regiment to whom I told the story. The next day I heard that when they got to the place they only saw a man lying dead, covered with blood, killed by a great pine cudgel at his side. Probably the three aggressors had taken advantage of the absence of one of their enemies to fall on the other.

When at length I got back to my regiment, several of the men asked me if I had found anything. I answered ' No,' and, taking my place near the fire, I hollowed out a bed in the snow, stretched my bearskin coat to lie on, a cape lined with ermine for my head. Before going to sleep, I had my potato to eat. Hiding it by my cape, I was as quiet as possible, terrified lest anyone should observe that I was eating. I had a little snow for drink, and then went to sleep, holding my bag containing the rest of my provisions fast in my arms. Several times in the night, as I woke, I put in my hand, carefully counting my potatoes ; so I passed the night without sharing with my starving companions the bit of luck I had had. I shall never forgive myself for this selfishness. I was awake and sitting on my knapsack before the reveille sounded in the morning. I saw that a terrible day was in store for us, on account

71

of the high wind. I made a hole in my bearskin coat, and put my head through it. The bear's head fell over my chest, and the rest over my back, but it was so long that it dragged on the ground. Before dawn we set out. We left behind us an enormous number of dead and dying. Further on it was worse still, as we had to stride over the dead bodies left on the road by the regiments going before us. It was worst of all for the rear-guard, as these were witnesses of all the horrors left by the whole army. The last corps were those commanded by Marshal Ney and Davoust, and the army of Italy under Prince Eugène. Daylight appeared when we had been marching for about an hour, and, as we had come up with the corps in front of us, we halted. Our *cantinière*, Mother Dubois, took advantage of the halt to feed her baby, when suddenly we heard a cry of anguish. The infant was dead, and as stiff as a piece of wood. Those nearest to her tried to comfort her by saying that it was the best thing both for the baby and herself, and, in spite of her cries and tears, they took the infant from her breast. They gave it to a sapper, who, with the child's father, went a short distance from the road. The sapper dug a hole in the snow, the father on his knees holding the child in his arms. When the grave was made, he kissed the baby, and placed it in its tomb. It was covered with snow, and all was at an end.

We stopped an hour later for a long halt at the edge of a wood. Here a large party of artillery and cavalry had encamped, for we found a great many dead horses, some of them cut in pieces. There were many more still living, though numbed, standing still to be killed; those that had died during the night were frozen so hard that it was impossible to cut the flesh. During this disastrous march I noticed that we were always placed as much as possible behind the cavalry and artillery; so that when we halted where they had passed the night, the horses they had left behind were ready for us.

While we were all resting, and each busy in arranging some fearful meal for himself, I retired furtively into the thickest part of the wood to eat the potatoes I had hidden so carefully. But a fearful disappointment was in store for me. When I tried to bite, I felt nothing but ice; my teeth slipped, and I could not get hold of a bit. I was sorry then that I had not shared the potatoes with the others, and I went back to them, holding in my hand the frozen one, covered with blood from my lips. They asked me what I had got, and I silently showed them the potato I held, and the others in my bag. They were snatched instantly from me; but the result, when they tried to bite, was no better than mine. They tried to thaw them at the fire, but they melted away like ice. While this was going on, other men came up to ask me where I had found the potatoes, and when I pointed to the wood they ran there, returning to say they had found nothing. They were very good to me, as they invited me to share a potful of horse's blood which they had cooked. I did not need two invitations. I have always felt very sorry for behaving as I did. The men believed that I found the potatoes in the wood, and I did not undeceive them. But all this is only a hundredth part of what came afterwards.

After an hour's rest we set out again, crossing a wood, where every now and then we came on open spaces, with houses in them occupied by Jews. Some of them are large, and built very much like our barns, only of wood. At each end is a large door. These houses take the place of posting houses. A carriage is taken in at one end, and, after changing horses, goes out at the other. The houses are built about three leagues apart; but most of them had disappeared, having been burnt at the army's first passage.

CHAPTER V.

WHEN we got out of the wood, near to a miserable little hamlet called Gara, I saw, a short distance off, one of the posting-houses I have been describing. I pointed it out to one of our sergeants, an Alsatian called Mather, and suggested to him that we should spend the night there, if we could possibly manage to get there first. We set off running, but found on arriving that it was crammed full with officers, men, and horses—about 800 people being there—so that there was not an inch of room for us.

While we were running, first one way and then another, trying to find places, the Imperial column and our own regiment passed, so we decided to spend the night under the horses tied up to the doors. Those who were camped round the house repeatedly tried to pull it down to make fires and shelters with the wood, and to get hold of the straw lying in a sort of loft. Some of this straw was used for beds by those inside the house, and, tightly packed though they were, they even made small fires to warm themselves and cook their horseflesh. They threatened to shoot those outside who tried to pull up the planks of the house. Some who had got on the roof, and had torn off

74

planks, were forced to jump down in danger of their lives.

It might have been perhaps eleven o'clock at night. Some of the unfortunate men were asleep, others were warming their limbs at the fire, when we heard an indistinct noise behind us. Fire had broken out in two places—in the centre and at the other end of the barn. When we tried to open the doors, the horses fastened to the inside reared and prevented our passing. It was impossible to get to the other door for the smoke and flames.

The confusion was supreme. The men from the further side of the barn threw themselves in a compact mass against the inside of the door near where we slept, to prevent others from getting in. To do this more effectually, they had fixed the door firmly with a cross-bar of wood. In less than two minutes the whole place was in flames; the fire had begun in the straw where the men slept, and rapidly spread to the dry beams above their heads. Some men near the door tried to open it, but failed, as it opened inwards. A terrible scene, impossible to describe, took place; smothered groans and terrible shrieks were heard from the building. The unfortunate wretches inside climbed one upon the other, endeavouring to get out through the roof; but flames were already issuing through the holes there, and no sooner did the men appear, their clothes on fire, and the hair burnt off their heads, than they were driven back again by the force of the fire.

Then cries and shrieks of rage were heard, the fire became a vast tossing mass, through the convulsive efforts the poor wretches made to escape. It was the picture of hell.

We saved seven men by dragging them through a hole made by a plank torn from its place. One of them was an officer of our regiment. His hands were burnt and his clothes torn, and the other six were worse off still. It was impossible to save any more in this way, as the others were already half suffocated by the smoke, and by the weight of other men on the top of them; we had to leave them to be burnt with the rest. Some few flung themselves off the roof, and begged us to finish them off by shooting them.

Other men who were camping near, half dead with cold by their wretched fires, now came running up, attracted by the light of the flames. They came, not to offer help— they were too late for that—but to warm themselves, and cook their horseflesh on the points of their swords and bayonets. In their opinion, the disaster was an intervention of Providence, as the men burnt in the barn were the richest in the army, having brought away more treasure than any others from Moscow. In spite of their hunger and weakness, we saw men running the risk of the flames to drag out the bodies of their wretched comrades, in order to hunt for what they could find. Others said, ' It serves them right ; if they had let us get on to the roof, this would not have happened.' Others, again, stretched out their hands to the warmth, saying, 'What a beautiful fire !' regardless of the fact that several hundreds of their comrades, perhaps even of their relatives, had given their bodies to feed the flames.

Before the dawn, I set out with my companion to rejoin the regiment. We walked on, thinking of all that had passed, stumbling over dead and dying men. The cold was even more intense than on the day before. We joined two men of the line who had their teeth in a bit of horse-flesh. They said, if they waited any longer, it would be frozen too hard to eat. They assured us as a fact that they had seen foreign soldiers (Croats) of our army dragging corpses out of the fire, cutting them up and eating them. I never saw this sort of thing myself, but

I believe it frequently happened during this fatal campaign.

What object could these men have, almost dying as they were, in telling us this story, if it were not true? It was not an occasion for lying. I am sure that if I had not found any horseflesh myself, I could have turned cannibal. To understand the situation, one must have felt the madness of hunger; failing a man to eat, one could have demolished the devil himself, if he were only cooked.

Since we left Moscow, a pretty Russian carriage drawn by four horses had followed the Guards' column. For the last two days, however, we only saw two; the others had either been killed and eaten, or had died of the cold and fatigue. In the carriage was a lady, probably a widow, still young, with her two daughters, of seventeen and fifteen years of age. They were from Moscow, of French origin, and had yielded to the entreaties of one of our superior officers to accompany him to France. Perhaps the officer intended to marry the lady, for he was no longer very young. Be that as it may, these unhappy ladies were, like us, exposed to the terrible cold, and to all the miseries of hunger and want, feeling it, no doubt, far more keenly than we did.

The day was breaking when we got to the place where our regiment had slept, and the army was already in motion. During the last two days the regiments were diminished by a third of their number, and it was only too evident, from the slow, painful progress of many of the men, that they would succumb before the day was over. I saw the carriage containing the unfortunate ladies emerge from a little wood on to the highroad; there it stopped close to me, and I heard cries and groans proceeding from it. The officer in charge of the ladies opened the door, got into the carriage, and presently lifted out a dead body to the sappers waiting outside. One of the poor girls had just died. She was dressed in gray silk, with a cape of the same colour trimmed with ermine. She was still beautiful, but very thin. We were all very much touched at this sight, in spite of our usual indifference to tragic scenes, and when I saw the officer in tears, I wept also.

As the sappers took the girl's body away, I glanced into the carriage, and there I saw the mother and the other girl fallen one over the other. They seemed to be quite unconscious, and, indeed, their sufferings were ended that evening. I think they were all three buried by the sappers in the same grave, near Valoutina. The Lieutenant-Colonel, reproaching himself for this misfortune, tried at Krasnoë and other battles to meet his death; and in January, a few days after our arrival at Elbingen, he died of grief.

This day (November 8th) was a terrible one. We were late at our halting-place, and, as we were supposed to reach Smolensk the following day, the hope of getting food and rest, and the rumour that we were to go into cantonments there, inspired many of our men to superhuman exertions, in spite of the frightful cold and every kind of privation.

Before reaching the place for bivouac, we had to cross a deep ravine and climb a hill. Some artillerymen of the Guard had stopped in the ravine with their guns, quite unable to get up the hill. The horses were entirely spent, and the men's strength gone. They were accompanied by some gunners of the King of Prussia's Guard; they had been through the campaign with us, attached to our artillery as a Prussian contingent. They had made their bivouacs by the side of their guns, lighting their fires as best they could, and hoping to continue their way in the morning. Our regiment and the Chasseurs were on the right of the road. I believe these were the heights of Valoutina, where a battle had been fought on August 19th that same year.

I was on guard at Marshal Mortier's. His quarters were a barn without a roof. A hasty shelter had been put up, however, to keep out the snow and cold as much as possible. Our Colonel and the Adjutant-Major were there also. We tore some wood off the fence to make a little fire for the Marshal, at which we could all warm ourselves. We had hardly settled down to cook a piece of horseflesh, when a man appeared, his head tied up in a handkerchief, his hands swathed in rags, and his clothes burnt. He cried out as he came up:

'Ah, Colonel, how miserable I am! I am suffering terribly!'

The Colonel turned round, asking him who he was, where he came from, and what was the matter with him.

'Ah, Colonel,' he said, 'I have lost everything, and I am frightfully burnt.'

The Colonel then recognised him, and said:

'That was your own fault; you should have kept with the regiment. You have disappeared for several days. What have you been doing? You ought to have shown an example, and been ready, like us, to die at your post. Do you understand, sir?'

But the poor devil did not hear or understand, and this was not the right time to lecture. The man was the officer we had saved from the fire at the barn, and who was supposed to possess a great many gold and precious things taken at Moscow. He had lost everything, however; his horse and his belongings had all gone. The Marshal and the Colonel began to talk of the fire, and of several officers who had perished there with their servants. As they knew I had been present, they asked me for details of the disaster, as the officer we had saved could say nothing—he was too much overcome.

It was perhaps nine o'clock, an intensely dark night,

and many of us were already asleep—a sleep continually broken by the cold and the pain we suffered from fatigue and hunger. The fire also was constantly going out. We thought of the next day, which should bring us to Smolensk, where we had heard our misery would be over, as food could be had there and we should take up our quarters.

I had just finished my miserable supper of horse's liver, with snow for drink; the Marshal had eaten some also, but he had besides a little biscuit and a drop of brandy —not a very delicate repast for a Marshal of France, but quite luxurious in our present unfortunate circum-stances.

As we were eating, the Marshal saw a man leaning on his musket at the entrance to the barn, and asked him why he was there. The man replied that he was on sentry duty.

'For whom?' said the Marshal; 'and why should you do it? You cannot keep out cold and hunger from us. Come in and sit down by the fire.'

He then asked for some sort of pillow for his head. His servant brought him a portmanteau, and, wrapping himself in his cloak, he went to sleep. As I was following his example, in my bearskin, we were roused by an extra-ordinary noise. This was the north wind travelling over the forests, bringing with it heavy snow and twenty-seven degrees of frost, so that it became quite impossible for the men to stay where they had camped. We heard them shouting as they ran about towards any fire they saw; but the heavy snow-storms caught them, and they could soon run no more, or if they tried to do so, they fell and never rose again. In this way many hundreds perished, and thousands died of those who had stayed where they were camped. We were most fortunate in getting shelter in our corner of the barn. Many men took refuge with us, and thus saved their lives.

DEVOTION

I must relate an act of devotion called forth by this disastrous night, when all the powers of hell seemed to be turned loose on us.

The Prince Émile of Hesse-Cassel was with us, and his contingent, composed of several regiments of cavalry and infantry. Like us, he bivouacked on the left side of the road, with the remainder of his unfortunate men, now reduced to five or six hundred. About a hundred and fifty dragoons were left; but these were almost all on foot, their horses being dead and eaten. These brave men, almost frozen with the cold, sacrificed themselves in this awful night to save their young Prince, not more than twenty years of age. They stood round him the whole night wrapped in their great white cloaks, pressed tightly one against the other, protecting him from the wind and cold. The next morning three-quarters of them were dead and buried beneath the snow, along with ten thousand others from different corps.

At daylight, to regain the road, we were obliged to go down to the ravine, where the evening before the artillery-men had made their bivouac. Not one was left alive; men and horses were all covered with snow—the men still round the fires, the horses harnessed to the guns, which we were forced to leave there.

It almost always happened that the weather became more endurable after a storm and excessive cold. It seemed as if Nature had wearied herself out in torturing us, and she must have breathing-space before she struck us again.

All who were still alive set out once more. To right and left of the road men half dead crept out of wretched shelters formed by pine branches, buried all night under the snow. Others came from further off in the woods, dragging themselves painfully along. We halted a little, waiting for them, talking to each other of the horrors of the night and the incredible number of men we had lost, and looking mechanically over that terrible field. Piles of arms were there in places, many others overthrown, but no one to take them up.

After collecting together as far as we could, we recommenced the march, our regiment forming the rear-guard. This was a most painful and weary day for us, as numbers of men could no longer walk, and we were obliged to hold them up under the arms, dragging them with us, to save them if possible by getting them to Smolensk.

We had to cross a little wood before reaching the town; here we came up with all the artillery collected together. The horses were a fearful sight; the gun-carriages and waggons were crowded with sick men dying from the cold. I remember that one of my old friends named Ficq, from the same part of the country as myself, was in this condition. I asked a Chasseur of the Guard of his regiment what had become of him, and he told me only a few minutes ago he had fallen dead on the road. Just at that place he said the road was narrow, and in a deep hollow, so that they could not carry his body to the side. All the artillery, therefore, had passed over him, as well as some others fallen in the same place.

I was walking now in a narrow footpath in the wood to the left of the road, and with me was one of my friends, a sergeant in the same regiment. We suddenly came upon a gunner of the Guard lying right across the path. By him was another gunner stripping his clothes from him. We could see that the man was not dead, as his legs moved, and every now and then he struck the ground with his fists. Without saying a word, my companion gave the wretched thief a blow in the back with the butt of his musket. We immediately abused him violently for his barbarous conduct. He answered that, although the other was not dead, he very soon would have died, as he had been quite unconscious when placed there to be out of the way of the artillery; and, besides, he was his mess-mate, and if anyone had the clothes he was the right man.

The same thing frequently happened to these wretched men who were supposed to have money about them. There were many who remained by those who had fallen : not to help them, but to behave as did the gunner.

For the honour of humanity, perhaps, I ought not to describe all these scenes of horror, but I have determined to write down all I saw. I cannot do otherwise, and, besides, all these things have taken such possession of my mind that I think if I write them down they will cease to trouble me. And if in this disastrous campaign acts of infamy were committed, there were noble actions, too, which do honour to our humanity; amongst others, I have seen men carry a wounded officer on their shoulders for many days.

As we emerged from the wood, we met about a hundred lancers mounted on good horses with new equipments. They came from Smolensk, where they had been all the time. They were horrified on seeing the wretched con-dition we were in, and we were no less surprised to see their well-being. Many of our men ran after them like beggars, asking if they had a bit of bread or biscuit to give them.

We now made a halt to wait for those who were bringing the sick. It was a most harrowing sight. Talk to them as we would of the hope of good food and lodging, they seemed not to hear anything. They were like clay figures, walking where they were led, standing still if they were left. The strongest among them took turns in carrying the arms and knapsacks, for these unfortunate men, who, besides having lost their strength and a part of their reason, had also lost their fingers and toes.

We now saw the Dnieper again on our left, and on the further bank caught sight of the thousands of men who had crossed the river on the ice. Foot soldiers and cavalry were there from different corps, running as fast as they could towards a distant village to get food and shelter for the night. We marched on painfully for another hour, and in the evening reached the banks of the fatal Boristhène; we crossed the river, and, worn out with fatigue and almost dying, we were at last beneath the walls of the town.

Thousands of men were there already, from every corps and of every nation. They were there waiting at the gates and ramparts till they could gain admission, and this had been refused them on the ground that, marching as they were without officers or order, and already dying of hunger, they might pillage the town for provisions. Many hundreds of these men were already dead or dying. When we arrived there with the rest of the Guard in an orderly fashion, and taking the utmost precaution for our sick and wounded, the gates were opened, and we entered. The greater number broke the ranks, and spread on all sides, anxious to find some roof under which to spend the night, and eat the food promised us.

To obtain any sort of order, it was announced that men isolated from the rest would get nothing; so after this the men were careful to rejoin their regiments, and choose a head to represent them, as several of the old regiments existed no longer. We of the Imperial Guard crossed the town with extreme difficulty, worn out with fatigue as we were. We had to climb the steep slope which separates the Boristhène from the other gate; this was covered with ice, and at every step the weakest of our men fell and had to be lifted up; others could not walk at all.

In this way we came to the side of the faubourg which had been burnt at the bombardment last August. We settled down as well as we could, in the ruins of those houses the fire had not quite destroyed. The sick and wounded who had had strength and courage enough to come with us were made as comfortable as possible. We were obliged to leave some of them, however, in a hut in a wood, near the entrance of the town, being much too ill to go any farther. Amongst them was a friend of mine, in a dying condition. He had dragged himself so far, hoping to find a hospital, for we had all hoped to stay in this town and the neighbourhood until the spring. Our hopes were disappointed, however, as most of the villages were burnt and in ruins, and the town of Smolensk existed only in name. Nothing was to be seen but the walls of houses built of stone; the greater part of the town had been built of wood, and had disappeared. The town, in fact, was a mere skeleton. If we went any distance in the dark, we came on pitfalls—that is, the cellars belonging to the wooden houses, now completely gone. These cellars were covered with snow, and if any man was so unfortunate as to step on one, he disappeared, and we saw him no more. A great many men were lost in this manner. Their bodies were dragged out again the next day, not for burial, but for the sake of their clothes, or anything else they might have about them. All those who died, whether on the march or while we stopped, were treated in the same way. The living men despoiled the dead, very often, in their turn, dying a few hours afterwards, and being subjected to the same fate.

Soon after our arrival, a little flour was given out to us, and about an ounce of biscuit, more, indeed, than we could have hoped for. Those of us who had a saucepan made hasty pudding; others made cakes, and cooked them in the ashes, devouring them half raw. Several of the men were dangerously ill afterwards, in consequence of the avidity with which they devoured the food. I was lucky enough not to suffer, although I had not tasted soup since November 1st, and the hasty pudding made of rye flour was as heavy as lead.

Many of the sick men who had made gigantic efforts to get here died, and as they occupied the best positions in our miserable ruins, their bodies were hastily removed, so that others could take their places.

After resting a little, in spite of the cold and falling snow, I went out to look for one of my comrades. He was my best and dearest friend; we had been together for seven years, and we had everything in common. His name was Grangier.* At Viasma he had gone forward with a detachment, escorting a waggon belonging to Marshal Bessières, and I had not seen him since. I heard that he had arrived two days ago, and was quartered in one of the faubourgs. The hope of seeing him again, and also of sharing his provisions and his quarters, decided me to go at once. Without a word to anyone, I took my knapsack and re-entered the town by the road we had taken, and after falling on the steep and slippery slope several times, I reached the gate by which we had entered.

I stopped to see after the men we had left near the guard at the gate; this guard was composed of men from Baden, who partly formed the garrison. But my surprise was great on seeing the friend we had left with the others, till we could fetch them away, lying at the door of the hut, with nothing on but his trousers; everything had been taken from him, even his boots.

* Sergeant-vélite in the same regiment as myself, the Fusilier-Grenadiers.—*Author's Note.*

HUMANITY

The Baden men told me that soldiers from the regiment had been to fetch the others, and, finding that this man was dead, they had themselves taken his clothes, and that afterwards they had carried away the two sick men, going round the town by the ramparts, hoping to find an easier road. While I was there several wretched men from different regiments came also, leaning on their muskets, hardly able to drag themselves along. Others, who were still on the farther side of the Boristhène, had fallen down in the snow, crying and imploring help. These German soldiers, however, either did not or would not understand. Fortunately, a young officer in command spoke French, and I begged him, in common humanity, to send help to these men over the bridge. He replied that since our arrival more than half his guard had been employed in that way, that there were hardly any men left, and that his guard-room was filled with sick and wounded, till there was no room to move.

However, as I entreated, he sent three men, who came back soon afterwards supporting an old Chasseur of the Cavalry of the Guard. They said they had left many others who would have to be carried, and that in the meantime they had put them near a large fire. The old Chasseur had nearly all his toes frozen, and had wrapped them up in a sheepskin. His beard, whiskers, and moustache were filled with icicles. They led him near a fire, where he sat down, and then he began to curse Alexander, the Emperor of Russia, the country, and the God of Russia. Then he asked me if brandy had been given out.

I said, 'No, not yet; there does not seem much chance of it.'

'Then,' he said, 'I had better die.'

The young German officer, on seeing the veteran suffer so terribly, could resist no longer, and, drawing a bottle of brandy from his pocket, he gave some to him.

'Thanks,' he said; 'you have saved my life. If I ever have an opportunity of saving your life at the cost of my own, you may be sure I shall not hesitate a moment. Remember Roland, Chasseur of the Old Guard, now on foot, or, to be exact, on no feet just at present. I had to leave my horse three days ago, and blew out his brains to put an end to his sufferings. I cut a piece off his leg afterwards, and I am going to eat a little now.'

Saying this, he unfastened the portmanteau he carried on his back, and, taking out some horseflesh, he offered some first to the officer and then to me. The officer gave him the bottle of brandy, and begged him to keep it. The old chasseur was grateful beyond all words. He again asked the officer not to forget him either in garrison or in the field, and finally said:

'The right sort never die.' But directly afterwards he reminded himself what a foolish speech he had made. 'For,' he said, 'there were many as good as me among the thousands who have died these last three days. I have been in Egypt, and, by God! it was no comparison with this. I hope to goodness we are at the end of our troubles; they say we are to take up our quarters here and wait for the spring, when we can take our revenge.'

The poor old fellow, rendered so talkative by a few mouthfuls of brandy, had no conception that we were only at the beginning of our troubles!

It was quite eleven o'clock, but I had not given up the search for Grangier, even during the night. I asked the officer to direct me to where he supposed Marshal Bessières was quartered; but either I was misinformed or I did not understand, and I mistook the road. I found myself with the rampart on my right, and the Boristhène flowing beneath; on my left was a piece of waste ground, on the site of houses burnt down. Here and there through the darkness I saw odd beams and rafters standing out like shadows on the snow. The road I had taken was such a bad one, and I was so tired, that, after stumbling on a little way, I regretted having come alone. I began to retrace my steps, and put off my search for Grangier till the next day, when I heard someone behind me, and, turning, I recognised one of the Baden soldiers carrying a little barrel looking like brandy on his shoulder. I called to him, but he did not answer, and when I followed him, he doubled his pace. I did the same. He then ran down a rapid slope, and I tried to follow him; but my legs gave way beneath me, and I rolled from top to bottom, getting to the door of a cellar as soon as he did. The weight of my body against the door opened it, and I went in before the Baden fellow, with my right shoulder badly bruised, however.

I had scarcely time to collect my wits and look about me, when I was startled by confused cries in different languages from a dozen people lying on straw round a fire. They were French, German, and Italian, and I saw at once they were a gang of thieves who banded themselves together, travelled before the army, and arrived first at any houses they found, or camped separately in the villages. As soon as the army arrived at any place, the thieves came out of their hiding, prowled round the bivouacs, stole as quietly as possible their horses and bags from the officers, and set out again very early in the morning before the army started. This was their plan every day. The gang was one of those which had prowled about ever since the great cold began, and multiplied as they went.

I was stunned by my fall, and lay still for a minute, when one of the thieves lit a bit of straw to see me better. It was impossible to discover what regiment I belonged to on account of my bearskin. As soon, however, as he caught sight of the Imperial eagle on my shako, he called out in a jeering way, 'Ah! the Imperial Guard! Out with you! out with you!' And the others repeated, 'Get out! Out with you!'

I was stupefied and not at all alarmed by their shouting, and I got up to beg them to let me stay till morning, as fate or luck had brought me there. But the man who had spoken first, and seemed to be the chief, replied that I must go at once, and they all chorused, 'Be off! Out with you!'

A German was laying his hands on me, when I gave him a blow in the chest that sent him sprawling among the others, putting my hand on the hilt of my sword at the same time (my musket had been left behind in my roll down the hill). The chief applauded me for the blow I had given, saying a German, a sauerkraut-eater, had no business to touch a Frenchman. As I saw that the man was disposed to take my part, I announced that I would not go away until the morning, and that I would rather be killed than die of cold on the road. One of two women there began to put in a word for me, but was immediately ordered, in curses and filthy language, to be silent. The chief told me again to go, asking me not to oblige him to use force, as, if he did, the question would soon be settled, and I should be sent flying to rejoin my regiment.

I asked him why he and his companions were not there also, and he told me it was none of my business, that he had nothing to do with me, that he was master here, and that I could not spend the night with him, as I should be in their way when they made their night excursions, taking advantage of the disorder of the town. I then asked for permission to stay and warm myself, and said that afterwards I would go. Not receiving any answer, I asked a second time; the chief said he would consent if I left in half an hour. He ordered a drummer, who seemed to be second in command, to see that this was done.

As I wished to make the best of my opportunity, I asked if anyone had any food or brandy to sell. 'If we had,' they said, 'we should keep it ourselves.'

However, the little cask I had seen on the Baden man's shoulders looked very like brandy, and I understood when he said in his own language that he had taken it from a *cantinière* in his regiment, who had hidden it when the army came into the town. I concluded from this that the man was a new-comer, one of the garrison, and had only joined the thieves the day before, choosing, as they had done, to leave his regiment for the sake of plunder.

The drummer who was to see me out talked mysteriously with the others, and then asked me if I had any gold to buy brandy with.

'No,' I said, 'but I have some five-franc pieces.'

A woman near me, who had wished to take my part before, stooped down and seemed to be searching for something on the ground near the door. Coming close up to me, she said in a low voice:

'Run away; believe me, they will kill you. I have been with them, against my will, since Viasma. Come back with help, I implore you, to-morrow morning, to save me!'

I asked her who the other woman was, and she replied, 'A Jewess.'

I was going to question her further, when a voice from the back of the cellar told her to be quiet, and asked her what she had been saying. She answered that she had been telling me to get brandy of a Jew in the new market.

'Hold your tongue!' he replied.

She was silent, and went to a corner of the cellar.

After what the woman had said, I saw there was no doubt that I was in a regular den of thieves. So I did not wait till they turned me out, and, pretending to look for a place to lie down in, I got near the door, opened it, and went out. They called me back, saying I could stay all night and sleep there. But I made no answer, and picking up my musket, which lay near the entrance, I tried to find a way out of the hole. Not succeeding, I was on the point of knocking at the cellar door to ask the way, when the Baden soldier appeared, probably to see if it was time to make an excursion. He asked me again if I would go back. I said no, but I begged him to show me the way to the faubourg. He signed to me to follow him, and crossing the ruins of several houses, he climbed up by means of the staircase. I followed him, and when we were on the ramparts he made several détours on the pretext of showing me the way, but I could see that he wanted me to lose all trace of the way to the cellar. However, I wished to remember it, as I intended to go back the next day with several others to save the poor woman who had begged my help, and also to get an explanation about several portmanteaus I had seen at the back of their cursed cellar.

CHAPTER VI.

A DISTURBED NIGHT—I FIND MY FRIENDS AGAIN—WE LEAVE
SMOLENSK—A NECESSARY CORRECTION—THE BATTLE OF
KRASNOË—MELLÉ THE DRAGOON.

MY guide disappeared suddenly, and I was at a total loss
as to my whereabouts. I was only sorry now that I had
ever left the regiment. However, I had to go in one
direction or another, and, as the snow had stopped falling,
I began to search for my footmarks. And then I remembered that I must keep the rampart on my right hand.
After walking for some minutes, I seemed to recognise the
place where I met the Baden soldier; but, to make quite
sure, I marked two deep crosses in the snow with the butt-
end of my musket, before going further.

It was now about midnight, and more than an hour
since I had fallen into the cellar, and during that time the
cold had increased terribly. I saw a great many fires on
my left, but dared not go in that direction for fear of falling into holes that the snow had hidden. I walked on,
feeling my way with my head down, looking out for safe
places for my feet. I now saw that the road sloped down-
wards, and further on I found it was almost blocked up by
gun-carriages, intended no doubt for the rampart. When
I had arrived at the bottom, it was so fearfully dark that I

lost all idea of direction, and I was obliged to sit down on a gun-carriage to rest, and try to think which way I ought to take.

In this dreadful predicament, as I sat with my head buried in my hands, I was dropping off into a sleep from which I should not have awakened, when I heard some extraordinary sounds. I got up, terrified to think of the danger I had just escaped. I listened with all my ears, but heard nothing more. So I think I must have been dreaming, or perhaps it was a warning from Heaven to save me. So taking fresh courage, I began to walk again, feeling my way, and striding over the numbers of obstacles in the road.

At last I left all the obstacles behind me, after nearly breaking my leg several times, and I rested a moment to take breath and get strength enough to climb a hill in front of me. Then I heard the same sounds which had awakened me before, but this time I recognised them for music. I heard the slow, prolonged notes of an organ some distance off: they produced an indescribable impression on me, alone as I was at such a place, and at such an hour. I set out, quickening my pace, in the direction of the sounds—up the steep ascent. When I got to the top, I took a few steps, and then stopped—just in time! another step, and I should have been done for— I should have fallen from top to bottom of the rampart, more than fifty feet, on to the banks of the Boristhène. Horrified at my narrow escape, I drew back a few steps, and stopped to listen, but I did not hear the sound again. I began walking once more, and, turning to the left, fortunately found the beaten track. Slowly and cautiously I advanced, holding my head well up, my ears open for any sound, and at last I made up my mind the music had been an hallucination. In our present dreadful circumstances, how could such music have been possible—and, above all, at such an hour?

Reflecting as I walked, my right foot, which already was half frozen, and giving me some pain, struck against something hard. I cried out with the pain, and fell all my length over a dead body, its face touching mine, then raised myself with great difficulty, and saw that it was the body of a dragoon, his helmet still strapped on, and his cloak, on which he had fallen. He had probably not been there long.

My cry of pain was heard by a man on my right, who called out to me to go to him, he had been waiting for so long. I was surprised, and very glad to find a human being when I thought I was quite alone, and I went in the direction of the voice. The nearer I got to it, the better I seemed to recognise it, and at last I cried:

'Is it you, Béloque?'*

'Yes,' he called back.

He was as much surprised as I at our meeting at this time of night, in such a desolate spot, and knowing no more than I did where we were. He had at first taken me for a corporal who had gone to get men on extra duty to help carry the sick who had been left at the gates. They had been got so far, but then it had been necessary to send for more help.

I told him how I had been lost, and of my adventure in the cellar, but I dared not say anything of the music I had heard, fearing he should say I was out of my mind. He begged me to stay with him, and I was glad to do so. Then he asked me why I had cried out, and I told him of my fall on to the dragoon, and how my face had touched his.

* Béloque was one of my friends, a sergeant-vélite like me.—
Author's Note.

' Were you very frightened, poor fellow ?'

' No,' I said ; ' but I hurt myself horribly.'

' It was lucky for you,' he said, ' that you were so badly hurt as to cry out, as you might have passed on and never found me.'

We stamped backwards and forwards to keep ourselves warm while we waited for the men who were to carry away the sick.

The poor fellows were lying on a sheepskin, propped up one against another, and covered with the cloak and coat of a dead man. They seemed in a terrible condition.

' I am afraid,' Béloque said, ' that we shall not have the trouble of taking them away.'

We heard them murmur and breathe from time to time, but these were the last efforts of dying men.

While the fearful death-rattle was going on near us, the aerial music began again, but this time much nearer. I called Béloque's attention to it, and told him of the strange things which had happened to me when I heard the sounds before. And then he said that at intervals he had heard the music too, and could not make it out. Sometimes it made an infernal racket, and if men were amusing themselves in that way, they must have the devil inside them. Then, coming closer to me, he said in a low voice :

' My friend, these sounds are very like death-music. Death is all round us ; and I have a presentiment that in a few days I shall be dead too.' Then he added, ' May God's will be done ! But the suffering seems too great. Look at those poor wretches !'—pointing to two men lying in the snow.

I said nothing, for I thought just as he did.

He stopped speaking, and we listened attentively in a silence only broken by the heavy breathing of a dying man. Suddenly my companion said :

' To my mind, the sounds seem to come from above.'

As he said so, the sounds did certainly seem to come from just over our heads. All at once the noise ceased, and an awful silence followed, broken only by a mournful cry—the last breath of one of our men.

Just then we heard footsteps, and a corporal came up with eight men, to carry away the two who were dying ; as there was now only one, he was removed at once— covered with his dead companion's clothes—and we all set out.

It was now past one o'clock : the wind had dropped, and the cold in consequence was not so great, but I was so worn out that I could walk no longer; and besides, I was so terribly tired that several times Béloque found me standing asleep in the road. He had told me where to find Grangier ; the men of his company in charge of the only cart the Marshal had left remaining had seen their comrades, and had recognised the cart placed at the Marshal's door. When we got to the place where we left the rampart, I parted from the funeral cortège, and decided to follow the new way pointed out to me.

I had not been alone a minute, when the cursed music started again. I stopped, and, raising my head to listen better, I saw a light in front of me. As I walked on towards the light, the road descended rapidly and the light disappeared. In spite of this, I continued, but was stopped almost directly by a wall in front of me, and was forced to retrace my steps. I turned first to the right, then to the left, and found myself in a street of ruined houses. I strode on quickly, still guided by the music. At the end of the street there was a building lighted up, from which the sounds evidently came. There I was stopped by a wall surrounding the building, which I now saw was a church.

Tired as I was, I wished to avoid going all round the wall to find an opening, and decided to climb over it, feeling the depth on the other side with my musket. As it was not more than three or four feet, I climbed to the top and jumped down, and striking some round object with my feet, I fell. I was not hurt, however, but on walking a few steps I felt the ground uneven under my feet, and had to steady myself with my musket. I then became aware of the fact that more than 200 dead bodies lay on the ground, barely covered with snow. As I stumbled along, picking my way among the legs and arms of the bodies, a melancholy chant arose—like the Office for the Dead. Béloque's words came back to me, and I broke out into a cold sweat, not knowing where I was and what I was about. I found myself at last leaning against the church wall.

I came to myself in a bit, in spite of the diabolical noise, and walked on with one hand against the wall, at length finding an open door through which came a thick smoke. I went in, and saw a great number of people, who in the dense smoke looked like shadows. Some of them were singing, and others playing on the organ. All at once a great flame burst forth and the smoke disappeared. I looked round to see where I was; one of the singers came up to me and cried out : ' It's our sergeant !' He had recognised my bearskin, and I saw, to my immense surprise, all the men of my company ! I was on the point of questioning them, when one of them offered me a silver cup full of brandy. They were all fearfully drunk !

One, rather less drunk than the others, said that they had been on extra duty when first they came, and that they had seen two men with a lantern coming out of a cellar ; that they had banded together to go there after the distribution of rations, to see if they could find something to eat, and then spend the night in this church. In the cellar they had found a small cask of brandy, a bag of rice, and a little biscuit, besides ten capes trimmed with fur, and some Rabbi's fur caps.

With the men of the company were several musicians of the regiment, who had started playing the organ—being half seas over, as they say. This explained the harmony which had puzzled me so much.

They gave me some rice, a few pieces of biscuit, and a Rabbi's cap, trimmed with magnificent black fox fur. I put the rice carefully away in my knapsack. The cap I placed on my head, and pulling a plank in front of the fire, I lay down on it. I had scarcely laid my head on my knapsack when I heard shouts and curses from the door, so we hastened to see what was the matter. Six men were driving a cart drawn by a worn-out horse. The cart was filled with dead bodies to be left behind the church, with the others I had seen there. The ground was much too hard to dig graves, and the cold preserved the bodies in the meanwhile. These men told us that, if this sort of thing went on, there would soon be no room anywhere for the bodies; all the churches were used as hospitals, and were filled with the sick, whom it was impossible to help. This was the only church not full of them, and the dead had been laid here for the last few days. From the time that the column of the Grand Army had made its appearance, they had been unable to supply transport for the men who died as soon as they arrived. After hearing all this I lay down again. These ambulance men asked us if they might spend the rest of the night with us; they unharnessed their horse and brought him into the church.

I slept pretty well for the remainder of the night, but was awakened before daylight by the shrieks of an unfortunate musician, who had just broken his leg in coming down from the organ-loft, where he had slept. The men below had taken away some of the steps during the night to make a fire. The poor devil had a terrible fall, it was impossible for him to walk; most probably he never left the church. When I got up, nearly all the men were roasting meat on the points of their swords. I asked them where the meat came from, and they replied it was the horse who had drawn the dead-cart, and that they had killed him while the ambulance men were asleep. I don't blame them for doing it: one must live somehow. An hour afterwards, when a good quarter of the horse had disappeared, one of the undertakers told his companions what we had done. They were furious, and threatened to inform the chief director of the hospitals. We went on eating calmly, saying it was a pity he was so thin, and that half a dozen like him would be wanted for rations for the regiment. They went off threatening us, and in revenge they threw the seven corpses they had in their cart right in the doorway, so that we were obliged to climb over them to get out.

These ambulance men had not been through the campaign, or felt the want of anything, and they did not know that for the last few days we had lived on any horses we could find.

When I got ready to go back to my regiment it was seven o'clock. I told the fourteen men that were there that they must collect together and arrive in good order. We first had some very good *purée de cheval au riz*. After that, giving them the bag containing the Jew's fur capes to carry, we left the church, which was already filling with new-comers—some miserable wretches who had spent the night where they could, and many others who had left their regiments, hoping to find something better. They prowled about in all the corners, looking for food. They did not seem to notice the dead bodies in the doorway, but walked over them as if they had been wood, so stiff were they frozen.

When we reached the road I told my men of my adventure in the cellar, and proposed to go there, and they agreed. We found the way quite easily, for we had as sign-posts first the man whom Béloque had left dead, and then the dragoon over whom I had fallen, and who, I now saw, was without his cloak and his boots. After passing the gun-carriages where I nearly fell fatally asleep, we reached the cross I had made in the snow. After descending the slope in rather slower fashion than I had done the day before, we stood before the door, which was shut. We knocked, but no one answered ; we burst the door in, but the birds had flown. We only found one man, so drunk he could not speak. I recognised him as the German who wished to turn me out. He was wrapped in a great sheepskin cape, which was taken from him by one of our musicians, in spite of his resistance. We found several portmanteaus and a trunk—stolen during the night—but all were empty, and also the cask brought by the Baden man, which had contained gin.

Before going on to the camp I noticed our position and was surprised to find that, although I had walked so much during the night, I had been no distance. I had simply walked round and round the church.

We then went back to the camp. As we went I met several men of our regiment, whom I joined to those already with me. Just afterwards I saw a non-commissioned officer in the distance, whom by his white knapsack I recognised at once as the very man I was looking for— Grangier. I had embraced him before he knew who I was, I had altered so much. We were mutually looking for each other, and if I had had the patience to wait, he said he would have taken me to his quarters and given me good soup, and straw to sleep on, for he had searched for me at this very place the evening before. He went with us to the camp, whither I brought my nineteen men in good order. Grangier then made me a sign, and opening his knapsack, he took out a piece of beef, ready cooked, which he said he had kept for me, and also a piece of bread.

I simply devoured the food, for it was twenty-three days since I had tasted anything like it. Then he asked me for news of a friend of his, whom he supposed dangerously ill. I could only tell him that he was in the town, but as we did not know the whereabouts of his regiment, he would be obliged to go through the gate by which we had entered, as many of the sick, unable to go further, had remained there. So we set off at once.

We soon reached the place where the poor dragoon lay. This time we found him almost stripped; he had been searched, no doubt, in the hope of finding a belt containing money. I showed Grangier the cellar, and then we arrived at the gate. The number of dead there was appalling; near the Baden sentry were four men of the Guard, who had died during the night. The officer on duty had forbidden the men to strip them, and he told us of two more he had in his guard-room. We went in to see them; they were both unconscious. The first was a Chasseur; the second, his face hidden in a handkerchief, was in our regiment. Grangier uncovered his face, and recognised the man he was in search of. We did all we possibly could to bring him round, relieving him of his sword and powder-flask and his collar, and trying to force a few drops of brandy between his lips. He opened his eyes without seeming to see us, and directly afterwards died in my arms. We emptied his knapsack, and found a watch and several little knick-knacks, which Grangier took charge of, to send as keepsakes to his family, if ever he were lucky enough to get back to France. We placed the Chasseur as comfortably as possible, and then left him to his melancholy fate ; what else could we do ?

Grangier then took me to his post, and when, soon afterwards, he was relieved by some Chasseurs, we asked them to look after the man we had just left. The sergeant immediately sent four men to fetch him.

We returned to the regiment, and the rest of the day we spent in getting our firearms into good order, in warming ourselves and talking. We killed several horses during the day, and divided them. Rations of rye and oatmeal were given out, consisting chiefly of straw with a little rye mixed.

At four o'clock the next morning we were ordered under arms and sent a quarter of a league from the town, where, in spite of the cold, we remained in order of battle until daylight. The same thing was repeated the few following days, as the Russian army was manœuvring on our left.

We had been three days already at Smolensk, and we did not know if we had to remain in this position or continue the retreat. To stay, they said, was impossible. Why, then, did we not leave a town where there were no houses to shelter us, and no provisions to feed us ? On the fourth day, as we returned from our position of the morning, I saw an officer of a line regiment lying in front of a fire. We looked for some time at each other, trying to recall each other's appearance and features under the rags and dirt with which we were covered. I stopped ; he got up, and, coming nearer to me, he said :

' I thought I was not mistaken.'

' No,' I said.

We had recognised and embraced each other without

pronouncing a name. It was Beaulieu,* my messmate in the Vélites when we were at Fontainebleau.

How much we had both altered, and how wretched our condition now! I had not seen him since the Battle of Wagram, when he had left the Guard, to pass as an officer into the line, with other Vélites.

I asked him after his regiment; for answer he pointed out the eagle to me in the middle of a pile of arms. There were thirty-three of them left. He and the Surgeon-Major were the only officers; of the others, a great many had been killed in battle, but more than half had died of cold and hunger; a few had been lost on the road.

Beaulieu was Captain, and he had received orders to follow the Guard. I stayed with him for some time, and, as he had nothing to eat, we shared the rice the men in the church had given me. In those days, when food was not to be had for gold, this was the greatest proof of friendship one could possibly give.

On the morning of the 14th, the Emperor left Smolensk with the Grenadiers and Chasseurs; we followed a short time after as rear-guard, leaving behind us the corps belonging to Prince Eugène, Davoust, and Ney, reduced to lamentably small numbers. On first leaving the town we crossed the Sacred Field, so called by the Russians. A little past Korouitnia† we came upon a deep ravine; here we had to wait while the artillery crossed it. I went in search of Grangier, and proposed that we should cross first, as we were getting frozen while standing still. When we were at the other side, I saw three men round a dead

* Beaulieu was from Condé, in Valenciennes, my native country. When I came out of prison in 1814, his sister, Mme. Vasté, told me that her unfortunate brother had been killed by a bullet at Dresden.— Author's Note.

† Korouitnia, a small village.—Author's Note.

horse; two of them staggered about as if they were drunk. The third, a German, lay on the horse; the poor wretch was dying of hunger, and, not being able to cut the flesh, was trying to bite it. He soon afterwards died where he was of cold and hunger. The two others, Hussars, were covered with blood about the hands and mouth. We spoke to them, but they did not answer; they looked at us, laughing in a horrible way, and then sat down close to the dead man, where they no doubt fell into the last fatal sleep.

We went on then, walking by the side of the highroad to come up with the right of the column, and then wait for our regiment near a fire, if we were lucky enough to find one. We met a Hussar—I think of the 8th Regiment; the poor fellow was struggling against death, continually rising and falling down again. We ran up to give him what help we could; but he fell once more, not to rise again. Thus, all along our way we were forced to step over the dead and dying. As we advanced with great difficulty, keeping to the right of the road to get past the convoys, we saw a man of the line sitting against a tree near a little fire; he was busy melting snow in a saucepan to cook the liver and heart of a horse he had just killed with his bayonet.

As we had rice and oatmeal with us, we asked him to lend us the saucepan to cook them, so that we could all eat together. He was delighted; so with the rice and straw-oatmeal we made some soup, seasoning it with a little sugar Grangier had in his knapsack, as we had no salt. While our soup was cooking, we roasted some bits of liver and kidneys from a horse, and enjoyed it greatly. We devoured our rice only half cooked, and hastened to join our regiment, which had passed us. That night the Emperor slept at Korouitnia, and we in a wood a short distance off. The next day we set out very early, so as to reach Krasnoë; but before we could get so far, the front of the Imperial columns was stopped by 25,000 Russians occupying the road. Stragglers at the front caught sight of them first, and immediately turned back to join the first regiments advancing; the greater part of them, however, united and faced the enemy. A few men, too careless or too wretched to care what they did, fell into the enemy's hands.

The Grenadiers and Chasseurs, formed into close columns, advanced against the mass of Russians, who, not daring to wait for them, retired and left the passage free; they took up a position on the hills to the left of the road, and turned their artillery on us. When we heard the cannon, we doubled our pace, as we were behind, and arrived just as our gunners were answering them. The Russians disappeared behind the hills as our fire began, and we continued our way.

An incident occurred at this time about which I cannot keep silence, and I have heard the same incident entirely differently related. What they say is this: That when, on first catching sight of the Russians, the first regiments of the Guard were grouped round the Emperor, marching as if no enemy were before them, the band played the air 'Où peut-on être mieux qu'au sein de sa famille?' and that the Emperor stopped the music, ordering to be played instead 'Veillons au salut de l'Empire!'

The incident did happen, but in quite a different fashion, as it was at Smolensk, on the day of our departure. The Prince Neuchâtel, then Minister of War, seeing that no orders for departure came from the Emperor, and that the whole army was in despair at being kept in such a wretched position, collected some men from the bands under the Emperor's window, and told them to play the air 'Où peut-on être mieux qu'au sein de sa famille?' They had scarcely begun, when the Emperor appeared on the balcony, and ordered them to play 'Veillons au salut de l'Empire!' The men were forced to play it as best they could, in spite of their pain, and immediately afterwards the order for departure on the next morning was given. How could it have been possible for the wretched men, even had they been to the right of the regiment, to have blown down their instruments, or used their poor frost-bitten fingers? This, on the other hand, was quite a possibility at Smolensk, as there were fires where they could get warm.

In two hours after the encounter with the Russians, the Emperor reached Krasnoë with the first regiments of the Guard—ours and the Fusiliers-Chasseurs. We camped behind the town. I was on guard with fifteen men at General Roguet's quarters: a miserable house in the town, thatched with straw. I put my men in a stable, thinking myself in luck to be under cover, and near a fire we had just lighted, but it turned out quite otherwise.

While we were in Krasnoë and the immediate neighbourhood, the Russians, 90,000 strong, surrounded us—to right, to left, in front, and behind, nothing but Russians—thinking, no doubt, they could soon finish us off. But the Emperor wished to show them it was not quite so easy a thing as they imagined; for although we were most wretched, and dying of cold and hunger, we still possessed two things—courage and honour. The Emperor, therefore, annoyed at seeing himself followed by this horde of barbarians and savages, decided to rid himself of them.

On the evening of our arrival, General Roguet received orders to attack during the night, taking with him part of the Guard, the Fusiliers-Chasseurs, the Grenadiers, the light companies, and skirmishers. At eleven o'clock a few detachments were sent on first to reconnoitre, and find out exactly where the Russians lay; we could see their camp-fires in the two villages they held. They seem to have expected us, for some were already prepared to receive us.

At about one o'clock in the morning, the General came to me, and said, with his Gascon accent :

' Sergeant, leave a corporal and four men here in charge of my quarters, and the few things I have left. Go back to the camp yourself, and rejoin the regiment with your guard. We shall have our work cut out for us presently.'

To tell the truth, I was very much disgusted at this order. I do not mean that I was afraid of fighting, but I grudged the time lost for sleep terribly.

When we got to the camp, preparations were already going on ; evidently serious things were expected. I heard several men say that they hoped an end would at last be put to their sufferings, as they could struggle no longer.

At two o'clock we began to move forward. We formed into three columns—the Fusiliers - Grenadiers (I was amongst them) and the Fusiliers-Chasseurs in the centre, the skirmishers and light companies on the right and left. The cold was as intense as ever. We had the greatest difficulty in walking across the fields, as the snow was up to our knees. After half an hour of this, we found ourselves in the midst of the Russians. On our right was a long line of infantry, opening a murderous fire on us, their heavy cavalry on our left made up of Cuirassiers in white uniform with black cuirasses. They howled like wolves to excite each other, but did not dare to attack. The artillery was in the centre, pouring grape-shot on us. All this did not stop our career in the least. In spite of the firing, and the number of our men who fell, we charged on into their camp, where we made frightful havoc with our bayonets.

The men who were stationed further off had now had

time to arm themselves, and come to their comrades' help.
This they did by setting fire to their camp and the two
villages near. We fought by the light of the fires. The
columns on the right and left had passed us, and entered
the enemy's camp at the two ends, whereas our column
had taken the middle.

I have omitted to say that, as the head of our column
charged into the Russian camp, we passed several hundred
Russians stretched on the snow; we believed them to be
dead or dangerously wounded. These men now jumped
up and fired on us from behind, so that we had to make
a demi-tour to defend ourselves. Unluckily for them, a
battalion in the rear came up behind, so that they were
taken between two fires, and in five minutes not one was
left alive. This was a stratagem the Russians often employed, but this time it was not successful.

Poor Béloque was the first man we lost; he had foretold
his death at Smolensk. A ball struck his head, and killed
him on the spot. He was a great favourite with us all,
and, in spite of the indifference we now felt about everything, we were really sorry to lose him.

We went through the Russian camp, and reached the
village. We forced the enemy to throw a part of their
artillery into a lake there, and then found that a great
number of foot soldiers had filled the houses, which were
partly in flames. We now fought desperately hand-to-
hand. The slaughter was terrible, and each man fought
by himself for himself. I found myself near our Colonel,
the oldest in France, who had been through the campaign
in Egypt. A sapper was holding him up by the arm, and
the Adjutant-Major Roustan was there too. We were
close to a farmyard filled with Russians, and blockaded
by our men; they could retreat only by an entrance into
a large courtyard close by a barrier.

While this desultory fighting was going on, I saw a Russian officer on a white horse striking with the flat of his sword any of his men who tried to get away by jumping over the barrier, and so effectually preventing his escape. He got possession of the passage, but just as he was preparing to jump to the other side, his horse fell under him, struck by a ball. The men were forced to defend themselves, and the fighting now grew desperate. By the lurid light of the fire it was a dreadful scene of butchery, Russians and Frenchmen in utter confusion, shooting each other muzzle to muzzle.

I tried to get at the Russian officer, who had now extricated himself from his horse, and was trying to save himself by getting over the barrier, but a Russian soldier got in the way and fired at me. Probably only the priming caught fire, otherwise there would have been an end of me; but the man who had fired reloaded his musket calmly, thinking, no doubt, that I was dangerously wounded. The Adjutant-Major, Roustan, ran to me and, seizing me by the arm, said:

' My poor Bourgogne, are you wounded ?'

' No,' I answered.

' Then,' he said, ' don't miss him.'

That was what I meant also, and before the Russian had time to reload, I shot him through. Mortally wounded, he did not, however, fall at once, but reeled back, and, glaring at me, fell over the officer's horse at the barrier. The Adjutant-Major gave him a thrust with his sword. Just then I found myself near the Colonel, who was completely worn out and fit for nothing more. He was alone except for his sapper. The Adjutant-Major came up, his sword covered with blood, saying that, to get back to the Colonel, he had been forced to cut his way with the sword, and that he had a bayonet wound in his thigh. As he spoke, the sapper, who was supporting the Colonel, was struck in the chest by a ball. The Colonel instantly said :

'Sapper, you are wounded ?'

'Yes, sir,' said the sapper, and, taking the Colonel's hand, he made him feel the hole the ball had made.

'Then go back.'

The sapper replied that he was strong enough to stay and die with him if necessary.

'And, after all,' said the Adjutant-Major, 'where could he go, in the midst of the enemy ? We do not know where we are, and I can see that we shall have to wait here, fighting, till daylight.'

We had indeed lost all idea of our locality, blinded by the glare from the fires.

Five minutes after the sapper had been wounded, the Russians, whom we had held blockaded in the farm, seeing that they ran a chance of being burnt alive, offered to surrender. They sent a non-commisioned officer through a perfect storm of balls to make the proposal. The Adjutant-Major therefore sent me with the order to stop firing.

'Stop firing !' said one of our wounded men; 'the others may stop if they please, but as I am wounded, and very likely dying, I shall go on as long as I have cartridges to fire with.'

He went on, therefore, sitting in the snow all stained with his blood, and even asked for more cartridges when he had fired his own. The Adjutant-Major, seeing that his orders were disregarded, came himself with a message from the Colonel. But our men, now perfectly desperate, took no notice, and still continued to fire. The Russians, seeing that there was no hope for them, and probably having no more ammunition, tried to rush out all together from the building, where they were fast getting roasted; but our men forced them back. They made a second attempt, not being able to endure their position, but scarcely had a few of their number reached the yard, when the building collapsed on the rest, more than forty of them perishing in the flames, and those in the yard being crushed as well.

When this was over, we collected our wounded together, and gathered round the Colonel with loaded weapons, waiting for daybreak. All this time the rattle of musket-shots was going on continually round us, mingled with the groans of the wounded and the dying. There is nothing more terrible than a battle at night, when often fatal mistakes take place.

In this way we waited for the light. As soon as it appeared, we looked about us, and could see the result of the night's fighting. The whole ground we had been over was strewn with the wounded and dying. I saw the man who had tried to kill me, and who was not yet dead, so I placed him more comfortably away from the white horse near which he had fallen. All the houses in the village (either Kircova or Malierva) and the whole of the Russian camp were covered with half-burnt corpses. M. Gilet had his leg broken by a ball, and died a few days afterwards. The sharp-shooters (skirmishers) and the light companies lost more men than we.

During the morning I met Captain Débonnez, who came from my country and commanded a company in the Guards. He was looking for me to see if I were all safe. He said he had lost the third of his company, besides a Sub-Lieutenant and his Sergeant-Major.

After this bloody contest the Russians abandoned their positions without going very far off, and we remained on the battle-field during the day and night of the 16th and

17th, keeping on the qui-vive, however, all the time, neither being able to rest a moment nor even to warm ourselves.

During the day, while we were all talking together of our miserable discomfort and of the night's battle, the Adjutant-Major, Delaître, came up. He was the worst man I have ever known and the cruellest, doing wrong for the mere pleasure of doing it. He began to talk, and, greatly to our surprise, seemed much troubled by Béloque's tragic death.

' Poor Béloque!' he said; ' I am very sorry I ever behaved badly to him.'

Just then a voice in my ear (what voice I never knew) said :

' He will die very soon.'

Others heard it also. He seemed sincerely sorry for all his bad behaviour to those under him, especially to us non-commissioned officers. I do not think there was a man in the regiment who would not have rejoiced to see him carried off by a bullet. We called him Peter the Cruel.

On the morning of the 17th, almost before it was light, we took up our firearms, and forming into columns, set out to take up our position by the side of the road, opposite to the field of battle. When we got there we saw a part of the Russian army on a little hill in front of us, near a wood, and therefore deployed in a line fronting them. On our left and behind us was a ravine which crossed the road. This hollow sheltered all those near it. On our right were the Fusiliers-Chasseurs, with the head of their regiment a gunshot from the town. In front of us, 250 yards off, was a regiment of the Young Guard, commanded by General Luron. Further still on the right were the old Grenadiers and Chasseurs. The whole was commanded by the Emperor himself, on foot. Walking with firm steps, as if on a grand parade day, he placed himself in the midst of the field of battle, opposite the enemy's batteries.

I was with two of my friends, Grangier and Leboude, behind Adjutant-Major Delaître. We were within half-range of the Russian artillery, and directly they caught sight of us they opened fire. Adjutant-Major Delaître was the first man to fall; a ball had taken off his legs, just above his knees and his long riding-boots. He fell without a cry, nor did he utter one at all. He was leading his horse, the bridle on his right arm. We stopped, as he filled up the path we walked on; we were forced to stride over him to get on at all, and as I was next after him I did so the first. I looked at him as I passed. His eyes were opened, and his teeth chattered convulsively. I went nearer to listen. He raised his voice and said:

'For God's sake take my pistols and blow my brains out!'

No one dared do this service for him, and without answering we went on our way—most luckily as it happened, for before we had gone six yards a second discharge carried off three of our men behind us, killing the Adjutant-Major.

Directly afterwards the Emperor arrived, and we began fighting. The enemy made terrible havoc in our ranks with their artillery. We had only a few pieces to reply with, and some of them were soon dismounted. Our men died without moving, and until two o'clock in the afternoon we maintained this dreadful position.

The Russians sent a part of their army to take up a position on the road beyond Krasnoë, and to cut off our retreat; but the Emperor anticipated them by sending a battalion of the Old Guard there.

While we stood thus exposed to the enemy's fire, our numbers continually diminishing, we saw to our left the remainder of Marshal Davoust's army in the midst of a swarm of Cossacks calmly marching towards us. With them was the canteen man's cart containing his wife and children. A ball intended for us struck them, and we heard the woman's shrieks, but we could not tell whether one of them was killed or only wounded.

Just then the Dutch Grenadiers of the Guard abandoned an important position, which the Russians instantly filled with their artillery, and directed their fire against us. Our position after this was untenable. A regiment sent to recover the ground was forced to retire ; another moved forward as far as the foot of the batteries, but was stopped by a body of Cuirassiers. It then retired to the left of the battery, forming into a square. The enemy's cavalry came on to the attack again, but were received by a heavy fire, which killed a great many. A second charge was made, and met with the same reception. A third charge, supported by grape-shot, was successful. The regiment was overwhelmed. The enemy broke into the square and finished off the remainder with their swords. These poor fellows, nearly all very young, having their hands and feet mostly frost-bitten, had no power to defend themselves, and were absolutely massacred.

We witnessed this scene without being able to help our comrades. Eleven men only returned ; the rest were all killed, wounded, or taken prisoners, driven by sword-thrusts into a little wood opposite. The Colonel himself,* covered with wounds, was made prisoner, with several other officers.

I must not omit to say that as we were getting into

* Colonel Luron.—*Author's Note.*

order of battle, the Colonel had given the word of command: ' Drapeaux, guides généraux sur la ligne!'

I was therefore *guide général* on the right of our regiment. But they omitted to give the order for our return, and as I made it a point of honour to remain at my post, there I stayed for more than an hour, holding the butt-end of my musket in the air, and in spite of the bullets flying round me, I did not move.

By two o'clock we had lost a third of our men, but the Fusiliers-Chasseurs were the worst off of all, as, being nearer to the town, they were exposed to a more deadly fire. For the last half-hour the Emperor had drawn back with the first regiments of the Guard to the highroad. We remained on the field alone with a very few men from different corps, facing more than 50,000 of the enemy. Marshal Mortier then ordered us to retreat, and we began to move, drawing off at walking pace as if we were on parade, the Russian artillery overwhelming us with grape-shot all the while. We took with us the least dangerously wounded of our men.

It was a terrible scene as we left the field, for when our poor wounded men saw that they were being abandoned, surrounded by the enemy, many of them dragged themselves painfully on their knees after us, staining the snow with their blood, and raising their hands to heaven with heart-rending cries, imploring us to help them. But what could we do ? The same fate was in store for us, for at every moment men fell from our ranks, and were in their turn abandoned.

I saw, as I passed the position occupied by the Fusiliers-Chasseurs, several of my friends stretched dead on the snow, horribly mutilated by grape-shot. A man named Capon, from Bapaume, was one of my best friends.

After passing the Fusiliers-Chasseurs, as we entered the

town, we saw on our left some pieces of artillery, firing at the Russians for our protection ; they were served and supported by about forty men, gunners and Light Infantry —all that was left of General Longchamp's brigade. He was there himself with the remnant of his men, determined to save them or die with them.

As soon as he caught sight of our Colonel, he came to him with open arms. They embraced as two friends who had not met for long, and who perhaps were never to meet again. The General, with his eyes full of tears, showed the two guns and the few remaining men to our Colonel.

' Look,' he said ; ' that is all I have left !'

They had been through the Egyptian campaign together.

After this battle, Kutusow, the General-in-Chief of the Russian army, was heard to say that the French, so far from being disheartened by their cruel sufferings, only rushed more madly on the guns which destroyed them. Wilson,* the English General who was present at this battle, called it the Heroes' Battle. The word ought to be applied to us, and to us only, who, with a few thousand men, fought against the whole Russian force of 90,000.

General Longchamps, with his poor remainder, was forced to leave his guns, all the horses being killed, and follow our retreat, taking advantage of what shelter he could find behind houses or banks as he went.

We were scarcely within the town of Krasnoë when the Russians, their guns mounted on sledges, took up a position near the outlying houses, and opened a fire of grape-shot on us. Three men of our company were wounded. A ball, which grazed my musket and split the stock, struck a young drummer on the head and killed him on the spot. The town of Krasnoë is divided in two by a deep hollow,

* He was serving in the Russian army.

which must be crossed. Arrived there, we saw at the bottom a herd of oxen dead of cold and hunger. So stiff were they frozen, that our sappers could scarcely cut them up with hatchets. Only their heads were visible, their eyes still open ; their bodies were covered with snow. These bullocks belonged to the army, and had not been able to reach us : the extreme cold and want of fodder had killed them.

A large convent in this wretched town and all the houses were filled with wounded, who shrieked in despair when they heard they were to be left to the Russians. We were forced to leave them thus to a savage and brutal enemy, who stripped and robbed these unfortunate men without pity for.their wounds or their condition.

The Russians still followed us, but slowly, and they were unable to do us much harm. Our road was through a deep cutting, and the bullets passed over our heads ; the cavalry on our right also prevented the enemy coming to close quarters.

At a quarter of a league's distance from the town things grew quieter. We walked on sadly and silently, thinking of our dreadful situation, and of our unfortunate comrades left in the hands of the enemy. I seemed still to hear them begging for help; and looking back, we could see some of the slightly wounded already stripped almost naked by the Russians, and left in that condition. We were luckily able to save the poor fellows—at least, for the time, and we spared all we could to cover them.

That night the Emperor slept at Liadouï, a village built of wood. Our regiment camped a little further off. As I passed through the village I stopped near a wretched hovel to warm myself at a fire. There I had the good fortune to meet Sergeant Guignard again—from my own village—and his Hungarian *cantinière*. They gave me a little oatmeal broth and some horseflesh. I was badly in want of the food, as I was shockingly weak, having eaten hardly anything for two days. The sergeant told me that their regiment had suffered considerably in the battle, and their numbers were much diminished, but not nearly as greatly as ours; that he had thought much of me, and was heartily glad to see me again with a whole skin. He asked me after Captain Débonnez, but I had not seen him since the 16th. I left him to go back to my regiment, encamped near the highroad. We spent a dreadful night; there was a high wind, and half-melted snow was falling, which wetted us through, and we had very little fire. All this, however, was nothing compared to what we went through afterwards.

During this dreadful night many of the sharp-shooters came to warm themselves at our fire. I asked them for news of several of my friends, especially of two from my part who were in the Vélites with me. One was M. Alexandre Legrand, of the Quatre fils Aymon at Valenciennes ; and the other, M. Laporte, from Cassel, near Lille, had been killed by a grape-shot.

At midnight one of our sentinels told me he could see a man on horseback appearing to come from our side. I ran at once with two of our men to see who it could be. I could distinguish the horseman perfectly, and in front of him a foot soldier, whom he was apparently forcing on before him. When they got near us I recognised a Dragoon of the Guard, who had made his way into the Russian camp to get food for himself and his horse. He had disguised himself by means of the helmet of a Russian Cuirassier whom he had killed the day before. He had brought away from the enemy's camp a bundle of straw and a little flour, and had wounded one sentinel and knocked down another, whom he made prisoner and brought along with him. This brave fellow was called Mellé, and he came from Condé. He stayed with us for the rest of the night. He said that he had run this risk for his horse, called Cadet, and not fo himself; at any cost he had determined to get the animal some food. ' If I save my horse, he will save me afterwards.' This was the second time he had got inside the Russian camp since leaving Smolensk. On the first occasion he had brought back a horse already harnessed.

He was fortunate enough to return to France with his horse. They had already been through the Prussian and Polish campaigns of 1806-7 together, in Spain in 1808, in Germany in 1809, in Spain again 1810-11, and in Russia 1812 ; afterwards in Saxony in 1813, and France 1814. The poor horse was finally killed at Waterloo, after being through more than twelve great battles commanded by the Emperor, and over thirty smaller engagements. I met Mellé again during this wretched campaign on a lake breaking a hole in the ice with a hatchet to get water for his horse; and another time I saw him at the top of a burning barn, in peril of his life, getting straw from the roof for him, for the horses were as badly off as we were. The poor animals had to gnaw at the trees to feed themselves, until in their turn they fed us.

After this others followed Mellé's example and got into the Russian camp for provisions. Many of them were seized, and died afterwards. Our destitution was now so great that our men left their regiments at the least sign of a road in the faint hope of its leading to some village—if one can give that name to the collection of wretched hovels made out of tree-trunks, and containing absolutely nothing. I could never discover what these peasants lived on. Our men would come back sometimes bringing

bits of bread as black as coal, and filled with long pieces
of straw and grains of barley, so terribly hard that no
teeth could bite into them ; and, besides, our lips were all
split and cracked by frost. During all this miserable
campaign I never saw a man bring so much as a cow or a
sheep with him. What these savages live on no one can
tell. They have no beasts, that is certain, or we should
have seen some. It is the devil's own country, for it is
hell all through.

CHAPTER VII.

THE RETREAT GOES ON—I TAKE A WIFE—DISCOURAGEMENT—
I LOSE SIGHT OF MY COMRADES—DRAMATIC SCENE—MEET-
ING WITH PICARD.

ON November 18, the day after the Battle of Krasnoë, we
set out very early from our bivouac. The march was a
sad and weary one, and terribly tiring. There was a
thaw; our feet were wet through; and all day the fog
was so thick we could see nothing. Our men were still
in some sort of order, but the fighting of the preceding
days and the forced abandonment of their imploring
comrades had demoralized them; the same fate, no
doubt, they thought was in store for them.

I was terribly tired that day. One of the men in our
company named Labbé, seeing that I could scarcely walk,
offered to carry my knapsack for me, as he had lost his
own the day before. I gave it to him, as I knew he was
honest; but it was like trusting my life in his hands, as
the knapsack contained more than a pound of rice and
oatmeal, picked up by chance at Smolensk, and kept by
me for some desperate emergency, when there would be
no more horses to eat. On that day the Emperor went
on foot, carrying a stick.

At night it froze again, and the roads became so slippery
that we fell down continually, and many were seriously

hurt. I walked last of the company, keeping an eye, as far as possible, on the man with my knapsack, and sometimes regretting that I had given it up, and resolving to get it back when we stopped for the night. When night came, it was so dark that it was impossible to see anything. I called out ' Labbé ! Labbé !' and I heard him answer, ' Here, sergeant !' but when I called again later, one of our men told me that he had just fallen down, and was probably following the regiment. I did not worry myself about it, as in a short time we should be obliged to come to a halt, and take up a position for the night. When we did so, the whole army was collected, except Marshal Ney's *corps d'armée*, which had dropped behind, and which we feared was lost.

Everyone did as best he could during this wretched night. Several of us non-commissioned officers joined together, and took possession of a barn (we were close to a village without being aware of it). Many of the men had entered with us, but those who came too late for that mounted on the roof. Just then we were told that further on there was a church (Greek) intended for our regiment's shelter, but that now it was filled with men from different regiments, who would let no one else enter.

On learning exactly where the church was, a dozen of us set out to find it. When we arrived, the men inside tried to prevent our entering. They were Germans, Italians, and a few Frenchmen, who tried to frighten us by presenting the points of their bayonets at us. We answered them in the same fashion, and forced an entrance. They drew back a little, and an Italian called out :

' Do as I do—load !'

' Ours are loaded—ready !' said one of our sergeant-majors, and we were on the point of a fierce encounter, when reinforcements arrived for us in the shape of some men from our regiment; so seeing they had nothing to gain by fighting, 'and that we were not disposed to let them stay with us, the men in the church decided to leave.

Unfortunately for them, the night grew much colder, with a high wind and a fall of snow, and the next morning on going out we found many of the poor wretches dead by the side of the road. Others had dropped down further on, while trying to find a place of shelter. We passed by these dead bodies in silence. We ought, no doubt, to have felt guilty and miserable at this sad spectacle, of which we were partly the cause; but we had arrived at the point of complete indifference to everything, even the most tragic events, saying to each other that soon we should be eating dead men, as there would be no more horses left.

An hour afterwards we got to Doubrowna, a little town partly inhabited by Jews, where all the houses were built of wood. Here the Emperor had passed the night with the Grenadiers and Chasseurs, and part of the artillery. They had been kept under arms all night by a false alarm. We crossed this town on our way to Orcha. After an hour's march, we had to pass over a deep ravine, which the baggage had enormous difficulty in crossing, and several horses died. At last, during the afternoon, we arrived at this little fortified town, garrisoned by men from different regiments. These were men who had stayed behind, and had come up in detachments to rejoin the Grand Army. There were amongst them some gendarmes and a few Poles. They were horror-struck at seeing our miserable condition, and at the enormous number of stragglers in such disorganization. Part of the Guard were kept in the town to establish a little order, and a small distribution of flour and brandy was made from some stores found there. We found a pontoon train, and a great deal of artillery, horses and harness; and by an extraordinary fatality we burned the boats forming the bridges, in order to make use of the horses to draw the guns. We little knew what was in store for us at the Bérézina, where the bridge would have been of untold service to us.

We were now only seven or eight thousand men in the Guard, the remnant of 35,000. Although most of us marched in order, a good many straggled painfully behind. As I have already said, the Emperor and part of the Guard stayed in the town, and the rest of the army camped outside. During the night Marshal Ney arrived with the remainder of his *corps d'armée.*

Two or three thousand remained to him out of 7,000. The Emperor's joy was unbounded when he heard that the Marshal was safe.

We stayed here over the 20th, and I spent the time looking for my friend with my knapsack, but in vain. On the 21st we set out without my having found him, and I began to despair, although I heard from many that he had been seen.

At a short distance from Orcha we heard musket-shots, and stopping for a moment, we saw some sledges intercepted by Cossacks. These men joined our ranks and we went forward again. I searched for my man and the knapsack among the sledges, but again fruitlessly. We stayed that night in a village called Kokanow, of which nothing remained but a barn and two or three houses.

On the 22nd, after a wretched night, we set out very early, walking with great difficulty over a thawed, muddy road. At mid-day we reached Toloczin, where the Emperor had slept. We halted at the other side of the town, and drew up by the side of the road. While we were there M. Césarisse, an officer in our company, told me that he had seen Labbé near a fire busy frying biscuits, and that he had ordered him to join his regiment. He answered that he was coming directly, but a horde of Cossacks came and took possession of the sledges, and most probably he had been taken also. So good-bye to my knapsack and its contents, which I had so set my heart on taking back to France! How proud I should have been to say, ' I brought this from Moscow!'

However, to make quite sure, I thought I would see for myself, and I turned back to the end of the village, which was full of men from all regiments, walking about independently and obeying no orders but their own. I saw the Cossacks in the distance carrying off their prisoners—and no doubt my poor knapsack also.

I was looking about me to right and left, when I caught sight of a woman, dressed in a soldier's cloak, looking curiously at me, and I could not help thinking I had seen her before. She recognised me by my bearskin, and being the first to speak, she said she had seen me at Smolensk. I remembered her as the woman in the cellar. She told me that the brigands had been taken at Krasnoë, before we got there; that they were in a house where they had beaten her, because she would not wash their shirts, and she had gone out to get water. She had seen some Russians and had run away. As for the brigands, they had fought desperately, trying to save their money, for they had much, she said, gold and jewels above all; but it had ended by their being killed, wounded, and plundered. She herself had been saved when the Imperial Guard arrived.

She would have told me much more if I had had time to listen to her. I asked her who was with her, and she said no one; that since the day her husband was killed she had been with the brigands; that she was now alone, but that, if I would take her under my protection, she would take good care of me, and I should be doing her a very great service. I consented at once, never thinking of the figure I should cut in the regiment when I arrived there with a woman.

As she went she asked me what had become of my knapsack. So I told her its history, and how I had lost it. She told me not to worry about it, as she had a well-filled bag herself. She also carried a basket on her arm, and she added that if I could find a house or a stable to change in, she could give me some fresh linen. I accepted this joyfully, but as we were looking for a suitable place we heard the call to arms, and I heard the drums beating. I told the woman to follow me, and wait for me on the road.

When I joined my company, the sergeant-major asked me if I had found Labbé and the knapsack. I said no, and that I had given up all idea of finding them, but that instead I had found a woman.

' A woman !' he exclaimed ; 'what is the good of that ? She can't wash your linen for you, as you have not got any.'

' She will give me some.'

' Ah,' he said, ' that's a different thing. And what about feeding her ?'

' She will do as I do.'

Just then the Emperor came past with King Murat and Prince Eugène. The Emperor then placed himself amongst the Grenadiers and Chasseurs and made them an address, telling them that the Russians were waiting for us at the crossing of the Bérézina, and had sworn that not one of us should pass over. Then, drawing his sword and raising his voice, he cried :

' Let us all swear to die fighting rather than not see our country again !'

The oath was taken. Bearskins and caps were waved at the points of bayonets, and shouts were heard of 'Vive l'Empereur!' Marshal Mortier made us a similar address, and was received with the same enthusiasm, and so on with all the regiments.

It was a splendid moment, and for the time made us forget our miseries. If the Russians had only been within our reach then, we should have made short work of them, even had their numbers been six times greater than ours. We remained in this position till the right wing of the column began to move.

I had not forgotten my 'wife,' and while waiting for the regiment to start I went in search of her, but she was nowhere to be seen. She had been engulfed in the torrent of Prince Eugène's thousands. They and the corps belonging to Marshals Ney and Davoust were in complete disorder; three-quarters of them were sick and wounded, and the rest utterly demoralized and indifferent to everything.

I found myself at this moment near Marshal Lefebvre. He was alone and on foot in the middle of the road, shouting in his German accent, 'Come, my men, let us get together! Better large battalions than a pack of brigands and cowards.' He spoke to the men who were continually straggling away without apparent reason from their corps, sometimes in front, sometimes behind.

I made several inquiries about my 'wife,' as I so badly wanted the change of linen she had promised me, but I never saw her again, and so I found myself bereft both of her and of my knapsack.

Walking thus with the rabble, I had got far in advance of my regiment, and I stopped to rest by a fire left from a bivouac.

Up to the Battle of Krasnoë, I had managed to keep up

my spirits, in spite of all the miseries I had to endure. I felt that the greater the danger and suffering, the greater the glory and honour, and my patience had astonished my comrades. But since the terrible encounters at Krasnoë, and, above all, since the news that two of my friends (besides Béloque and Capon) had been, one killed and the other mortally wounded—(sic).

To complete my misery, a sledge came up and stopped close to me. I asked who the wounded man was, and they told me it was an officer of their regiment. It turned out to be poor Legrand, who related to me the way he had been wounded. His comrade, Laporte, from Cassel, near Lille, had stayed behind invalided at Krasnoë; but hearing that his regiment was fighting, he set out to join it. Hardly, however, had he taken his place in the ranks, when he had both his legs broken. Legrand, seeing Laporte arrive, came to speak to him, and the same shot wounded him in the right leg. Laporte remained dead on the battlefield, and Legrand was taken to the town; he was placed in a wretched Russian cart drawn by a miserable horse, but the cart broke up the first day. Fortunately for him, close by was a sledge, into which he was moved; four men of his regiment were with him, and he had travelled in this manner for six days. I bade farewell to the unfortunate Legrand, and wished him a safe journey; he answered that he trusted himself to the care of God and the friendship of his brave comrades. One of the men then took the horse by the bridle, another gave it a blow, and two pushed from behind; with great difficulty the sledge was thus set in motion. As I saw it off, I thought with such equipment it could hardly go much further.

After this I never felt the same; I was depressed, and a prey to gloomy forebodings. My head ached and burned;

I was in a fever. No doubt it was greatly owing to fatigue, as we were now obliged to start very early in the morning, and walk till very late. The days were so short ; it was not light till eight o'clock, and it was dark by four in the afternoon. This was the reason of so many unfortunate men losing their way, for it was always night when we arrived at the bivouac, and all the remains of the different corps were in terrible confusion. At all hours of the night we heard the weak, worn-out voices of new arrivals calling out ' Fourth Corps !' ' First Corps !' ' Third Corps !' ' Imperial Guard !' and then the voices of others lying down with no strength left, forcing themselves to answer, ' Here, comrades !' They were not trying any longer to find their regiments, but simply the *corps d'armée* to which they had belonged, and which now included the strength of two regiments at most, where a fortnight earlier there had been thirty.

No one now knew anything about himself, or could mention which regiment he belonged to. Many, after walking the whole day, were forced to wander about half the night to find their particular corps. They hardly ever succeeded ; then, not being aware of the hour of departure in the morning, they slept too late, and on waking found the Russians upon them. Thousands of men were taken prisoners, and perished in this way.

I kept near the fire, standing and trembling all over, and leaning on my musket. Three men were sitting round the fire in silence, mechanically watching people passing in the road, seeming disposed to stay where they were, simply for want of strength to move. I began to be uneasy at not seeing my regiment pass, when I felt someone pull at my bearskin cloak. It was Grangier come to tell me that the regiment was passing ; but my eyes were so worn out that I could not see him, even looking straight at him.

'And the woman ?' he said.

'Who told you anything about her ?'

'The sergeant-major.   But where is she ?'

'I don't know; but I do know that she has a knapsack full of linen, which I want badly, and if ever you meet her you might tell me.   She is dressed in a soldier's gray cloak, with a sheepskin cap on her head.   She wears black gaiters, and she carries a basket on her arm.'

Grangier thought (as he afterwards told me) that I was light-headed, and, taking me by the arm, he led me down the road, saying:

'We must get on, or we shall not catch up with the regiment.'

We came up with it, however, after passing the thousands of men from all kinds of regiments who walked confusedly, hardly able to drag themselves along.   We foresaw, on looking at them, that the journey, if long, would be a fatal one to most of us.

The march was indeed a long one; we passed a place where the Emperor was supposed to sleep, although he had got far in advance of it.   A great number of men stopped here, for it was very late, and we heard that two leagues separated us yet from our bivouac in a large forest.

The road here was very wide, and bordered on each side by birch-trees.*   There was plenty of room for us and the carts and waggons; but when evening came on there was nothing to be seen all the length of the road but dead horses, and the further we advanced, the more the road became blocked with carts and dying horses : whole teams succumbed at once from fatigue.   The men who could go no further stopped and made bivouacs underneath large trees; here they said they had wood at hand to make fires

* Birches in Russia grow to a great height.—*Author's Note.*

from the broken carts, and horseflesh to eat, and these they would not find further on.

For a long time I had walked alone in the midst of a miscellaneous rabble, forcing myself on to reach the camping-place arranged. The road became more difficult at every step, as it had begun to freeze again on the top of the half melted snow, and I fell continually. In the midst of these miseries the night suddenly fell.

The north wind had redoubled its fury. I had lost sight of my comrades; several men, lost like myself, strangers to me, who did not belong to my regiment, by superhuman efforts dragged themselves along to come up with their own regiments. They did not answer when I spoke to them; they were too weak even for that. Others fell down dying, never to rise again. Soon I was alone, with only dead bodies along the road to guide me. The trees had quite disappeared; it was perhaps seven o'clock. The snow, now falling heavily, prevented my seeing the direction in which I was going, and the violent wind had already filled up the traces of the advancing column.

Up till that time I had worn my bearskin cloak with the fur outside, but now, seeing what an awful night was in store for me, I stopped a moment, and turned the fur inside. Owing to this I was able luckily to withstand the cold of this disastrous night, falling to twenty-two degrees of frost. I arranged the cloak over my right shoulder in the direction of the wind, and I walked thus for an hour, during which I am certain I only went a quarter of a league; for, often seized by a blinding storm of snow, I had to turn round and thus retrace my steps without being aware of it. It was only the sight of the dead bodies of men and horses, and the mass of broken vehicles I had passed before, that convinced me I was in the wrong direction. I had then to take my bearings again.

Either the moon or a faint Northern Light appeared in the sky at intervals. Black clouds shot swiftly across this light, but when it was clear it enabled me to distinguish one object from another. I saw far off a black mass which I imagined to be the immense forest we had to cross before reaching the Bérézina, for now we were in Lithuania. I made a guess that this forest was perhaps a league off.

Unfortunately a terrible sleepiness, the certain fore-runner of death, began to come over me. I felt quite exhausted; my legs refused to carry me further. I had fallen down half asleep several times, and had I not been roused each time by the cold, all would have been over with me.

The road was here completely blockaded by dead men and horses, preventing me from dragging myself along, for I had no longer the strength to lift my feet from the ground. Whenever I fell it seemed as if I were dragged down by the unfortunate men stretched on the snow. Often these men would try to catch hold of the legs of those who passed, imploring their help, and many, in stooping to give help, fell themselves, not to rise again.

I walked on aimlessly for about ten minutes. I staggered as if I were drunk; my knees trembled under my weight. I thought my last hour had come at last, when all at once I stumbled over a sword on the ground, and fell all my length, stupefied, my chin having struck the butt-end of my musket. Coming to myself a little and getting on my knees, I picked up my musket, and was preparing to stand, when I saw a stream of blood coming from my mouth, and with a cry of despair, trembling with terror, I fell back again.

I had been heard by a miserable man lying a few yards off, and in a feeble voice he begged me to help him—I! so much in need myself. 'Stop! help us!'

The voice ceased; but I remained. still trying to find out who had spoken. Hearing nothing more, I began to think my senses had deceived me, and I called out as loud as I possibly could:

'Where are you?' adding to myself, 'If I only had a companion, we could walk on for the rest of the night encouraging each other.'

Then I heard the voice again, sadder and feebler this time:

'Come here and help.'

At that moment the moon came out, and I saw two men about ten yards off—one stretched at full length, and the other sitting near him. With great difficulty I struggled over a ditch filled with snow, and got near them. The man sitting laughed like a madman when I spoke to him, and said, 'Don't you know—you mustn't forget!' and began laughing again.

I recognised the terrible laughter of death. The other man was still living; turning his head a little, he said these last words to me:

'Save my uncle—help him. I am dying!'

I spoke to him, but he said no more. Then I turned to the other, and encouraged him to rise and come with me. He looked at me without speaking, and I saw that he was wrapped in a great fur-lined cloak which he tried to throw off. I endeavoured, without success, to help him to rise; but on taking hold of his arm I noticed that he wore officer's epaulets. He began talking incoherently about reviews and parades, and ended by falling on one side with his face in the snow. I was obliged to leave him; if I had remained I must myself have succumbed to the same fate. Before I left I picked up a pouch lying on the ground, in the hope of finding something inside, but it was full of rubbish and papers only. Having regained the road, I walked slowly along, listening as I went, as now I constantly seemed to hear cries of distress.

Soon I began to walk faster, in the hope of coming to some bivouac, and at last I got to a point in the road completely blocked up with dead horses and broken carts. The bodies of men from various regiments were scattered round. Several belonged to the Young Guard, recognisable by their shakos. In this immense cemetery and this awful silence I was alone, a prey to the most gloomy thoughts— of my comrades from whom I was separated, my country, my relations—and I began to cry like a child. The tears relieved me, and gradually my courage came back.

Close to me I found a small hatchet, such as every company carries in a campaign. I tried to cut off a piece from one of the horses, but the flesh was frozen so hard that this was impossible. I had spent the remainder of my strength, and I fell exhausted, but the exertion had warmed me a little. I had picked up with the hatchet a few pieces of ice, which I now found to be blood from the horse. I ate a little of it, and put the rest carefully in my knapsack; and feeling stronger, I set out again, trusting to God's mercy; taking care to avoid the dead bodies, I went on, stopping and feeling my way whenever a cloud passed over the moon.

After walking for some time, I noticed at a short distance off something I took for a waggon. When I got nearer I saw it was a canteen cart belonging to a regiment of the Young Guard. The horses which had drawn it were not only dead, but partly cut in pieces for eating. Around the cart were seven dead bodies almost naked and half covered with snow; one of them was still covered with a cloak and a sheepskin. On stooping to look at the body, I saw that it was a woman. The instinct of self-preservation was at this time the first with me, and, forgetting that I had ineffectually tried the same thing a short time before, I set to work to hack off a piece of one of the horses. I found that this time again I was utterly unable to do it, and so I decided to spend the night in the cart, which was covered. I approached the dead woman to take the sheepskin for a covering, but it was impossible to move it. Noticing, however, that she wore a leather strap round her body, buckled on the other side, and that the strap must be unfastened, I put my musket under her body to act as a lever ; but I had hardly done so, when a piercing cry came from the cart. ' Marie,' it said, ' Marie, give me something to drink ! I am dying !'

I was stupefied. The same voice repeated directly afterwards, ' Ah, my God !'

Mounting on the body of the horse in the shafts, I steadied myself by the top of the cart. I asked what was the matter. A feeble voice answered with some difficulty, ' Something to drink.'

I thought at once of the frozen blood in the pouch, and tried to get down to fetch it ; but the moon suddenly disappeared behind a great black cloud, and I as suddenly fell on the top of three dead bodies. My head was down lower than my legs, and my face resting on one of the dead hands. I had been accustomed for long enough to this sort of company, but now—I suppose because I was alone—an awful feeling of terror came over me. It was like a nightmare. I could not move, and I began screaming like a madman, as if something were holding me. But, in spite of all my efforts, I could not move. I tried to help myself up by my arm, but I found my hand on a face, and my thumb went into its mouth !

At that moment the moon came out and showed me all my dreadful surroundings. I shuddered all over, left hold of my support, and fell back again immediately.

But a change came over me now; I felt ashamed of my weakness, and a wild sort of frenzy, instead of terror, took possession of me. I got up, raving and swearing, and trod on anything that came near me—faces, arms, and legs, not caring which; and I cursed the sky above me, defying it, and taking my musket, I struck at the cart—very likely I struck also at the poor devils under my feet.

When I felt calmer, I decided to spend the night in the cart, as some sort of shelter from the cold; and taking a piece of the frozen blood from the pouch, I climbed inside, feeling for the man who had asked me for drink, and who had ever since uttered feeble cries. When I got near him, I saw that his left leg was amputated.

I asked him the name of his regiment, but he did not answer. So, finding his head, I put a bit of the ice into his mouth. The man next him was as cold and hard as marble. I tried to move him, so as to take his place, and be able to leave the next day with those who were still behind, but I could not do it. I now saw that he had only a few moments to live, so I covered him with two cloaks belonging to the dead man, and searched in the cart for anything I might find useful. Finding nothing, I turned round to speak to the man again. I got no reply, and, passing my hand over his face, I found it quite cold, and the piece of ice I had given him still between his lips. His sufferings were over.

I now prepared to leave, but waited to take another look at the dead woman, thinking it might be Marie the *cantinière*, whom I knew well as coming from my native country. I looked at her carefully by the light of the moon, and satisfied myself that it was not she.

With my musket under the right arm like a hunter, two pouches, one of red leather and the other of gray canvas, which I had just found, slung across me, a piece of the frozen blood in my mouth, and my hands in my pockets, I started off. It was perhaps nine o'clock; the snow had stopped falling, the wind had abated in strength, and the cold was not quite so intense. I continued to walk in the direction of the wood.

At the end of half an hour the moon disappeared again. This was terrible for me. I stopped for a few minutes, stamping my feet on the ground, to prevent their being frozen, and waiting for the light to come out again; but I was disappointed in this, as the moon appeared no more.

My eyes, however, became accustomed to the dark, and I could soon see well enough to go on, but all at once I discovered I was not on the same road. In naturally trying to avoid the north wind, I had turned my back to it. My opinion was confirmed by my not seeing any of the army débris on the road.

I cannot say for how long I had been walking in this new direction, when I saw that I had got to the edge of a precipice. I made the discovery too late, however, to save myself, and I rolled down for at least forty feet, although my fall was broken by bushes on the way. This time I thought that I was quite done for, and, closing my eyes, I resigned myself to God's will. When I reached the bottom I was stunned for a time, but, after all my adventures, I had ceased being astonished at anything, and I soon got up and began to search for my musket, which I had lost in my fall; however, I decided to leave it and wait for daylight. As I drew my sword from its sheath and felt my way, I now became aware of a waggon close to where I had fallen, and the bodies of two dead horses; and feeling something warm under my feet, I found I was standing on the ashes of a half-extinct fire. So I lay down, and bathing my hands in the ashes to warm them, I luckily found a few pieces of coal, and was able by blowing to revive a few sparks. But where could I get wood to relight the fire? I dared not leave the ashes, for fear my sparks might be extinguished for good. I tore off a piece of my shirt, already in rags, made a match of it and lighted it. Then, feeling all round me, I fortunately came upon some tiny fragments of wood, and with much difficulty got them alight. Very soon flames crackled up, and in a minute or two I had quite a large fire.

I could now see for several yards round me, and I caught sight of some large letters on the waggon, 'Garde Impériale. État Major.' Over the inscription was the eagle. As far as I could see, the ground was covered with helmets, shakos, swords, cuirasses, broken chests, empty portmanteaus, bits of torn clothing, saddles, costly schabraques, and quantities of other things. But hardly had I glanced round me, when I became possessed with the idea that this place might be near a Cossack bivouac, and I felt terribly frightened, and dared not keep my fire up any longer. If Frenchmen had been anywhere near, I should have seen some bivouac fires. This place, above all others, sheltered as it was from the wind, would have been chosen for a bivouac. I was at a loss whether to stay or go.

While I reflected my fire had diminished, and I dared not put on more kindling. But at last the desire for warmth and rest overbore the feelings of fear. I picked up as much wood as I could find and piled it up near me. I also collected a number of schabraques to sit on, and wrapping myself in my bearskin cape, with my back against the waggon, I arranged myself for the night.

In putting wood on the fire I had found some horse-flesh—enough to stay the hunger which now devoured me.

Although covered with snow and ashes, it was more than I had dared to hope for. Since the evening before, I had eaten nothing but half a dead raven I had found, and a few spoonfuls of gruel mixed with grains of oats and rye, and salted with powder.

I hardly waited for my cutlet to be warmed through before I bit into it, in spite of the ash which covered it. In this way I made my miserable dinner, looking round me from time to time, to make sure that things were safe.

My situation was slightly better than before. I was not obliged to keep on walking, I was sheltered from the wind and cold, I had a fire for warmth, and food; but I was so terribly tired that I fell asleep while I was eating— sleep broken, however, by fear, and by dreadful pains in my legs. I felt as if I had been beaten all over. I do not know how long I slept, but on awaking there was still no appearance of daylight. In Russia the nights now are so long, and in summer there is scarcely any night at all.

I had fallen asleep with my feet in the ashes, and when I woke they still felt warm. I had learnt by experience that warmth refreshes tired limbs, and soothes pain, so I picked up and collected all the wood I could find, put it on my fire, and relit it.

I could now see round me again, and on my left caught sight of some object I took for an animal. As there are so many bears in Russia, I felt sure this must be one, especially as it walked on all fours. When it got to a distance of five or six yards off, I saw that it was a man. To guard against a surprise, I drew my sword, and, advancing towards the man, I cried, ' Who are you?' at the same moment placing the point of my sword against his back, as I saw him to be a Russian, a real Cossack with a long beard.

He raised his head and threw himself down like a slave, trying to kiss my feet, and saying, ' Dobray Frantsouz,'* and other words which I understood to mean that he was frightened. If he had only known it, I was as much frightened as he. He knelt upright to show me a sword-cut he had had on his face. I noticed then, even in this position, his head reached to my shoulders, so that his full height would be over six feet. I signed to him to come near the fire ; then he made me understand that he had another wound—a ball had struck him in the stomach. The sword-cut on his face was frightful. It began at the top of the head, and cut open his face to the chin, losing itself in the beard. He lay down on his back to show me the bullet wound, and I could see in this position that he was unarmed. Then, without saying anything more, he turned on to his side. I sat opposite to him to watch him. I did not wish to sleep again, as I intended before daylight appeared to set fire to the waggon and leave at once ; but suddenly the terrible thought struck me that the waggon might be full of powder !

I jumped up, tired as I was, cleared at one bound the fire and the poor devil lying beside it, and set off running, but stumbling over a cuirass in the way, I fell all my length on the ground. I was fortunate enough not to hurt myself ; I might well have done so with all the fire-arms lying about. I got up and walked backwards, my eyes fixed on the waggon, as if I expected an explosion every instant. At last I recovered from my terror, and came back to the place I had left so foolishly, for I was quite as safe there as twenty yards off.

I took off the pieces of burning wood and carefully carried them to the place where I had fallen ; then I took the cuirass to gather snow in and put out the fire. But I

* ' Bon Français.'—*Author's Note.*

had hardly begun this work, when I heard a flourish of trumpets, and after listening attentively, I recognised it for the Russian cavalry, announcing that they were not far off. I saw the Cossack raise his head at the sound. I tried to read his thoughts by his expression, for the fire was now bright enough for me to see his features, which were truly hideous. He squinted, and his eyes were deeply set beneath a low, prominent forehead; his hair and beard were red and thick like a mane, giving him a wild and savage appearance. His shoulders were of Herculean proportions. He was probably suffering terribly from his wound, for he writhed as he lay, and from time to time ground his teeth. I was listening to the sound of the trumpets in a dazed sort of way, when all at once I heard another noise just behind me. I turned round, and, to my horror, saw the waggon opening like a tomb, and coming out of it an enormous individual, white as snow from head to foot, like the commander's ghost in the 'Festin de Pierre,' holding up the top of the waggon with one hand, and having a drawn sword in the other. I looked silently at this spectre, walking a few steps backward, and drawing my sword while waiting for it to speak first. It was trying, without success, to unfasten the great white cloak it wore with the hand which held the sword, as the other was engaged in holding up the top of the waggon.

At last, breaking the silence, I asked in rather a trembling voice:

'Are you a Frenchman?'

'Yes, of course I am French! What a d——d silly question! There you stand like a church candle! You see what a fix I am in, and you don't attempt to help me out of this coffin. I seem to have frightened you, my good fellow.'

142

' Yes, you did frighten me ; but I thought you might be another of these beauties '—pointing to the man at the fire.

I helped him out as I spoke, and he threw off his cloak. Imagine my surprise and delight when I recognised one of my old friends of the Grenadiers of the Old Guard, a comrade called Picart—Picart by name and *Picard* by nation—whom I had not seen since the Emperor's review at the Kremlin !   He and I had made our first campaign together ; we had been at the battles of Jena, Pultusk, Eylau, Tilsit, and later, in 1809, at Mora, on the Spanish frontier, and other campaigns since then, although not in the same regiment.   Picart scarcely knew me again, I had altered so much and looked so miserable.   We gazed at each other in amazement—I to see him looking so clean and well, and he to find me so thin, and looking, as he said, like Robinson Crusoe.   At last he said:

' Tell me, sergeant, my old friend, by what luck or misfortune do I find you here, alone and at night, with that villainous Cossack.   Just look at him !   See his eyes ! He has been here since five o'clock yesterday, and then he disappeared.   I can't think why he has come back. And you ?   What brought you here in the middle of the night ?'

' Before I tell you, have you a bit of something to eat about you ?'

' Yes, sergeant, a little biscuit.'

And he opened his knapsack and drew out a piece of biscuit the size of his hand, which I devoured at once.   I had not tasted bread since October 27.*   As I ate I said :

' Picart, have you any brandy ?'

' No, *mon pays !*'

* Except a little bit given me by Grangier at Smolensk, on November 12.—*Author's Note.*

' I thought I smelt something like it.'

' You are right,' he said. ' Yesterday, when the waggon was pillaged, there was a bottle of brandy; but they quarrelled over it, and it was broken and the brandy spilt.'

I said I should like to see the place where it happened, and when he showed me I gathered up some snow *à l'eau de vie*, just as before I had collected horse's blood *à la glace*.

' That's good,' said Picart. ' I never thought of doing that. I think we can manage to get drunk, as there were several bottles in the waggon.'

The biscuit and brandied snow had done me a great deal of good, so I related to Picart all that had happened to me since the evening before. He could scarcely believe me; but when I told him of the misery the entire army was suffering, including his regiment and all the Imperial Guard, he was distressed beyond words. The readers of this diary will be surprised that Picart knew nothing of what had been going on. I will tell them the reason of this.

CHAPTER VIII.

SINCE the Battle of Malo-Jaroslawetz, Picart had been separated from his regiment, as he had been sent in the escort of a convoy composed of part of the Imperial equipage. This detachment was always two or three days' march in advance of the army, and in consequence had not suffered anything like the same privations as the rest. As there were only 400 of them, they had often been able to find provisions, and, besides, had means of transport. At Smolensk they had found enough flour and biscuits to last for several days. At Krasnoë they had the good luck to arrive and get away twenty-four hours before the Russians got there. At Orcha again they had found flour. In any village they came to there were always houses enough available for shelter, if only post-houses at some distance from each other. We, on the other hand, had to march 150,000 strong to begin with, afterwards only half that number, and had had only forests and marshes to sleep in, only horseflesh to eat—and very little of it—water to drink, and sometimes not even that. My old comrade's sufferings only began when he joined me.

Picart told me that the man lying by our fire had been wounded by some Polish Lancers in an attack during the afternoon. This is the account he gave of it :

' More than 600 Cossacks and other cavalry attacked our convoy. We were sheltered, however, by our carts, formed into a square, and letting the enemy come quite close to us, at our first discharge we stretched eleven of them on the snow ; a greater number still were wounded and carried off by their horses. They fled, but met some Polish Lancers of General Dombrouski's corps,* who put them to utter rout. The man by the fire was brought back a prisoner, and several others with him, but I don't know why they left him. After the affair I told you of, there was a good deal of confusion. Those in charge of the waggons tried to get through the defile near the forest before each other, so that the shelter of the trees might guard them against a surprise. Some of them, hoping to find a crossing higher up, were deceived by the aspect of the snow, and fell into a deep crevasse—the first waggon turned completely over with the two *cognias*.†

' The other waggons avoided the same fate by turning to the left, but I do not know if they arrived safely or not. They left me here to take care of this d——d waggon, and two Chasseurs with me, saying that they would send some men and horses to fetch it or its contents away. An hour afterwards, however, as it was getting dark, nine men, stragglers from different regiments, passed by.

* The corps commanded by General Dombrouski, a Pole, had not been as far as Moscow. It was marching just now to Borisow to cut off the Russians from the bridge over the Bérézina.—*Author's Note.*

† *Cognia* in Polish, and in Russian also, means *horse.*—*Author's Note.*

146

Seeing the overturned waggon, and only three men to guard it, they broke into it, on the pretext of finding food, in spite of everything we said to the contrary.

'Seeing that all our efforts were unavailing, we followed their example, taking and putting aside anything we could find. But it was now too late, as all the best things had been taken, and the horses were cut up into twenty pieces. I managed to secure this white cloak for myself. I cannot understand how the Chasseurs with me contrived to get away without my seeing them.'

I told Picart that the men who had pillaged the waggon belonged to the Grand Army, and if he had only asked them for news they could have told him as much, or more, than I.

'After all, Picart, it was just as well that they took what they did, for the Russians will be here very soon.'

'You are right,' said Picart; 'and we had better put our arms in order.'

'First of all, I must find my musket,' I said. 'I have never lost it before. I have carried it for six years, and I am so familiar with it that at any hour of the night, in the middle of a pile of others, I know it by touching it—even by the noise it makes in falling.'

As no fresh snow had fallen, I fortunately was able to find it. Picart helped me by lighting my way with a piece of resinous wood.

After having looked to our boots—an important consideration—we cooked a piece of horseflesh, of which Picart had a good store. After eating, and drinking a little brandied snow, we put some meat into our knapsacks, and, standing to warm ourselves before the fire, we considered the next step to be taken.

'Well,' said the good fellow, 'which way now for us?'

'That infernal music's in my ears still,' I said.

'Perhaps we are making a mistake. Very likely it's the first bugle, or our Horse-Grenadiers' reveille—you know the air :

'Fillettes, auprès des amoureux
Tenez bien votre serieux,' etc.

I interrupted Picart by telling him that there had been no first bugle or reveille for the last fortnight ; that we had no more cavalry ; that with the few that still remained a squadron called the Doomed Squadron had been formed, commanded by the oldest Marshal in France, that the Generals were Captains, and the Colonels and other officers served as private soldiers ; that just the same thing had happened to a battalion now called the Doomed Battalion ; that, in short, of 40,000 men in the cavalry, only 1,000 remained.

Without leaving him time to reply, I told him that what we had heard was the signal of departure for the Russian cavalry, and it was that which brought him out of the waggon.

'Oh, *mon pays*, it wasn't only that which made me clear out : I had been watching you some time trying to set me on fire !'

Picart had hardly finished speaking, when he seized me by the arm suddenly, saying, ' Silence ! Lie down !' I threw myself·on the ground at once. He followed my example, and covered the fire with a cuirass. I looked up, and saw the Russian cavalry defile above us in the utmost silence. This lasted for quite a quarter of an hour.

As soon as they had gone, Picart said, ' Follow me,' and, linking arms, we started walking in the direction they had come from.

After going for some time, Picart stopped, saying quite softly :

148

'Now we can breathe; we are safe, at least, for a time. We've been lucky, for if that wounded bear' (the Cossack) 'had seen his people, he would have bellowed like a bull to attract them, and God knows what would have happened then! But that reminds me: I have forgotten something most important—a saucepan at the back of the waggon—more useful for us than anything else. We must go back for it.' As he saw I was unwilling, he said: 'Come quick, or we may die of hunger!'

We got back to our bivouac. We found the fire almost extinct, and the poor devil of a Cossack rolling about in the snow in the most terrible sufferings, with his head almost in the fire. We could do nothing to relieve him, but we laid him on some sheepskin schabraques, so that he might die more comfortably.

'He will not die just yet,' said Picart. 'Look at his eyes: they shine like two candles.'

We had placed him sitting up, holding him by his arms, but as soon as we let him go he fell down again, his face in the fire. We dragged him out only just in time to prevent his being burnt. We left him then to look for our saucepan, which we found so battered that it was past using. Picart, however, strapped it all the same on to my back.

We then tried to get up the steep bank, and reach the wood before daylight, where there would be shelter both from the cold and the enemy. After twice rolling down from the top to the bottom, we managed to make a footing in the snow. We reached the top at the exact place from which I had fallen the evening before, and where the Russian cavalry had filed past. We stopped for an instant to take breath and make out our bearings.

'Straight on,' said Picart. 'Follow me.'

He started off as he spoke, and I followed; but hardly

had he gone twenty yards when he disappeared in a hole six feet deep. He stood up without speaking, and I helped him out with his musket ; but as soon as he was safe he began swearing against the God of Russia and the Emperor Napoleon, whom he called ' Conscript.'

' He is a regular fool of a conscript to have waited so long in Moscow. A fortnight was long enough to eat and drink everything we found there ; but to stay there thirty-four days just waiting for winter to come on ! I call that folly. If he were here, I could tell him to his face that isn't the way to lead men. Good God ! the dances he has led me the last sixteen years. We suffered enough in Egypt —in the Syrian deserts ; but that's nothing compared with these deserts of snow !' and he began blowing on his hands.

' Come, my poor fellow,' I said, ' this is not the time to stand and talk — we must do something ; let us see if we can't find a better way to the left.'

Picart had drawn out the ramrod of his musket, and walked about sounding the snow in front of him. It was just as deep all round. In the end we got across near where he had fallen in. Once on the other side, we went on, still sounding as we went. Halfway to the wood we came upon another deep ditch, like that one in which we had spent the night. We crossed it, and with very great difficulty reached the other side. We were so tired that we were forced to stop and take breath.

To the right we saw some black clouds coming on us with frightful rapidity. The clouds coming with a north wind foretold a terrible storm, and a cruel day in store for us. The wind roared through the pines and birch-trees, and drove us just the way we did not want to go. Sometimes we fell into holes concealed by the snow. At last, after an hour's walking, we arrived at our haven just as the snow began to fall in great flakes.

The storm burst with such force that trees broken or torn up by the roots fell on all sides, and we were compelled to leave the forest. We kept on the edge of the wood, with the wind to our left, but were stopped by a great lake which we could have easily crossed, as it was frozen hard, if it had been in the right direction. The quantity of snow falling prevented our seeing, and we were forced finally to stop altogether, sheltering behind two large birch-trees, until the weather had mended a little.

For a long time we stood there, stamping our feet to keep out the frost, when I noticed that the wind had abated a little. I mentioned this to Picart, and proposed going further on. We had skirted a good way along the lake, when suddenly Picart stopped and looked steadily before him. He then seized my arm and whispered :

' Hold your tongue !' Then, dragging me behind a bush, he said in a low voice, ' Don't you see ?'

' I don't see anything. What is it ?'

' Smoke. A bivouac.'

I looked, and saw it too. An idea came to me, and I said :

' Perhaps the fire belongs to the bivouac of the cavalry we saw this morning.'

' I think very likely it does,' he said ; ' we must behave as if we were sure of it. We made a great mistake this morning in not loading our muskets while we were near the fire. Now our hands are numbed, and the barrels full of snow, we can't do it.'

The snow fell very lightly now, and the sky was clearer. All at once I caught sight of a horse gnawing the bark of a birch on the edge of the lake. I pointed it out to Picart, and as the horse was not harnessed, he thought it might be a wounded one, abandoned by the Russian cavalry.

While we were talking, the horse suddenly threw up his head and began to neigh, then quietly came straight up to us and snuffed at Picart as if he knew him. We dared neither move nor speak. The confounded horse stopped there, his head against Picart's fur cap, who dared hardly breathe, fearing that his master might come to look for him. Seeing, however, that he had a wound in the chest, we concluded that he was abandoned, and no doubt the bivouac also. We moved forward, and reached a cleared semicircle covered with shelters and fires, and seven horses killed and partly eaten. We guessed that more than 200 men must have passed the night here.

'It was the Russians,' said Picart, warming his hands in the ashes. 'I remember that yellow horse; he was my mark in the attack. I think I got his master a commission for the next world.'

After a thorough look round we revived the fire in front of the shelter, which the leader of the party had apparently occupied.

The snow had stopped, and a dead calm had succeeded the wind. We now began to make soup, but thought it wiser to keep back our own store of meat, as there was plenty to be had here. Picart cut some fresh meat with my little axe, enough for soup, and also some to take away with us. We tried to break through the ice for water, but had not enough strength or patience for the job. Now we were quite warm, and the prospect of having some good soup filled me with joy. When one is in real trouble, how little it takes to make one happy! Our saucepan was of no use in its dilapidated condition, but Picart, who was full of resource, and whom nothing put out, set to work to put it right. He cut down a pine-tree to about a foot and a half from the ground, and using the stump as an anvil, and another thick piece as a hammer (wrapped in rag to dull the sound), he began his tinker's work, singing and keeping time with his blows. These were the words he sang, just as he used to sing them during the night-marches to his company:

> ' C'est ma mie l'aveugle,
> C'est ma mie l'aveugle,
> C'est ma fantaisie ;
> J'en suis amoureux.'

As I listened to his powerful voice ringing out, I was obliged to say, ' *Mon vieux camarade*, you quite forget: this is hardly the time for singing.'

Picart looked at me, smiling, and without answering he started again :

> ' Elle a le nez morveux
> Et les yeux chassieux.
> C'est ma mie aveugle,
> C'est ma fantaisie ;
> J'en suis amoureux !'

He stopped, seeing that I was afraid of his singing, and showed me the saucepan, now fit to use.

' Do you remember,' he said, ' the day of the Battle of Eylau, when we were on the right of the church ?'

' Yes, of course I do,' I said ; ' we had weather just like to-day. I have reason to remember it, for a brutal Russian bullet carried away my saucepan. Have you forgotten it, Picart ?'

' By Heaven, no !' he said ; ' that's why I remind you of it, and ask you if a little patience and industry would not have mended your pan ?'

' Certainly not, no more than Gregoire's and Lemoine's heads which it carried off, too.'

' How the devil do you remember their names ?'

' I cannot forget them ; Gregoire was a Vélite like me, and a good friend, too. That day I had some biscuits and haricots in the saucepan.'

'Yes,' said Picart, 'which were splashed all over us. Great God! what a day that was!'

While we talked the snow melted in the pan. We put as much flesh in as it would hold, so that we might have some cooked meat to take away with us.

My curiosity prompted me to look into the canvas bag which I had picked up the evening before. I found in it only three cotton handkerchiefs, two razors, and several letters in French, dated from Stuttgart, written to Sir Jacques (*sic*), a Baden officer in a Dragoon regiment. The letters were full of affection from a sister to a brother. I kept them for some time, but they were lost when I was taken prisoner.

Picart sat down before the fire at the entrance to our shelter, his back turned to the north, and opened his knapsack. He drew out a handkerchief, with some salt tied up in one corner, and a little oatmeal in another. It was long enough since I had seen so much, and my mouth watered merely to think of soup salted with real salt, when for the last month all the seasoning I had taken was powder.

I was terribly tired, and the warmth of the fire made me sleepy. I told Picart that I should drop off.

'All right,' he said, 'drop off. Get into the shelter, and I'll look after the soup, and I can clean and load our arms. How many cartridges have you?'

'Three packets of fifteen.'

'Very good. I have four, so that makes a hundred and five; more than enough to do for twenty-five Cossacks, if they should come this way. Get along; go to sleep.'

I did not need telling twice, and, wrapping myself in my bearskin cloak, with my feet to the fire, I fell asleep. I was sleeping soundly, when Picart awoke me, saying:

'*Mon pays*, you have been sleeping like an angel for two

hours. I have had supper; now it's your turn to eat and mine to rest, for I want it badly. Here are our muskets cleaned and loaded. Mind you keep good watch, and when I am rested a bit we will get on.'

He wrapped himself in his white cloak and lay down, while I took the saucepan between my knees and began with a tremendous appetite on the soup. I do not think I ever enjoyed, or ever shall enjoy, anything so much.

After my supper, I got up to take my turn at the watch; but I had not been there for more than five minutes, when I heard the wounded horse neigh loudly several times, and then gallop off on to the middle of the lake. Then he stopped and neighed again. Several other horses answered him, and he started off in the direction of the sound. I hid myself behind a clump of firs, and saw the horse join a detachment of cavalry which was crossing the lake. There were about twenty-three of them. I called Picart, already sleeping so soundly that I could not make him hear, and I was obliged to pull his legs. At last he opened his eyes.

' Well, what is it ?'

' Quick, Picart! Get up! Russian cavalry on the lake. We must get back to the wood.'

' You ought to have let me sleep. I deserved it.'

' I am sorry, *mon vieux*, but you told me to warn you, and no doubt a lot more may be coming.'

' Oh yes,' he said, ' that's true. What a devilish trade this is! Where are they ?'

' Rather to the right, and out of range.'

Five others passed directly afterwards, half a gun-shot off. We saw the first few stop, and, dismounting, make a circle near a place on the lake, where they had probably broken the ice before to water their horses, for we saw them strike the new ice with the butts of their lances.

We decided to pack and be off as soon as possible; to strike the road again, and, if possible, rejoin the army. It was about eleven o'clock; thus we had until dark—*i.e.*, about four o'clock. The army, I knew, could not be far off, as the Russians were waiting for us at the crossing of the Bérézina, where all our scattered troops would have to collect.

We hurried our preparations as much as possible. Picart filled his knapsack with meat, and I did the same with the canvas bag. He decided to regain the road by the way we had come, following the outskirts of the forest. If we were surprised by the Russians, we should have the wood for shelter; and if we were not molested, we should be on a road we could not easily lose.

We started then—he with more than fifteen pounds of fresh meat, and I carrying the saucepan filled with the meat already cooked. Picart told me that he always liked carrying the food on a march in preference to other things, as after a few days it diminished greatly in quantity; he quoted Æsop as a proof of what he said. As he was talking, we heard musket-shots from the opposite side of the lake. 'Back! Into the wood!' said Picart; but the noise soon ceased, and we set out again.

The storm, so long quiet, now threatened to break out afresh. Great clouds covered the forest, making it so dark that we dared not enter it for shelter. As we stopped to consider our next move, we heard more firing, this time much nearer. We now saw two troops of Cossacks trying to surround seven of our infantrymen, who were coming down a hill, apparently from a little hamlet on the opposite side of the lake. We could see them fire on the enemy, and then retreat to the side of the lake, evidently trying to gain the forest, where they could set the Cossacks at defiance.

There were more than thirty of the Cossacks; half of

them came down to the edge of the lake opposite to us, to cut off our men's retreat. Our fire-arms were ready loaded, and I had thirty cartridges ready to receive them if they came over to our side, and perhaps to help our men to get off. Piçart, who kept his eyes fixed on them, said :

'*Mon pays*, you must load, and I will engage to bring them down like so many ducks. As a beginning, we'll both fire together.'

Our men, however, continued to retreat. Picart recognised them as the same men who had pillaged the waggon the day before; but now there were only seven, instead of nine. The cavalry were now only about forty yards off, so Picart, slapping me on the shoulder, said : 'Attention to the word of command ! Fire !' The men stopped astonished, and one of them fell from his horse. When the Cossacks saw this they scattered, and only two remained with the wounded man, who was now sitting on the ice, supporting himself by one hand. Picart, anxious to lose no time, fired a second time, and wounded a horse. Then they all fled, leaving their wounded comrade, and sheltering themselves behind their horses, which they led by the bridles. We next heard savage cries on our left hand, and saw our unfortunate comrades surrounded by Cossacks on all sides. On our right we could see the two men return for the wounded one, and as he was unable to walk, they dragged him by the legs over the ice.

We specially noticed a Cossack on the look-out for us, gazing at the place where he had first seen us. Picart could contain himself no longer; he fired, and the Cossack was struck on the head, for we saw him reel in his saddle, drop his head forward, and, with his arms stretched out, fall from his horse. He was dead.*

* Picart was one of the best shots in the Guard. In camp at target practice he always carried off the prizes.—*Author's Note.*

At the noise of the shot the Cossacks who surrounded our comrades turned round astonished. Our infantry fired at them, and four Cossacks fell at once. Then we heard shouts of rage, and a stubborn fight followed. We were just about to help in a vigorous manner, when the storm, which had threatened for so long, broke. The snow, which had been falling all the time, grew so thick as completely to blind us. We found ourselves in a thick cloud, obliged to cling to each other to avoid being blown down by the wind. All at once the cloud disappeared, and six yards off we saw the enemy, who yelled out on seeing us. We could not fire, our hands were so frozen by the cold; but we faced them with the bayonet, and regained the wood, while they galloped off.

On entering the wood, we saw the three infantrymen pursued by five Cossacks from the other side of the lake. We fired on them, but without success, and were beginning again, when all at once we saw them sink in the lake and disappear, two Cossacks with them. The unfortunate men had passed over the place which the Russians had broken in for their horses, and the new ice was not strong enough to bear any weight. A third Cossack, seeing the others disappear, tried to stop his horse, and made him rear upright. The horse's hind-legs slipped, and he fell over with his rider, and they, too, disappeared after the others.

We were horror-struck, and our pursuers remained motionless on the ice, not attempting to help their comrades. We could hear piercing cries from the hole in the ice, and several times saw horses' heads appear; then the water bubbled up and spread over the ice.

Ten cavalrymen with their commander came up, and, approaching the fatal spot, plunged their lances in; apparently finding no bottom to the lake, they looked over to our side, and then galloped off again. We lost sight of them, and all was quiet.

We were now left alone in this deserted spot, leaning on our firearms, and looking at the bodies of the wretched men. After a silence of some minutes, Picart said:

'I have a longing for a pipe. I have a good mind to look for some tobacco among these men; I shall be very unlucky if I don't find any.'

I said this was an imprudent thing to do, as we did not know where the first of the cavalry had gone to; and as I spoke we saw a number of horsemen and peasants carrying long poles towards the ice where the unfortunate men had been engulfed. A cart with two horses followed them.

'Good-bye to my tobacco,' said Picart.

We now thought it advisable to go to the farthest side of the wood; there we found a shelter, probably belonging to a last night's bivouac, where we could hide ourselves and watch the Cossacks. They partly stripped the bodies of our men, and the peasants came afterwards and stripped them naked. I had the greatest difficulty while this was going on to keep Picart from shooting at them.

The rest of them, with the peasants, went on towards the hole in the ice, and began to make preparations for dragging out the submerged men. When we saw them at work, there was nothing more for us to wait for. It was not quite so cold, and might be about mid-day. We noticed two Cossacks patrolling the outskirts of the wood, following our footprints in the snow. At sight of them, Picart flew into a rage, and said:

'If they have seen us, there is nothing more for us to do; they will follow us wherever we go by our footmarks. Let us hurry on, and get into the wood as soon as we can, and if they're not more than two, we can account for them.' He stopped directly afterwards. 'Confound them!

I had counted on them for tobacco. The cowards! They were too frightened to follow us.'

We kept as much as possible to the forest; but the fallen trees here and there barred our way, and we had to come out occasionally. Once we looked back, and saw the two men, one behind the other, about thirty yards off. One of them no doubt saw us, as he spurred on his horse, then waited for his companion to come up. We retired into the wood, where we could see them without being seen, and we walked as quickly as possible—sometimes in the wcod, sometimes outside—in order to draw the two men farther and farther from their companions.

After half an hour's walking, we were stopped by a wall of snow ending in a ravine, so we were forced to take a few steps back towards the forest to hide ourselves. The Cossacks were now close to us, but Picart, who knew the art of war, whispered: 'I want them at the other side of the ditch; they will be further off from the others.'

When the Cossacks saw that they could not get through, they went down the ravine so as to come up on the other side of the snow wall. We had in the meantime found a passage for ourselves. We took advantage of the moment when they were in the ditch for getting out of the forest; but just as we thought we had got rid of them, and I waited for a breathing-space, for my legs were beginning to fail under me, Picart turned his head, and saw our two friends behind, trying to take us by surprise, when we thought they were in front. We re-entered the forest quickly, and, making several détours, we returned and saw them walking very softly. Again we took to the forest, running in and out to deceive them, and finally returning to hide behind a group of little pine-trees covered with snow.

When the first man was about forty yards off, Picart

said : ' The honour of the first shot is yours, sergeant ;
but wait till he comes nearer.'

As he spoke, the Cossack signed to his comrade to
advance. He turned his horse to the right, facing the
bush we were behind. When he was four yards off I
fired, and wounded him in the breast. He cried out, and
would have fled, but Picart rushed forward, seized the
bridle of his horse, and struck him with the point of his
bayonet, saying, ' Look out, *mon pays ;* take care of the
other.' As he spoke, the other came up and discharged
his pistol at the head of Picart, who fell under the horse
he was holding. I ran at the man who had fired, but,
seeing me, he threw away his pistol, turned, and galloped
off to the plain, a hundred yards from us. I could not
fire at him, as my musket was not reloaded, and with my
benumbed hands it was impossible to do it.

Picart was now on his feet, but the Cossack I had
wounded fell from his horse as if dead. Picart lost no time.
He gave me the horse to hold. Walking twenty paces
off, he aimed at the other man, sending a ball whistling
by his ear, which he avoided by laying himself almost
flat on his horse, and then made off at a gallop. Picart
reloaded his musket, and then said to me, ' The victory
is ours, but we must be quick ; let us use the conqueror's
rights, and see if this man has anything for us. We can
go off with the horse.'

I asked Picart if he was not wounded, but he said it
was nothing ; we would talk of that later. He took two
pistols, one of them loaded, from the dead man, and said,
' I believe he is shamming ; I saw him open his eyes.'

In the meantime I tied the horse to a tree, and took
the man's sword and a pretty little case set in silver,
which I recognised as belonging to a surgeon in our army.
This I hung round my neck, but I threw the sword into

the brushwood. The Cossack wore two French uniforms under his cloak, a Cuirassier's, and a red Lancer's of the Guard, with an officer's decoration of the Légion d'Honneur, which Picart promptly secured. He wore besides several very fine waistcoats folded in four, making a thick breast-plate, which no ball could have pierced. In his pockets we found more than 300 francs in five-franc pieces, two silver watches, and five crosses of honour, all taken from the dead and dying, or from carts left behind. If we had stayed longer we should probably have found more.

Picart picked up his lance and unloaded pistol. He hid them in a bush, and we set off. Picart walked in front, leading the horse, and as I followed it occurred to me to feel inside a portmanteau fastened on the horse, which I could see had belonged to an officer of Cuirassiers of our own army. When I got my hand inside I felt something very much like a bottle. When I told Picart, he cried, ' Halt !' The portmanteau was opened in a couple of minutes, and I drew out a bottle filled with something the colour of gin. Picart swallowed some of it without troubling to smell it, and then passed it to me. ' Your turn, sergeant.' An exquisite sensation impossible to describe came over me after I had drunk some. We agreed that this was the most precious of all our finds. We must be very careful of it ; and as I had in my pouch a little china cup I had brought from Moscow, we decided that it should be the measure each time we drank.*

We plunged into the forest, and after a quarter of an hour's painful progress, on account of the quantity of fallen trees, we reached a road five or six feet wide, going

* I still have the little cup ; it is at home, under a glass case, with a little silver cross found in the crypt of the Church of St. Michael, and under the Emperors' tombs.—*Author's Note.*

precisely in the direction we must take to rejoin the high-road where the army must have passed.

Feeling now easier in my mind, I raised my head and looked at Picart. His face was all covered with blood. Blood had formed in icicles on his moustache and beard. I told him that he was wounded on his head. He said 'yes,' he had discovered it when his cap had caught on a branch, and blood had flowed down his face; it was nothing of any consequence. 'And besides,' he continued, 'this is not the time to bother about it; it will do this evening.'

I proposed that, to get on faster, we should both mount the horse. 'Let us try,' he said. We therefore took off the wooden saddle he had on his back, leaving only a cloth underneath, and we both got astride, Picart in front, and I behind. We drank some of our spirit and started, holding our muskets across like balancing-poles. We trotted on, sometimes we galloped; often our way was barred by fallen trees, and the idea occurred to Picart to cut down a few more which looked on the point of falling, and thus to form a barrier against the cavalry if they came after us. He dismounted, and with my axe he felled some small pine-trees across the road, which would effectually provide twenty-five men with work for an hour. After he had mounted again, we trotted on for a quarter of an hour, when he stopped and said:

'*Coquin de Dieu !* this tartar has a hard trot !'

I said he was taking his revenge on us for having killed his master.

'Ah, sergeant,' he said, 'the drop of drink has made you merry, I see.'

Picart arranged the flaps of his white cloak carefully on the horse's back to make his seat easier, and we went on for a quarter of an hour at a walking pace. Some time the horse was half buried in the snow. We now saw a road crossing ours, which we concluded must be the high-road, but we had to be careful before entering it. We jumped down, and leading the horse, we retired into the forest, in order to examine the road without being seen. We soon recognised it as being the road leading to the Bérézina, by the vast number of corpses half covered by snow, and footmarks coming towards us; and the traces of blood on the snow looked as if a convoy of French prisoners, escorted by Russians, had passed not long since.

There was therefore no doubt that we were behind the Russian van-guard, and that very soon others would come after us. What were we to do? To follow the high-road was the only course open to us. Picart's opinion was this:

'An idea has occurred to me. You shall be the rear-guard, and I the van-guard. I will guide the horse forward if I see nothing coming; you, my friend, with your head turned towards his tail, can look out behind.'

It was not easy to put Picart's idea into practice. We had to sit back to back, like a double eagle, as he said, with two eyes in front and two behind. We each took a small glass of gin, reserving the rest for a case of necessity, and we put the horse to a walk, setting off again in this silent and lonely forest.

The north wind was bitterly cold, and the rear-guard suffered severely from it, hardly able as he was to keep his position; but, fortunately, the atmosphere was clear, and one could see objects quite a long way off; the road we followed was also a straight one, so that we had no fear of being surprised at a sudden bend. We progressed in this way for half an hour, when we met in the wood bordering the road seven peasants, who appeared to be waiting for us. They each wore a sheepskin coat, and their boots were made of the bark of trees. They came up to us, wished us good-day in Polish, and seemed pleased to find that we were French. They made us understand that they had to go to Minsk to join the Russian army, as they belonged to the militia; they had been forced to march against us by blows from the knout, and Cossacks were stationed in all the villages to drive them out.

We went on our way, and when they were out of sight I asked Picart if he had understood what the peasants said. Minsk was one of our great depots in Lithuania, containing storehouses of food, and where a large part of the army was to meet. He said he had understood perfectly, and if it was true, *Papa Beau-père** had played us a nasty trick. As I did not understand, he explained that the Austrians must have betrayed us.† He was going on at some length, when he suddenly pulled the horse up, saying, ' Look out, there! Isn't that a column of troops?' I saw something black, which disappeared again; but directly afterwards the head of a column appeared as if coming from a deep hollow.

It was easy to see they were Russians. We had just time to turn to the right and enter the forest, but we had hardly gone four paces, when the horse sank breast-deep into the snow and threw me off. I dragged Picart with me into six feet of snow, and we had the greatest trouble in getting out again. The brute of a horse got off, but he cleared a passage for us through the woods, and we took advantage of it at once. After twenty yards we could go no further owing to the thickness of the trees,

* The Emperor of Austria.
† Picart knew what he was about in speaking of Austrian treason, as I learnt since that an alliance had been made against us.—*Author's Note.*

so we were obliged to return—there was no choice. We found our horse munching the bark off a tree, to which we tied him. We went some distance off behind a thick bush, and got ready to defend ourselves. While we waited Picart asked whether our bottle was either lost or broken. Luckily it was all right, so we each had a cup, which we wanted badly. While I undid the bottle, Picart looked to the priming of our guns, and took the snow out of the hammers.

After waiting for about five minutes, the head of the column appeared, preceded by ten or twelve armed Tartars and Kalmoucks, some with lances, others with bows and arrows, and peasants to right and left of the road, armed with anything they could lay their hands on. In the centre of the group were more than 200 prisoners of our army, hardly able to drag themselves along. Many of them were wounded; some had their arms in slings, others had frozen feet, and leant on thick staves for support. Several had fallen, and in spite of the blows from the peasants and from the lances of the Tartars, they did not move. I cannot describe the pain we suffered at seeing our comrades so ill-treated. Picart said nothing, but I feared every instant that he would rush out from his cover at the offenders. Just then an officer galloped up, and, addressing the prisoners in French, he said:

' Why don't you walk faster ?'

' We cannot,' said a soldier lying in the snow, ' and, for my part, I would rather die here than further on.'

The officer said that he must have patience, that carts were coming, and that the most seriously ill would be put into them.

' You will be better off than you were with Napoleon, for at the present moment he is a prisoner with all his Guard and the rest of his army, and the bridges over the Bérézina are cut.'

'Napoleon a prisoner with his Guard!' replied an old soldier. ' May God forgive you, sir! You do not know them. They would only be taken dead. They swore it! They cannot be prisoners!'

' Come,' said the officer, ' here are the waggons.'

We now saw two of our waggons and a travelling forge filled with sick and wounded men. Five men were thrown out, whom the peasants at once stripped absolutely naked. These were replaced by five others, three of whom were unable to move by themselves. We heard the officer order the peasants to return the clothes they had taken to the prisoners most in need of them. As they did not hurry themselves to obey his orders, he gave each of them several smart blows with a whip. We then heard him say to some soldiers who were thanking him :

' I am French myself. I have been in Russia for twenty years. My father died there, but my mother is still alive. I hope now that we shall get back to France and our property there. I know quite well you have not been conquered by force of arms, but by this unendurable Russian climate.'

' And the want of food, besides,' replied a wounded man. ' If it were not for that, we should be at St. Petersburg.'

' Perhaps so,' said the officer.

The convoy moved slowly on.

When it was out of sight we went for our horse, and found him with his head in the snow searching for grass. By chance we came upon the remains of a fire. We relit it and warmed our frozen limbs. We jumped up every moment, and looked to right and left, when all at once we heard a groan, and saw a man coming towards us almost naked. He had on a coat half burnt, a dilapidated forage-cap on his head. His feet were wrapped in rags, and string was tied round them, and round a ragged pair of gray trousers. His nose was almost frozen off, his ears covered with wounds. Only his thumb remained on the right hand; all the fingers had dropped off. This was one of the poor wretches abandoned by the Russians. We could not understand a word he said. When he saw our fire he almost threw himself upon it; he seemed as if he would devour it, kneeling down in front of the flame without a word. We got him with difficulty to swallow a little gin. More than half of what we gave him was wasted, for his teeth chattered so he could hardly unclose them.

His groans ceased, his teeth had almost stopped chattering, when he suddenly turned pale, and seemed to collapse without a word or sigh. Picart tried to raise him up, but he only lifted a corpse. This scene took place in less than ten minutes.

Everything my old comrade saw and heard seemed to impress him very much. He took his musket, and without a word to me turned on to the highroad, as if there was nothing more to trouble about. I hastened after him, leading the horse, and when I caught him up I told him to mount. He did so without speaking, and I after him, and we pressed forward, hoping to get out of the forest before nightfall.

After an hour's trotting, seeing nothing but dead bodies along the road, we came to what we took for the end of the forest. We found, however, that it was only a large clearing in semicircular form. In the centre was a fair-sized house with a few huts round it. This was one of the posting-stations, but, unfortunately for us, there were horses tied to the trees. Their riders came out of the house, and formed in order on the road; then they trotted off. There were eight of them, in white cloaks and very

high-crested helmets. They were like the Cuirassiers we
fought against at Krasnoë, in November. Luckily, they
went off in the opposite direction from the road we were
making for.

On re-entering the forest, we found it impossible to
advance twenty yards. No human being could ever have
set foot there, the trees were so crowded together, the
brushwood was so thick, and there were so many fallen
trunks half buried in the snow. We were forced to come
out, and run the risk of being seen by following the forest
outside. Our poor horse sank at every step into the
snow, and night was drawing on before we had gone half
our distance. To rest for a few minutes, we entered a
road leading into the forest. We dismounted, and flew
at once to our precious bottle. This was our fifth attack,
and we could now see its contents diminishing.

As there were a good many felled trees about, we
decided to get as far to the other side of them as possible,
and we halted against a pile of wood which would prove
a shelter. After Picart had rid himself of his knapsack,
and I of my saucepan, he said, ' Now for the main thing—
a fire. Quick! an old bit of linen.'

My old shirt was a wonderful thing for catching a blaze.
I tore off a bit and gave it to Picart; he made it into a
wick, and putting it with a bit of powder into the priming-
pan of his gun, he fired. The linen caught fire, but a
terrible report was the consequence, repeated again and
again by echoes, and I feared it would betray us.

My poor friend Picart was not the same man since he
had seen the prisoners and heard the officer's account
of the Emperor's surrender. It had made a great effect
on him; he even complained at times of a bad pain in
his head, which was not at all the result of the Cossack's
pistol. I cannot explain it. He forgot that he had loaded

his musket, and after the report he just sat still without speaking, and finally only abused himself for a conscript and an old blockhead. Several dogs were set barking. Then he said he expected they would come and track us out like wolves. I tried to reassure him by saying that we need fear nothing at that late hour.

We soon had a good fire, as we found some really dry wood; we also found, to our joy, some straw, probably hidden by peasants. Providence seemed to smile on us again, and Picart said, ' Cheer up, *mon pays;* we are saved just for this night! God will do the rest to-morrow, and if we are lucky enough to find the Emperor, it will be all right.'

Picart, along with all the veterans, who idolized the Emperor, thought that once with him everything was bound to succeed, and that, in fact, nothing was impossible.

We made a comfortable litter for our horse with straw, and gave him something to eat as well, all the time keeping him ready harnessed, and with the portmanteau strapped on his back, ready for the first alarm. Picart took a piece of cooked meat from the saucepan to thaw it, and said :

' Do you know, I am thinking a great deal of what the Russian officer said.'

' What do you mean ?'

' Why, that the Emperor and the Guard were taken prisoners. I know, of course, that it's not that—couldn't possibly be—but I can't get it out of my wooden head. It sticks there, and I shall have no peace till I am with the regiment. Just now let's eat and rest a little, and afterwards '—he went on in Picardy patois—' we'll drink a *tiote goutte.*'

The temperature was almost mild just then ; we ate the horseflesh without much appetite, and Picart talked by himself, swearing all the time.

'I have forty gold napoleons in my belt, and seven Russian gold pieces, not counting the five-franc pieces; I would give the whole with all my heart to be with the regiment again. That reminds me,' he said; 'the pieces are not in my belt, but are sewn inside my white service waistcoat, and, as one never knows what may happen, they will belong to you.'

'Well,' I said, 'now for my last will and testament. I have 800 francs in notes and in gold. You may dispose of it all, if it is God's will I should die before finding the regiment.'

While warming myself, I put my hand mechanically into the little canvas bag I carried, and found something hard like a bit of cord and as long as two fingers. On examining it I found it was tobacco. What a discovery for poor Picart! When I gave it to him, he let fall a bit of meat he was eating, and took a quid of tobacco instead, to wait with, he said, while he found his pipe. As it was hardly the time to search for it, he contented himself with his quid, and I with a little cigar which I made à l'Espagnole with a piece of paper.

We had been resting for about two hours, and it was not yet seven o'clock. We had therefore eleven or twelve hours yet to wait before continuing our march.

Picart had been walking a few yards off for a moment, and I was getting uneasy about him, when I heard a rustling in the brushwood in the opposite direction from that he had taken. I took my musket and put myself ready, when Picart appeared.

'It is all right, *mon pays*—quite right,' he said in a mysterious voice, signing to me to keep silence. Then he told me that two women had just passed along the road, one carrying a bundle and the other a pail. They had stopped to rest for a few minutes, chattering like magpies. 'We will follow them,' he said; 'probably we shall come to a village or some hut where we shall get shelter and greater safety than here, for listen to those confounded dogs barking!'

'But,' I said, 'we shall be sure to find Russians!'

He said we would risk that. So we set off again in the night, in the midst of a forest, not knowing where we were going, and with only a few footmarks in the snow to guide us. The footsteps ceased suddenly, and when we found them again, they turned off to the right. This put us out, as they led us away from the highroad. Very often, too, we almost lost sight of them, and Picart had frequently to go down on his knees and search for them with his hands.

Picart led the horse by the bridle, and I followed, holding his tail. A little further on we found two roads, both of them with footmarks, and we stopped, not knowing which to take. We thought of making the horse go first, and trusting to him to guide us; but at last God took compassion on our misery. We heard a dog bark, and a little further on we came to a fairly large building. Imagine the roof of one of our barns placed on the ground, and you will have an idea of the kind of building now before us. We walked round it three times before we could discover a door, hidden as it was by a thatched roof reaching down to the ground. Picart went under the roof, and found a second door, at which he knocked gently. No one answered. He knocked again. Still no answer. Thinking the house was deserted, he was about to push open the door, when a feeble voice was heard; the door opened, and an old woman appeared, holding a piece of resinous wood lighted in her hand. At seeing Picart, she dropped the wood in terror and fled. My companion picked up the wood, still alight, and advanced some steps. I fastened the horse up near the door, and on going in found Picart in a cloud of smoke. In his white cloak, with the light in his hand, he looked like a penitent. He broke the silence by the best greeting he could muster in Polish, and I repeated it after him. An old man heard us, and came forward. When he saw Picart, he exclaimed:

' Ah, Frenchmen, that is well !'

He said it in Polish, and repeated it in German. We told them that we were Frenchmen of Napoleon's Guard. At that name the Pole bowed, and would have kissed our feet. At the word ' French,' repeated by the old woman, two younger women came out of a little recess, and showed the greatest joy. Picart recognised them for the two women whose footsteps we had followed.

After being with these good people for about five minutes the heat of the cottage, to which I was so unaccustomed, nearly suffocated me. I retreated to the door, where I fell down unconscious.

Picart ran to help me, but the old woman and one of her daughters had already lifted me up, and placed me on a wooden stool. They relieved me of the saucepan and of my bearskin cloak, and made me lie down on a camp-bed covered with skins. The women seemed very sorry for us, seeing our great misery, and especially for me, as I was so young, and had suffered so much more than my comrade. My sufferings had made me so wretched that it was pitiful to see me. The old man had busied himself in bringing in our horse, and they did all they could for us. Picart remembered the gin in my pouch, and made me swallow a little, and I began to feel much better.

The old woman took off my boots for me. I had not had them off since Smolensk—that is to say, since November 10th ; it was now the 23rd. One of the girls filled a great basin with warm water, and, kneeling down, took my feet gently one after the other and washed them, pointing out that I had a wound in the right foot. It was an old chilblain of 1807, at the time of the Battle of Eylau. I had not felt it since then, but now it opened again, and I suffered cruelly from it.*

The other girl, who seemed to be the elder, performed the same office for Picart. He submitted calmly, but seemed embarrassed. I said he had had an inspiration from God when he thought of following the girls' footsteps.

'Yes,' he said; 'but when I saw them in the forest, I never thought we should be received like this. I did not tell you,' he continued, 'that my head ached like the devil—and I still feel it. I believe that dog of a Cossack's ball did more damage than I thought. We'll see.'

He untied the cord under his chin, which held the sheep-

---

* The Battle of Eylau began on February 7th, 1807, at daybreak ; we had slept the night before on a plain behind the town, a quarter of a league away. This plain was covered with snow and with dead bodies, the rear-guard having been engaged there just before our arrival. It was scarcely daybreak when the Emperor ordered us to move forward. This we had great difficulty in doing, as we walked through ploughed fields, and snow up to our knees. He placed the Guard near the town—a part of it near the cemetery, and a part on a lake fifty yards off. Balls and shells falling on the lake cracked the ice, and threatened to submerge those who stood on it. All day we stood in this position, our feet in the snow, and half crushed by the shells and grape-shot. The Russians were four times as strong as we were, and they also had the advantage of the wind, which blew dead against us, driving the snow, and the smoke from our powder and theirs, into our faces. Up till seven o'clock we remained in this position. At three in the afternoon our regiment was sent to resume the position of the morning, which the Russians wanted to take. All night, as during the battle, the snow never ceased to fall. That day my right foot was frozen, and was only cured at Finkeistein, before the battles of Essling and Friedland.—*Author's Note.*

skin ear-coverings in their places; but hardly had he done this when the blood began to flow.

'Just look!' he said. 'But that's nothing—it's only a scratch; the bullet must have slipped down the side of my head.'

The Pole helped him off with his shoulder-belt. He had almost forgotten how to take off that and his fur cap, he had slept in them for so long. The girl who had washed his feet washed his head too. Everyone gathered round to serve him. The poor fellow was so much touched by their care for him that great tears rolled down his face. Scissors were needed to cut his hair, and all at once I remembered the surgeon's little case which I had taken from the Cossack. We found everything we wanted there for dressing the wound—two pairs of scissors, and several other surgical instruments, with lint and bandages. After cutting the hair off, the old woman sucked the wound, which went deeper than we thought. Then we put on some lint, a bandage, and a handkerchief. We found the ball in the midst of some rags which filled his cap. It had gone right through the left wing of the Imperial eagle on the front of the cap. To his great joy, he also found his pipe, a regular cutty, not three inches long, and he began to smoke it at once.

When our feet were washed, they dried them with lambskins, which served afterwards as a carpet; and on my chilblain they put some ointment, assuring me it would soon make me all right. They gave me a bit to take away in a piece of linen; this I put in the surgeon's case with all the instruments I had used for Picart. We already felt much better, and we thanked the Poles for all the care they had taken of us. They told us how grieved they were not to be able to do more. On a journey one must lodge one's enemies and wash their feet. How much more one's friends! Just then the old woman screamed and ran out. Her great dog had run off with Picart's cap. They wanted to beat him, but we begged him off. I proposed to Picart that we should examine the portmanteau still on the horse's back, so we carried it near the stove. First we found nine handkerchiefs embroidered in silk. 'Quick!' said Picart; 'two each for our princesses, and one for the old mother, and the others we will keep.' This was done immediately, to everyone's great satisfaction. Then we found three pairs of officer's epaulettes, three silver watches, seven crosses of honour, two silver spoons, two dozen Hussars' gilt buttons, two boxes of razors, six bank-notes of 100 roubles each, and a pair of linen trousers stained with blood. I hoped to find a shirt, but was disappointed. I had greater need of that than of anything else, as the warmth had revived the vermin which devoured me.

The girls opened their eyes wide as they looked at our presents, unable to believe they were really theirs. The gilt buttons gave them greater pleasure than anything else, and also some gold rings, which I enjoyed putting on their fingers. The girl who had washed my feet noticed, I am sure, that I gave her the best. Very likely the Cossacks cut off the dead men's fingers to take the rings.

To the old man we gave a large English watch and two razors, besides all the Russian small money, amounting to more than thirty francs. We noticed that he fixed his eyes continually on a commander's cross with the Emperor's portrait, so we also gave that to him. I cannot describe his pleasure. He pressed it several times to his lips and his heart, and finally fastened it round his neck by a leather band, making us understand that only death should part him from it.

We asked for some bread, and they brought us what

they had not dared give us before, they said, it was so bad. We really could not eat it. It was made of a black paste, full of grains of barley, rye, and bits of straw, rough enough to tear one's throat to pieces. They said this bread came from the Russians, that three leagues off the French had beaten them that very morning, and had taken a large convoy from them. This news had been brought to them by the Jews who were flying from all the villages on the road to Minsk. They had also sold them this bread, which was quite uneatable, and although I had not eaten any bread for more than a month, I could not manage to get my teeth into it. For a long time, too, my lips had been so cracked by the frost that they bled constantly.

When the peasants saw that we could not eat the bread, they brought us a piece of mutton, a few potatoes, some onions, and some pickled cucumber. They gave us, in fact, everything they had, saying that they would do their best to get us something better. We put the mutton into the saucepan to make some soup. The old man told us that half a league off there was a village filled with refugee Jews, and as they had carried off all their food with them, he hoped he could find there something better to eat than what they had set before us. We wished to give him some money, but he refused it, saying that what we had given him and his daughters would be quite sufficient, and that one of them had already gone off with her mother and the big dog.

They had made a bed for us on the ground, of straw and sheepskins. Picart had already gone to sleep, and I soon followed his example. We were awakened by the loud barking of the dog. ' Good !' said the Pole, ' my wife and daughter have come back.' They brought us some milk, a few potatoes, and a little cake of rye-meal, which they had procured by heavy payment, but brandy, *nima*.*

The little there was had been taken by the Russians. We thanked these kind people who had walked nearly two leagues, with the snow up to their knees, in the middle of the night, too, in terrible cold, and exposed to the attacks of wolves and bears, which abound in Lithuanian forests. We made some milk soup and drank it at once. I felt much better after I had eaten, and then sat reflecting, my head in my hands. Picart asked me what I was thinking of.

'I am thinking,' I said, 'that if I were not with you, and bound by honour and my oath, I should stay here in this forest with these good people.'

'Cheer up,' he said. 'I have had a lucky dream. I dreamed I was in the barracks at Courbevoie, eating a piece of *Mère aux bouts'* pudding, and drinking a bottle of Suresnes wine.'†

While Picart was speaking, I noticed that his face was very red, and that he frequently put his hand to his forehead. I asked him if his head pained him. He said it did, but that was caused very likely by the heat, or by having slept too long, but he seemed to me to be in a fever. His vision of the barracks at Courbevoie confirmed me in this opinion. 'I want to go on with my dream, and try to find *Mère aux bouts* again,' he said. 'Good-night!' He was asleep in two minutes.

* *Nima* in Polish and Lithuanian means 'no,' or 'there is none.'— *Author's Note.*

† *Mère aux bouts* was an old woman who came at six o'clock every morning to the barracks at Courbevoie, and sold us, for ten centimes, a piece of pudding six inches long. We feasted on this every day before our drill, and drank ten centimes' worth of Suresnes wine, to help us to wait for the soup at ten o'clock. What Vélite or old Grenadier of the Guard has not known *Mère aux bouts?—Author's Note.*

I, too, tried to rest, but my sleep was constantly broken by the pains in my legs, the result of my continued over-walking. The dog began to bark soon after Picart went to sleep; he roused the people of the house, and the old man, who was seated on a bench near the stove, got up and seized a lance fastened to a long pine-branch, his only means of defence. He ran to the door, followed by his wife, and I did the same, taking care not to wake Picart, and armed myself with my musket and bayonet. We heard someone trying the outer door, and in reply to the old man's question of who was there, a nasal voice answered, ' Samuel !' The wife then told her husband that it was a Jew from the village. I resumed my place on hearing that a son of Israel was at the door, taking care to collect all our possessions around me, so little confidence had I in the new-comer. I slept for two hours, when Picart awoke me to take my share of the mutton soup. He still complained of a bad pain in his head, saying he had dreamt of nothing but Paris and Courbevoie, and, for-getting that he had already related his dream to me, told me that he had been dancing at the barrière du Roule,* and had drunk with the Grenadiers who were killed at the Battle of Eylau.

As we sat down to eat, the Jew gave us a bottle of gin, which Picart took possession of at once, and speaking in German, he asked its history. When he tasted it, all the thanks the Jew got was the exclamation that it was not worth the devil. It was bad gin made from potato-spirit.

The idea came to me that we might make use of the Jew as a guide; we had quite enough with us to tempt his love of gain. Picart approved of my plan, and just as he was

* Place where the old Grenadiers of the Guard met their mistresses and danced.—*Author's Note.*

prepared to propose it, the horse raised himself, terrified, trying to break his tether, and the dog gave tongue, and at the same moment some wolves began howling at the door. Picart took his musket to chase them away, but our host warned him against this, on account of the Russians. He contented himself, therefore, by taking his sword in one hand, and in the other a piece of flaming pine. Then opening the door, he ran at the wolves and put them to flight. He came in again, saying that the air had done him good, and that his headache had nearly gone. The wolves afterwards came back, but we took no notice of them.

As I had expected, the Jew asked us if we had anything to sell or exchange. I said to Picart that now was the time for proposals, as we wanted to be put on our way to Borisow, or to the first French outpost. I asked him how far we were from the Bérézina, and he answered nine leagues by the high road; but we made him understand that we wished to get there by a shorter route, and I proposed that he should guide us if we could arrange it. We gave him the three pairs of epaulettes, and a banknote worth 100 roubles, the whole the value of 500 francs; I made the conditions, however, that the epaulettes should be left in charge of our host, who would hand them over to him on his return, and that I would give him the banknote on arriving at our destination—that is, at the first French outpost. When he returned the epaulettes would be given to him on presentation of a silk handkerchief which I showed to the assembled company. The handkerchief was to be given to the younger daughter, who had washed my feet, and the Jew agreed to give our host and hostess 25 roubles. The son of Israel accepted the conditions, observing, however, that he should be running a great many risks in thus leaving the high road.

Our host said how sorry he felt that he was not ten years
younger, so that he might guide us for nothing, and defend
us also against any Russians who might come; saying this,
he shook his halberd. He gave the Jew a great many
instructions as to the road, and he at last consented
to guide us, after satisfying himself that everything we
had given him was of full value.

At nine in the morning we started. It was November 24th.
The Polish family stood on the highest piece of ground
they could find, following us with their eyes, and waving
to us with their hands. Our guide went first, leading our
. horse. Picart talked to himself, sometimes standing and
going through the musket-drill. All at once he stopped,
and, on turning round, I saw him motionless, porting arms
as if on parade. Suddenly he thundered out, 'Vive
l'Empereur!' I went up to him, and, taking him by the
arm, I said, 'What is the matter with you, Picart?' fearing
that he had gone mad.

'What!' he answered, as if only just awake, 'isn't the
Emperor inspecting us?'

I was distressed to hear him, and answering that it was
not to-day, but to-morrow, I took his arm, and hurried
him along to catch up with the Jew. Large tears were
falling down his face.

'What,' I said, 'an old soldier crying!'

'Let me cry,' he said; 'it will do me good. I feel
miserable, and if we don't get to the regiment to-morrow,
it's all up with me.'

'Cheer up! We shall be there to-morrow, I hope, or
the next day at latest. How's this?· You are taking on
just like a woman.'

'That is so,' he said; 'I can't explain it. I was either
sleeping or dreaming; but I am better now.'

'That's right, *mon vieux*. It's nothing; it has often

happened to me before. But since you came I have felt quite hopeful.'

As I talked, I saw our guide stop continually to listen. Suddenly Picart threw himself full length in the snow, and shouted in a commanding voice, ' Silence !'

' Now,' I said to myself, ' he's done with—my old comrade has gone mad ! What will become of me ?'

I looked at him petrified. He then got up, and shouted again, ' Vive l'Empereur ! The guns ! Listen ! We're saved !'

' What do you mean ?' I said.

' Yes, listen,' he went on.

I listened, and really heard the sound of distant guns.

' Ah, now I can breathe again !' he said ; ' the Emperor is not a prisoner, as that fool of an emigrant said yesterday. It had got regularly on my brain, and I should have died of rage and mortification. Now let us go in that direction ; it's a safe guide.'

The Israelite assured us that the guns were in the direction of the Bérézina, and my old comrade was so delighted that he began to sing :

Air du *Curé de Pomponne.*

' Les Autrichiens disaient tout bas ;
Les Français vont vite en besogne
Prenez, tandis qu'ils n'y sont pas,
L'Alsace et la Bourgogne.
Ah ! tu t'en souviendras, la-ri-ra,
Du depart de Boulogne' (*bis*).*

Half an hour later we could not advance any further, so difficult had our march become ; our guide believed he had missed the way. We heard the booming of the guns continually ; it might be about mid-day. All at once the

* This song had been composed on leaving the camp at Boulogne in 1805, to go to Austria for the Battle of Austerlitz.—*Author's Note.*

sound of the guns ceased, the wind got up again, and the snow began falling in such quantities that we could not see each other, and the poor son of Israel gave up leading the horse. We advised him to mount the beast, which advice he took. I began to feel terribly tired, and uneasy in my mind, but said nothing; while Picart swore like a madman because he could not hear the guns, and at the wind which prevented our hearing. The trees were now so close together that we could not possibly penetrate through them. Every moment something caught our feet, and we fell headlong on the ground half buried in the snow; and after much painful walking we found ourselves at the place we had left an hour before.

We now stopped for a few minutes, drank some of the bad gin which the Jew had given us, and discussed our next move. We decided that we must return to the high-road. I asked the guide if he could take us back to where we had spent the night, in the event of our not being able to find the road. He said he could, but that we must make landmarks where we passed. Picart accomplished this by 'blazing' the young birches and pines as he went along. When we had gone about half a league, we came upon a cottage; it was only just in time, as my strength was now failing me. We decided to halt there for half an hour while we fed the horse, and ourselves also. By a stroke of luck, we found there a quantity of dry wood for burning, two benches made of rough wood, and three sheepskins; these we thought we would take away with us, in case we were obliged to spend the night in the forest.

We warmed ourselves while we ate a piece of horseflesh. Our guide would not touch it, but drew from under his sheepskin cloak a wretched-looking cake of barley-flour mixed with straw, which he begged us to share with him. He swore to us by his father Abraham that he had nothing

183

with him but that and a few nuts. We therefore divided it into four; the Jew took two parts, and we each had one. We also drank a little of the bad gin. When I offered some to him he refused, as he would not drink out of our cup, but he accepted some poured into the hollow of his hand.

Then he told us that the next hut was a good hour's walk off, so we resolved to set out at once for fear of being overtaken by the darkness. The road was so narrow that we had the greatest difficulty in getting along, but Samuel, our guide, had pluck, and kept on assuring us that it would become wider farther on.

As a finishing stroke to our misfortunes, the snow began to fall again heavily, and completely hid the way from us. Our guide burst into tears, saying that he did not know where we were. We tried to retrace our steps, but this was worse, as the snow flew straight in our faces, and now the best thing we could do was to stand against a group of pine-trees, waiting till it pleased God to stop the snow-storm. It lasted for more than half an hour longer. We were almost perished with cold. At times Picart swore, and then he would hum :

> 'Ah ! tu t'en souviendras, la-ri-ra,
> Du depart de Boulogne !'

The Jew continually cried out, ' My God ! my God !' For my part, I said nothing, but my thoughts were gloomy, and had it not been for my bearskin and the Rabbi's cap, which I wore under my shako, I should have yielded to the cold.

As soon as the weather grew a little better, we tried to find our way, but a complete calm had followed the storm, so that we could not distinguish the north from the south. We were now completely lost. We walked on at random in great circles, continually coming back to the same place.

Picart swore continually, but now it was at the Jew. However, after walking for some time, we found ourselves in an open space, about 400 yards in circumference, and we hoped to find a road here, but after wandering round it several times, we discovered nothing. We looked at each other, hoping for an idea from someone. My old comrade leant his musket against a tree, and, looking all round him, he drew his sword from its sheath. Hardly had he done so, when the poor Jew, thinking he was going to be killed, set up a piercing shriek, and, leaving the horse, prepared to fly; his strength, however, failed him, and he fell on his knees, imploring mercy of God and of us; quite needlessly, however, as Picart had only drawn his sword to cut down a small birch-tree and consult it as to our direction. He looked fixedly at the part of the tree still in the ground, and then said calmly, ' That is the direction we must take. The bark on this side, which must be the north, is a little red and rotted, and the other side, that of the south, is white and perfect. Let us walk towards the south.'

We had no time to lose, as our greatest dread was that night should overtake us. We tried to beat out a path for ourselves, taking care not to lose the direction of our starting-point.

Just then the Jew, who was in front of us, uttered a cry, and we saw him stretched full length on the ground. He had fallen down in trying to drag the horse between two trees where there was not room to pass. The poor *cognia* could neither go forward nor back. We had to stop and disentangle the man from the horse; the burden the horse carried, as well as his harness, had been pressed backwards on to his hind-quarters.

I was much put out at this loss of time. I would
willingly have left the horse behind, but at the end of half
an hour's efforts we discovered a fairly wide path, which
the Jew recognised as being the continuation of the road
we had lost. He knew the road by some beehives in the
trees, too high, unfortunately, for us to reach.*

Picart looked at his watch, and saw that it was nearly
four o'clock, therefore we had no time to lose. We now
found ourselves close to a frozen lake, known to our guide.
We crossed it without difficulty, and, turning to the left,
continued our journey. Very soon we saw four men, who
stopped on seeing us. We naturally got on guard at once,
but it was soon apparent that they were more frightened
than we, and after consulting together they came towards
us, wishing us good-day. They were four Jews, known to
our guide, belonging to a village on the high road. As
the village was occupied by the French army, they could
not possibly remain there without dying of cold and
hunger. The provisions were all gone, and not a single
house was left for shelter, even for the Emperor. From
them we learnt, to our joy, that the French army was
only two leagues off. They advised us, however, to go no
further that day, as we might easily miss the road. We
could pass the night in the first hut we should come to,
not far off. They left us, bidding us good-night, and we
fortunately soon found our resting-place for the night,
There was a quantity of straw and wood in the hut, and
we immediately lit a good fire in an earthenware stove we
found there. It would have taken too long to make soup,

* In Poland, Lithuania, and a part of Russia, large trees are chosen ;
and about ten feet from the ground a hole of about a foot deep and
wide is made. Here the bees deposit their honey, and often it is
stolen by the bears, who are very numerous in these forests, and
very greedy. Thus the hives frequently become traps to take them.—
Author's Note.

so we contented ourselves with a piece of roast meat, and then decided to watch in turn two hours at a time, with loaded weapons near us.

I do not know how long I had been asleep, when I was awakened by the horse, frightened in his turn by the howling of the wolves outside. Picart took a long pole, and tying some straw and resinous wood to the end, he lit it and rushed on the animals, holding his flaming pole in one hand and his sword in the other, and for the moment they fled. He returned triumphant, but he had scarcely lain down again when they came back with redoubled fury. He then took a great piece of lighted wood, and, throwing it a dozen yards off, he told the Jew to take out a quantity of dry wood to keep up the blaze. After this we heard no more howling.

At about four o'clock Picart woke me with an agreeable surprise. Without telling me, he had made soup with some oatmeal and flour he had left, and had roasted a good piece of horseflesh. We both set to with a good appetite. Picart had given the Jew his share, and we took care of the horse also. We had filled several wooden tubs with snow, which was now melted; we purified it by putting in a quantity of lighted charcoal. This served for our drink, for soup, and for watering the horse, who had drunk nothing since the evening before. After looking to our boots, I took a piece of charcoal, and wrote the following inscription on a plank in large letters:

' Two Grenadiers of the Emperor Napoleon's Guard, lost in this forest, passed the nights of November 24th and 25th in this hut. The day before they enjoyed the hospitality of a kind Polish family.' This inscription I signed.

We had scarcely gone fifty yards, when our horse stopped short. Our guide said he thought he saw something on the road, and on going nearer there were two wolves sitting waiting for us. Picart fired, and the wolves disappeared. Half an hour afterwards we were safe.

We first came across a bivouac of twelve men, German soldiers attached to our army. We stopped near their fire to ask for news. They looked at us without answering, and then consulted among themselves. They were in the last stage of destitution. Three dead bodies were lying near them. As our guide had now kept his bargain, we gave him what we promised him, and after asking him again to thank the good Poles for us, we bade him good-bye and a safe journey. He strode off quickly and disappeared.

We now prepared to gain the high road, only ten minutes' walk off, when five of the Germans surrounded us, begging us to leave our horse behind to be killed, and assuring us we should have our share. Two of them took hold of his bridle, but Picart, who had had enough of this, said, in bad German, that if they did not leave hold of the bridle he would cut their faces for them with his sword, and he drew it out of its sheath. The Germans took no notice, and Picart repeated what he had said. No answer. He then gave the two holding the bridle a smart blow with his fist which stretched them in the snow. He asked me to hold the horse, and said to the others: 'Come on, if you have any pluck.' Seeing, however, that no one moved, he took three pieces of meat out of the saucepan and gave them to the men. Those lying on the ground got up at once for their share. I saw that they were almost dead of hunger, and to make up for our rough treatment of them, I gave them a piece already cooked, weighing more than three pounds. They threw themselves on the food ravenously enough, and we continued on our way. A little farther on, we came on two fires almost extinguished, several men, half dead, lying around them. Two of them spoke to us ; one cried, ' Comrades, are you going to kill the horse ? I only want a little blood !'

We did not answer. We were still a gun-shot from the highroad. When at last we reached it, I said aloud to Picart, ' We are saved !'

A man near us, wrapped in a half-burned cloak, said, raising his voice, ' Not yet !' He moved off, looking at me and shrugging his shoulders. He knew what was going on better than I did.

Soon afterwards we saw a detachment of about thirty men, engineers and *pontonniers*. I recognised them as the men we had met at Orcha, where they formed part of the garrison.* This detachment, commanded by three officers, and which had joined us only four days ago, had not suffered. They looked strong and well, and were travelling in the direction of the Bérézina. I asked an officer to direct us to the Imperial quarters, and he replied that it was still in the rear, but had begun to move, and that we should soon see the head of the column appear. He warned us to look well after our horse, as the Emperor had given orders to take all that were found for the use of the artillery and the wounded. While we waited for the column we hid ourselves in the wood.

I cannot possibly describe all the sufferings, anguish, and scenes of desolation I had seen and passed through, nor those which I was fated still to see and endure ; they left deep and terrible memories, which I have never forgotten.

This was November 25th, perhaps about seven o'clock in the morning, and as yet it was hardly light. I was musing on all I had seen, when the head of the column

* The *pontonniers* and the engineers saved us, and to them we owed the construction of the bridges over the Bérézina.—*Author's Note.*

appeared. Those in advance seemed to be Generals, a few on horseback, but the greater part on foot. There were also a great number of other officers, the remnant of the Doomed Squadron and Battalion formed on the 22nd, and barely existing at the end of three days. Those on foot dragged themselves painfully along, almost all of them having their feet frozen and wrapped in rags or in bits of sheepskin, and all nearly dying of hunger. Afterwards came the small remains of the Cavalry of the Guard. The Emperor came next, on foot, and carrying a baton. He wore a large cloak lined with fur, a dark-red velvet cap with black fox fur on his head. Murat walked on foot at his right, and on his left the Prince Eugène, Viceroy of Italy. Next came the Marshals, Berthier— Prince of Neufchâtel—Ney, Mortier, Lefebvre, with other Marshals and Generals whose corps had been nearly annihilated.

The Emperor mounted a horse as soon as he passed : so did a few of those with him, the greater part of them having no more horses to ride. Seven or eight hundred officers and non-commissioned officers followed, walking in order and perfect silence, and carrying the eagles of their different regiments, which so often had led them to victory. This was all that remained of 60,000 men.

After them came the Imperial Guard on foot, marching also in order. The first were the Chasseurs. Poor Picart, who had not seen the army for a month, gazed in silence ; but it was easy to see how much he felt. He struck the ground many times with the butt of his musket, then his breast and forehead with his clenched hand. Great tears fell from his eyes, rolled down his cheeks, and froze in his moustache. Then, turning to me, he said :

' I don't know, *mon pays*, if I am awake or dreaming. It breaks my heart to see our Emperor on foot, his baton in his hand. He, so great, who made us all so proud of him !' He went on : ' Did you notice how he looked at us ?'

The Emperor had turned his head towards us as he passed. He looked at us as he always looked at the men of his Guard when he met them alone. He seemed, in this hour of misfortune, to inspire us by his glance with confidence and courage. Picart declared that the Emperor had recognised him, which was quite possible. My old comrade, fearful of looking ridiculous, had taken off his white cloak and carried it over his left arm, and although his head still pained him, he had put on his fur cap, not liking to appear in the sheepskin the Poles had given him. Poor Picart forgot all his own miseries, and now only thought of the Emperor, and of the comrades he longed to see.

At last the old Grenadiers appeared. These were the first regiment ; Picart belonged to the second. We were not long in catching sight of them, however, as the first column was a short one—in my opinion quite half were missing. When at last his own regiment came up to us, Picart advanced to join it.

Then someone said :

' Look ! Isn't that like Picart ?'

' Yes,' answered Picart, ' it is I ; and I will not leave you again, except to die.'

The company immediately took possession of him (for the sake of the horse, of course). I walked with him for some time longer, to get a piece of the horse's flesh if they killed him, but a shout was heard :

' The horse belongs to the company, like the man !'

' I belong to the company, certainly,' said Picart ; ' but the sergeant, who claims a bit of the horse, killed his master in the first place.'

'Very well, then,' said a sergeant who knew me, 'he shall have some.'

This sergeant took the place of a sergeant-major who had died the day before.

The column came to a halt, and an officer asked Picart where he came from, and how he happened to be in front, as those who had escorted the convoy had come back three days ago. The halt lasted for some time. Picart related his adventures, stopping continually to ask after several comrades whom he failed to see in the ranks. They were all dead. He dared not ask after his bed-mate, who was also from his own country. But at last he ventured.

'And where is Rougeau?'

'At Krasnoë,' said the drummer.

'Ah! I understand.'

'Yes,' continued the drummer, 'he died from a ball which cut both his legs off. Before he died he made you his executor. He gave me for you his cross, his watch, and a little leather bag containing money and different things. He begged me to tell you that they were for his mother. If, like him, you were so unfortunate as not to see France again, you were to commission someone else.'

The drummer, named Patrice, then took all the things out of his knapsack before all the company, saying to Picart:

'I give them to you just as I received them from his hands. He took them out of his knapsack—which we replaced under his head—and directly afterwards he died.'

'If I have the good fortune to get back to Picardy,' said my friend, 'I will carry out my comrade's last wishes.'

They began the march, and I bade good-bye to my old

friend, saying we should meet again at bivouac in the evening.

Then I waited by the side of the road until my regiment came by, as I heard it formed part of the rear-guard.

After the Grenadiers came more than 30,000 men, almost all with their feet and hands frozen, a great number of them without firearms, as they were quite unable to make use of them. Many of them walked leaning on sticks ; generals, colonels, other officers, privates, men on horseback, men on foot, men of all the different nations making up our army, passed in a confused rabble, covered with cloaks and coats all torn and burnt, wrapped in bits of cloth, in sheepskins, in everything they could lay their hands on to keep out the cold. They walked silently without complaining, keeping themselves as ready as they could for any possible struggle with the enemy. The Emperor in our midst inspired us with confidence, and found resources to save us yet. There he was—always the great genius ; however miserable we might be, with him we were always sure of victory in the end.

I had more than an hour to wait before the column had passed by, and after that there was a long train of miserable wretches following the regiments mechanically. They had reached the last stage of destitution, and could not hope to get across the Bérézina, although we were now so near it. Then I saw the remains of the Young Guard, skirmishers, flank-men, and some of the light companies, escaped from Krasnoë. All these regiments mingled together marched in perfect order. Behind them came the artillery and several waggons. The bulk of the artillery, commanded by General Négre, had already gone before. Next came the Fusiliers-Chasseurs. Their numbers were greatly diminished. Our regiment was still separated from me by some pieces of artillery, drawn by poor beasts with no power left in them. After that I saw my regiment marching to left and right of the road to join the Fusiliers-Chasseurs. The Adjutant-Major, Roustan, saw me the first, and cried out, ' Hallo, poor Bourgogne! Is that you? We thought you were dead behind us, and here you are alive in front! This is first-rate. Have you met some of our men behind?' I told him that for the last three days I had been in the woods to avoid being taken by the Russians. M. Césarisse said to the Colonel that he knew I had stayed behind since the 22nd, and that he was surprised beyond everything to see me again. My company came at last, and I took my own place in it before my friends were aware of it.* When at last they saw me, they came round me asking questions which I had not strength to answer; I was as overwhelmed to find myself once more amongst my comrades as if I had been with my own family. They told me they could not imagine how I had become separated from them, and that if they had only known I was ill and could not follow, it should not have happened. As I glanced over the company, I saw that their numbers also were terribly diminished. The Captain was missing. He had lost all his toes by the frost, and just at that moment they did not know where he was, although they had found a wretched horse for him to ride. Two of my friends took hold of me under the arms, seeing that I could scarcely walk.†

We joined the Fusiliers-Chasseurs. I never remember in all my life having such a terrible longing for sleep, and yet we were obliged to go on. My friends supported me

* They marched with their heads bent, their eyes fixed on the ground, hardly seeing anything; the frost and the bivouac fires had nearly ruined their sight —*Author's Note.*

† Grangier and Leboude.—*Author's Note.*

under the arms again, telling me to go to sleep. This we did for each other in turn, for sleep overcame us all. Frequently it happened that we stopped short, all three of us having gone off. The cold, fortunately, was much less that day, otherwise most of us might have been frozen to death.

In the middle of the night we reached Borisow. The Emperor stayed in a country house on the right of the road, and the Guard bivouacked round it. General Roguet, who commanded us, took possession of a green-house for the night. I and my friends were behind it. During the night the cold increased very much. The next day (the 26th) we took up a position on the banks of the Bérézina. The Emperor was at Studianka, a little village on a hill in front.

We saw the brave *pontonniers* working hard at the bridges for us to cross. They had worked all night, standing up to their shoulders in ice-cold water, encouraged by their General.* These brave men sacrificed their lives to save the army. One of my friends told me as a fact that he had seen the Emperor himself handing wine to them.

The first bridge was finished at two o'clock in the afternoon. It was a painful and difficult piece of work, as the trestles sank continually in the mud. Marshal Oudinot's corps crossed immediately to attack the Russians, who had tried to prevent our passage. The cavalry of the 2nd Corps had already swum across, not waiting for the bridge to be finished, and every man took a foot soldier behind him. The second bridge, for the artillery and cavalry, was finished at four o'clock.†

* General Eblé.—*Author's Note.*

† This second bridge broke soon afterwards, when the artillery began to cross. A great many perished.—*Author's Note.*

Directly we arrived at the banks of the river I lay down wrapped up in my fur, and then found myself trembling all over with fever. I was delirious for a long time. I fancied I was at my father's house, eating potatoes, bread and butter *à la flamande*, and drinking beer. I do not know how long I was in this condition, but I remember my friend bringing me some hot broth in a bowl, which I drank eagerly, and I was soon in a perspiration, in spite of the cold. Besides my bearskin cloak, my friends had covered me with a great piece of waterproofing they had torn off a waggon. The rest of the night I lay quiet without moving.

On the next day (the 27th) I felt rather better, but terribly weak. That day the Emperor crossed the Bérézina with part of the Guard, and about a thousand men belonging to Marshal Ney's corps. Our regiment remained on the banks. Suddenly I heard my name called; I turned my head and saw M. Péniaux, director of the Emperor's stage posts and relays, who had searched me out. They told him that I was ill, and he came at once, not to give me anything—he had nothing to give, except encouragement. I thanked him for his kindness, and said I did not expect even to cross the Bérézina, or to see France again; but I begged him, if he were more fortunate than I, to tell my parents of my sad situation. He offered me money, but I declined it. I would willingly have exchanged 800 francs for the potatoes and bread-and-butter I dreamed I had eaten at home.

Before he left me he pointed out the house where the Emperor had stayed, saying he had been unfortunate, as the house was a flour warehouse, but the Russians had taken it all, so that he had nothing to offer me. He shook me by the hand and left me to cross the bridge.

As soon as he had gone, I remembered that he had

spoken of some flour in the Emperor's house, so I rose, and, weak as I was, I dragged myself in that direction. The Emperor had only just left the house, and yet they had already taken off all the doors. I went through several rooms, and the traces of flour could be seen in them all. In one of them the boards in the floor were very badly laid down ; there was more than an inch between them. I sat down and scraped out with my sword as much dirt as flour, which I collected and put into my handkerchief. After working more than an hour, I got out about two pounds in weight, an eighth of which was dirt, straw, and little bits of wood. That did not matter in the least; I went out happy. As I made my way towards our bivouac I saw a fire, where several men from the Guard were warming themselves. Amongst them was a musician from our regiment, who had a tin bowl on his knapsack. I signed to him to come to me, and as he seemed unwilling to leave his place, I pointed to my parcel, making him understand there was something inside it. He rose with difficulty, and when he was near enough I said, in a voice which the others could not hear, that if he would lend me his bowl, I would make some cakes which we could share. He consented directly, and as there were several fires near, we looked out for one in a quiet place. I then made a paste and four cakes from it ; the half I gave to my musician, and took him back with me to the regiment, still camped on the bank of the river. I divided the rest of the cakes with the men who had helped me along the road ; they thought them very good, still hot as they were from the baking. After drinking some of the muddy water of the Bérézina, we warmed ourselves, waiting for the order to cross the bridges.

Near our fire was a man belonging to the company attired in *full uniform !* I asked him what that was for, and he only laughed at me. The poor fellow was ill ; that laugh was the laugh of death, as he succumbed during the night.

A little further off was an old soldier with two chevrons —fifteen years service, that is. His wife was *cantinière*. They had lost everything—carts, horses, baggage, besides two children, who had died in the snow ; all this poor woman had left to her was despair and a dying husband. The poor creature, still a young woman, was sitting on the snow, holding her dying husband's head on her knees. She did not weep ; her grief seemed beyond that. Behind her, leaning on her shoulder, was a beautiful young girl of thirteen or fourteen years, the only child remaining to her. This poor child was sobbing bitterly, her tears falling and freezing on her father's cold face. She wore a soldier's cape over her poor dress, and a sheepskin on her shoulders to keep out the cold.* None of their own comrades were there to comfort them. Their regiment was utterly destroyed. We did all that we possibly could for them, but I was not able to find out if these unhappy people were saved. Whichever way one turned, these terrible scenes were taking place. Old carts and waggons furnished us with wood enough to warm ourselves, and we made the most of this opportunity. My friends wanted to hear how I had spent my three days of absence. They told me on their side that on the 23rd, when they were marching across the forest, they caught sight of the 9th Corps drawn up by the roadside, shouting ' Vive l'Empereur !' They had not set eyes on this corps for five months. These men, who had scarcely suffered at all, and had never wanted food, were distressed at seeing their comrades' destitution. They could hardly believe that this was the Moscow

* The girl, and also her mother, wore Astrakan caps on their heads. —*Author's Note.*

army, then so splendid, now so miserable, and so sadly reduced in numbers.

The 2nd *Corps d'Armée*, commanded by Marshal Oudinot, and the 9th by Marshal Victor, Duke of Bellune, also the Poles under General Dombrowski, had not been to Moscow, but had remained in Lithuania. For the last few days, however, they had been engaged against the Russians, had repulsed them, and taken a large quantity of baggage ; as the Russians retired they had burnt the bridge. This was the only bridge over the Bérézina, and had stopped our advance, keeping us penned up between two forests in the middle of a marsh. We were a medley of Frenchmen, Italians, Spaniards, Portuguese, Croats, Germans, Poles, Romans, Neapolitans, and even Prussians. I saw some canteen men whose wives and children were in great despair, weeping. We noticed that the men seemed to suffer more, both morally and physically, than the women. The women bore their sufferings and privations with an astonishing courage, enough to reflect shame on certain men, who had no courage and resignation to endure their trials. Very few of these women died, except those who fell into the Bérézina in crossing the bridge, or some who were suffocated.

We were quiet when night came, every one in his bivouac, and no one came to cross the bridge during the night of the 27th-28th, a most astonishing thing. I slept, as we had a good fire, but in the middle of the night I was seized with fever again, and became delirious. The sound of firing woke me at about seven o'clock. I got up, took my firearms, and without speaking to anyone I went up to the bridge and crossed it alone. I met no one but the *pontonniers*, who camped on the two banks to repair the bridge in case of any accident.

The first thing I saw when I reached the other side was

a large wooden hut. The Emperor had slept there, and had not come out yet. I was shivering with fever, so went up towards a fire where several officers were engaged in studying a map. I received such a cold welcome, however, that I hastily retired. One of our men, who had observed me, now came up to tell me that our regiment had crossed the bridge, and was in the second line of battle behind Marshal Oudinot's corps. As the cannon roared, and the bullets came rattling over to where we were standing, I started off to join the regiment, saying to myself that I had better be shot than die of cold and hunger, so I walked forward into the wood. On the way I overtook a corporal of my company dragging himself painfully along, so we helped each other and arrived at the regiment together. There we saw a fire, and as the corporal was shivering with fever, I led him up to it. Hardly had we arrived, when a ball struck my poor comrade in the chest, and stretched him dead at my feet. I could not help crying out, ' Poor Marcelin ! How lucky you are !' Just then the rumour ran that Marshal Oudinot was wounded.

When the Colonel saw one of his men fall, he ran to the fire, and noticing how ill I was, he ordered me to go back to the end of the bridge and wait for men who had not come up, and bring them to the regiment. The greatest disorder prevailed at this place. All the men who had not taken advantage of the night to cross had thrown themselves in a mass on to the banks of the river as soon as they heard the artillery, in order to cross by the bridges.

A corporal of our company named Gros-Jean, who came from Paris, asked me with tears in his eyes if I had seen his brother. I said no. Then he told me that he had been with him ever since the Battle of Krasnoë, as he was ill with fever; but just now, by some dreadful fatality, they had been separated. Thinking he had gone on in front, he had been inquiring of his comrades on all sides, and not finding him, he was going back over the bridge, for if he did not find him he would die. Wishing to dissuade him from such a fatal resolution, I begged him to stay with me at the head of the bridge, where we should very likely see his brother as he passed. But the poor fellow stripped off his arms and knapsack, saying that, as I had lost my own, he would make me a present of them if he did not return, and that there were plenty of muskets over at the other side. He then made as if he would go, but I stopped him. I pointed out to him the number of dead and dying already on the bridge, these last preventing others passing over by catching hold of their legs, and all rolling together in the Bérézina. They appeared for a moment amongst bits of ice, only to disappear altogether and make way for others. Gros-Jean did not even hear me. Fixing his eyes on this scene of horror, he thought he perceived his brother on the bridge, struggling to clear a pathway for himself through the crowd. So, listening only to the voice of despair, he climbed over the dead bodies of men and horses which blocked up the way from the bridge,* and rushed on. Those he first met tried to thrust him back, but he was strong, and did not give way. He succeeded in reaching the unfortunate man whom he had taken for his brother; but, alas! it was not he. I followed all his movements with my eyes. Seeing his mistake, he redoubled his efforts to reach the

* At the outlet of the bridge was a marsh, a slimy, muddy place, where many of the horses sank, and could not get out again. Many of the men, also, being dragged by the weight of the others to the outlet, sank down exhausted when left to themselves in the marsh, and were trampled upon by others coming on behind.—*Author's Note.*

further end; but he was knocked over on to his back, on the edge of the bridge, and nearly thrown into the water. They walked over his body, his head, but nothing vanquished him. He collected all his strength for a new effort to rise, and seized hold of a Cuirassier's leg, who, in his turn, got hold of another man's arm. The Cuirassier, however, was hindered by a cloak over his shoulder; he staggered, fell, and rolled into the Bérézina, dragging after him Gros-Jean and the man whose arm he held. They sank then, adding to the number of men underneath the bridge and on each side of it.

The Cuirassier and his companion disappeared under the ice; but Gros-Jean, more fortunate, had seized one of the supports of the bridge, against which he found a horse. Climbing on to the horse by his knees, he begged for help, for a long time speaking to deaf ears. Finally some engineers threw him a rope, which he was clever enough to catch and tie round his body; and thus from one support to another, over dead bodies and lumps of ice, he was drawn over to the further side. I did not see him again; but I heard the next day that he had found his brother, a little distance off, but in a dying condition. Thus perished these two poor brothers, and also a third in the 2nd Lancers. When I got back to Paris I saw their parents, who begged me for news of their children. I left them one ray of hope by saying that their sons had been taken prisoners, but I felt certain they died.

While these sad events were taking place, the Grenadiers of the Guard, accompanied by an officer, went round the bivouacs, asking for dry wood to warm the Emperor. Everyone willingly gave the best they had. Even dying men raised their heads to say, 'Take what you can for the Emperor.' By this time it might be ten o'clock, and the second bridge, built for the cavalry and artillery, had just broken in under the weight of the latter ; a number of men sank with it, and most of them perished. The disorder and confusion were thus doubly increased, for, as everyone rushed to the other bridge, it became an absolute impossibility to get across. Men, horses, carts, canteen men, with their wives and children, were all mingled in frightful disorder, crushed against each other ; and in spite of the shouts of Marshal Lefebvre, who stood at the end of the bridge to keep all the order possible, he could not remain there. He was swept on with the others and forced to cross, to avoid being suffocated or crushed to death. I had managed to get together five men of our regiment, three of whom had lost their firearms in the confusion, and I had ordered them to make a fire. I kept my eyes fixed all the time on the bridge, and saw a man in a white cloak ; he was pushed by those behind him, and fell over the body of a horse stretched on the ground. With extreme difficulty he got up, staggered a few steps, fell again, rose a second time, only to fall again by our fire. He remained thus for a little while, and, thinking that he was dead, we were about to lay him on one side and remove his cloak, when he raised his head and looked at me. It was the gunsmith of our regiment. He said sadly :

'Ah, sergeant, what misfortunes I have had ! I have lost everything—horses, carts—all I had ! I have only one mule left which I brought from Spain, and I have just been forced to leave him. I was carried across the bridge, but I nearly died.'

I told him that he would be very fortunate, and ought to thank Heaven, if he got back to France alive.

So many men now crowded round our fire that we were obliged to leave it and make another some little way back. The confusion and disorder went on increasing, and reached their full height when Marshal Victor was attacked by the Russians, and shells and bullets showered thickly upon us. To complete our misery, snow began to fall and a cold wind blew. This dreadful state of things lasted all day and through the next night, and all this time the Bérézina became gradually filled with ice, dead bodies of men and horses, while the bridge got blocked up with carts full of wounded men, some of which rolled over the edge into the water. Between eight and nine o'clock that evening Marshal Victor began his retreat. He and his men had to cross the bridge over a perfect mountain of corpses. On the night of the 28th-29th it was possible for all the unfortunate wretches on the opposite bank to get across, but, paralyzed by the cold, they stayed behind to warm themselves by the warmth of the burning waggons, which had been set on fire on purpose to make the men go across.

I remained in the rear with seventeen men and a sergeant named Rossière, led by one of the men, as he had become almost blind, and was shivering with fever.* I was sorry for him, and offered to lend him my bearskin to cover him, but so much snow had fallen during the night that it had saturated the cloak. The snow then melted with the heat of the fire and dried up again. When I took hold of the skin in the morning, it was as hard as iron and useless for wearing, and I had to leave it behind. Wishing, however, to make it useful to the last, I laid it over a dying man. We had passed a wretched night. Many of the men in the Imperial Guard had died. At about seven o'clock on the morning of the 29th I went

* I learned afterwards that the sergeant had the luck to return to France ; as he had plenty of money, he got a Jew to take him as far as Koenigsberg, but when he arrived in France he went mad and blew out his brains.—*Author's Note.*

towards the bridge, hoping to find some more of our men. The unfortunate men who had not taken advantage of the night to get away had at the first appearance of dawn rushed on to the bridge, but now it was too late. Preparations were already made to burn it down. Numbers jumped into the water, hoping to swim through the floating bits of ice, but not one reached the shore. I saw them all there in water up to their shoulders, and, overcome by the terrible cold, they all miserably perished. On the bridge was a canteen man carrying a child on his head. His wife was in front of him, crying bitterly. I could not stay any longer, it was more than I could bear. Just as I turned away, a cart containing a wounded officer fell from the bridge, with the horse also.* They next set fire to the bridge, and I have been told that scenes impossible to describe for horror then took place. The details I had witnessed were merely slight sketches of the horrible picture that followed.

I was now told that the regiment was moving. I made the men take up their arms, and counted them to the number of twenty-three, without the gunsmith. As the regiment moved off, each man joined his company.

We were at last on the march; it might be, perhaps, nine o'clock. We crossed a wooded piece of ground interspersed by marshes, which we traversed by means of bridges made of pine-wood, fortunately not burned by the Russians. We waited now and then for those in the rear to come up with us. The sun was shining, and I sat down on Gros-Jean's knapsack and went off to sleep; but

---

* Thus perished M. Legrand, the brother of Dr. Legrand, of Valenciennes. He had been wounded at Krasnoë, and had just got as far as the Bérézina. Just after the scene I have described, and while the Russians were firing at the bridge, I was told that he was badly wounded before being thrown into the water.—*Author's Note.*

an officer, M. Favin, catching sight of me, pulled me by the ears and the hair, others kicked me from behind, all without waking me. Several of them got hold of me and forced me to rise, and well for me that they did, or I should have slept the sleep of death. I felt very cross, however, at being roused.

Many who we thought had perished came on from the Bérézina. They embraced and congratulated each other as if it were the Rhine they had crossed, still 400 leagues off. They felt so happy that they were sorry for those left behind. They advised me to walk a little in front, so that I should not fall asleep again. This advice I took.

CHAPTER IX.

I HAD been walking in advance of the regiment for about half an hour, when I met a sergeant of the Fusiliers-Chasseurs whom I knew. He seemed very happy about something (a most unusual thing), so I asked him if he had anything to eat.

' I have found some potatoes,' he said, ' in this village.'

I raised my head and saw that we were actually in a village at that moment. Walking with my eyes fixed on the ground, I had not noticed it. When I heard the word 'potatoes' I stopped him to ask in which house he had found them, and I ran there as fast as my legs would carry me. After much searching, I had the luck to find three little potatoes under an oven, about the size of nuts. I half cooked them on an almost extinct fire I found a little distance off the road. When they were done enough, I ate them with a bit of horseflesh, but I hardly tasted them, as the fever I had on me for the last few days had destroyed my appetite entirely, and I was sure that if it continued I should soon be dead.

When the regiment passed I took my place, and we marched as far as Ziemben, where the Emperor, with part of the Guard, had already arrived. We could see him gazing at the road to Borisow on our left, where we were

told the Russians would come. Several of the horse-
Guards were sent on in front, but no Russians were to be
seen that day. The Emperor slept at Kamen with half
the Guard, and we, the Fusiliers, Grenadiers, and
Chasseurs, spent the night close by.

On the 30th the Emperor and his suite slept at
Plechnitzié. We bivouacked some distance off. We
arrived there on the following day, and heard that Marshal
Oudinot had only just escaped being made prisoner there;
that 2,000 Russians, with two field-pieces, had entered
the place, and that the Marshal, although wounded,
had entrenched himself in a house with twenty-five men,
both officers and privates, many of them wounded. The
Russians, astounded at these preparations for defence with
so small a number of men, had retired on to some heights
overlooking the house, and laid siege to it till the arrival
of the Emperor with the troop of the Rhine Confederation
and part of the Guard. As we passed, we looked at the
house, pierced through by balls in many places. It
seemed strange to us how 2,000 Cossacks had not
sufficient courage to take an old wooden house defended
by only twenty-five men.

On the next day, December 1st, we left early in the
morning, and after an hour's march we reached a village,
where the Fusiliers-Chasseurs had spent the night. They
were waiting to set out with us. I made inquiries if there
was anything to buy there, and was told by a sergeant-
major that there was some gin to be had from a Jew.
He took me to the place, and seeing the Jew with a long
beard, I asked him politely in German if he had any gin
for sale. ' No,' he answered rudely, ' I have none ; the
French have taken it all.' I said nothing, but I knew
perfectly well he was telling a lie, and that he was only
afraid of not being paid.

Just then a girl of fourteen or fifteen jumped down from a great stove she had been sitting on, and coming up to me, she said : ' If you will give me your silver lace, I will let you have a glass of brandy.' I said yes, so she took off the silver braid belonging to my haversack, worth thirty francs, which I had brought from Moscow. She hid it immediately in her dress, and gave me a miserable bit of cord instead. If I had allowed her, she would have taken the surgeon's pocket - case I had got from the Cossack, as she caught sight of the silver fittings. She then brought me a glass of very bad gin, but I felt so sick I could hardly swallow it. She also gave me a small oval-shaped cheese, the size of a hen's egg, smelling of aniseed. I put it carefully in my haversack, and went out.

I was hardly in the open air, when the abominable spirit flew to my head. I was obliged to cross a broad deep ditch on a tree thrown over to serve as a bridge. I danced across this without falling, and rushed in the same way amongst my comrades. More than that, I took hold of their arms, singing and trying to make them dance. Several of them, even officers, gathered round me, asking me what was the matter. I only sang and danced the more. The sergeant-major of our company took me a little way apart, and asked me where I came from. I told him that I had had some drink. ' Where ?' ' Come with me,' I said. He followed, and we crossed the tree, holding each other by the hand. On the other side a friend of mine took my arm. This was a sergeant-major named Leboude, a Liègeois. He had just heard what I had been doing. When we got to the Jew's house, I told them if they had any gold or silver lace they could get some gin. ' If that's all,' said the Liègeois, ' here it is.' He had a very nice Astrakan cap, with a gold braid round it. The young Jewess took matters into her own hands again, and ripped off the braid. They gave us some gin, and we came away; but we were hardly out of the house, when the same kind of frenzy came over me, worse than before. It took hold of the Liègeois also, and he and I danced together. The sergeant-major looked at us, telling us to march back and rejoin our regiment. Instead of answering, we each took one of his arms, and danced towards the tree over the ditch. There the Liègeois slipped and fell, dragging the sergeant-major into the ditch, and me also. Under the snow in the ditch were more than two hundred dead bodies, thrown there during the last two days. At this sudden collapse the sergeant-major shrieked with rage and terror, swearing loudly at us. We were none of us hurt, however, and the Liègeois began to sing and dance afresh.

We had not the strength to get out again. Ice was everywhere under the snow, and when we got away from the dead bodies, it was too slippery to walk. If a company of Westphalians had not passed at that moment, there we should have stayed. They threw us ropes at first, but our hands were too much frozen to hold them. At last they put down the side of a cart, making a kind of ladder, and they helped us to mount by it. The fall had sobered the Liègeois and me a little. We rejoined the regiment, which had halted near a wood, and resumed our march. A mile farther on we met Prince Eugène, the vice-King of Italy, at the head of a small number of officers and a few Grenadiers of the Royal Guard, grouped round their colours. They were completely exhausted with fatigue. We made a good distance on that day, leaving a great many far behind. We found a deserted village, where we slept, and plenty of straw to lie down in. Horseflesh we had in abundance, but no saucepans to stew it or make soup in. We were therefore obliged, as on the preceding days, to eat some of the meat roasted; but at least we could sleep under shelter and make fires. During the night I was obliged to go out into the air several times, as I was quite unaccustomed to the heat of the houses.

On the next day we started early; this was December 2nd. My fever came on again, and my legs almost gave way under me, so that after an hour's march I found myself behind the others. I went through a small village filled with stragglers, but I passed through without stopping. A little further on I saw large numbers of men gathered outside some houses busy roasting horseflesh. General Maison passed by and stopped, telling everyone to follow him if they wished to escape the Russian cavalry, now not far off. Most of the men, however, were too much famished and too demoralized to listen; they would not leave their fires till they had eaten, and many of them were prepared to defend the piece of meat they held against the enemy. I went on my way. Further on I met several men of my company, and begged them not to leave me; they promised me they would follow me anywhere—that they were quite indifferent where they went. In the evening we stopped near a wood for the night. Already several men from different corps were there, especially of the Italian army, and a few Grenadiers of the 1st regiment of the Guard, of whom I asked news of Picart. They said they had seen him the day before, but that he seemed quite mad, and they thought his brain was affected.

I had never till now thought of looking in poor Gros-Jean's knapsack, which he had given me at the Bérézina bridge. Now, as I felt certain he could not return, I opened it before two men of our company who were with me, and were, moreover, in his squadron. I found nothing of any importance, except a handkerchief containing oatmeal mixed with rye. One of the men happening to have a saucepan lid, we cooked the meal. I also found an old pair of shoes, but there was not a shirt, of which I was in great need; the rest was quite useless to me.

There was, fortunately, a great deal of wood about, so we made a large fire. The cold was endurable while the night lasted, but in the morning (the 3rd) a north wind got up, bringing with it twenty degrees of frost. We were forced to begin our march, as it was impossible to remain still. We started after eating some horseflesh, just following in the steps of those who walked before us, who knew no more than we did where they were, or in what direction they were going. The sun shone brilliantly, and the cold decreased a little; so we made good progress, stopping every now and then at houses with deserted bivouac fires. As far as I can remember, we slept in a posting-station.

The sun which we had enjoyed the day before was the forerunner of a terrible frost. I cannot write of this day, for I truly do not know how I got through it. When my comrades spoke to me, I answered as if I were mad. The cold was intolerable. Many took the first road they came to, in the hope of finding houses of some kind as shelter. We lost our way at last in following some Poles, who were going to Varsovia. One of them who spoke French assured me that we were more than a league from the road to Wilna. We tried to retrace our steps, and we lost ourselves again. We met three officers, followed by more than a hundred unfortunate men from different corps and of different nations, half dead with cold and want. When they heard from us that they were lost, many of them cried like children.

We were now near a pine-wood, so we decided to bivouac there with the men we had met. They had a horse, which we killed and divided amongst us. Two fires were made, and everyone cooked his meat at the point of his sword or a stick. When we had finished our meal, we gathered round the fires, and arranged that a quarter of the number should keep watch, as we feared we might be taken by the Russians, who were following the army on both sides of the road. An hour later the snow began to fall, and a high wind got up, driving us under the shelters we had made. The wind grew furious, driving the snow into the shelters, and entirely preventing us from sleeping, though we wanted it badly enough. I slept, however, seated on my knapsack, with my fur-lined collar on my head to keep off the snow. How many times during this miserable night I longed for my bearskin coat!

I did not sleep long, as a violent gust of wind carried away the shelter. I and my two men were forced to walk about to keep ourselves from freezing. When the dawn came at last, we set out on our march, leaving seven men behind in the bivouac, three of whom were already dead, and four unconscious.

At about eight o'clock we reached the high road, and after countless difficulties we arrived at Molodetschno at three in the afternoon, amid a rabble of men of all corps, especially of the army of Italy. The Emperor had slept here. We tried to find shelter for the night in some barn or stable, but found we were too late. We had to be content with a half-burnt house with no roof, and three-quarters filled with men already; but we considered ourselves lucky in getting any kind of shelter against the fearful cold, which went on increasing until we got to Wilna.

I heard later that it was from this place that the Emperor despatched his twenty-ninth bulletin, which caused such a sensation in France, announcing the destruction of our army. It was broad daylight when we started on the 5th. Mechanically we followed 10,000 men in front of us, marching in confusion, without knowing where they went. We crossed several marshes, where we should have all probably sunk and perished, but for the severe frost. Those who lagged behind were in no danger of losing their way, for the numbers of fallen men on the road served as guides. We arrived the next day at Brenitza. The Emperor had slept there, and had already left. This day we were more fortunate. I was able to buy a little flour, and we made some hasty-pudding; but we had not the luck to find a roofless house again, and were obliged to spend the night in the street. It was so bitterly cold that we got no sleep. The next morning we set off for Smorgony. The road was full of officers of different corps, and the remnants of the Doomed Squadron and Battalion, wrapped in worn-out furs, and half-burnt garments. Some had not even these, having, no doubt, parted with them for their friends. Many of them walked leaning on sticks, their beards and hair a mass of ice; others, no longer able to walk, looked vainly at the miserable men passing along the road, trying to find some part of the regiments they had commanded a fortnight before, and get help or an arm to lean on. It was all over, I fear, with those who could not walk.

The roads were like battlefields, there were so many dead bodies; but as the snow fell all the time, the horror of the sight was softened. We had lost all sense of pity, besides; we were insensible even to our own sufferings, let alone those of others. The men who fell imploring help were not listened to. Thus we arrived at Smorgony, on the 6th. On entering the town, we heard that the Emperor had left the evening before, at ten o'clock, for France, leaving the command of the army to King Murat. Many of the foreigners took advantage of this circumstance to blame the Emperor, but the step he took was a perfectly natural one, as, owing to Malet's conspiracy, his presence was necessary in France, not only for the administration, but to organize a new army. Amongst the numbers of dying men constantly arriving were others who were well dressed and vigorous, evidently foreigners, and these all exclaimed loudly at the Emperor's conduct. I have often thought since that these men were agents from England, come to create disaffection in the army.

In the crowd I lost one of the men who had been with me, but I had no time to look for him, I was so afraid of losing shelter for the night. Seeing an officer from Baden, who belonged to the garrison of the town, I followed him with my other man. He went to a Jew's house where he was quartered, and, seeing us after him, made no objection to our entrance. We sat down near a warm stove. One must go through the misery and suffering we had experienced to understand the delight of being in a warm house and having the prospect of a good night.

In the same room there was a young officer on the staff, ill with fever and lying on a wretched sofa. He told me that he had been ill ever since Orcha, and as he could go no farther, there was probably an end of him, as he would certainly be taken by the Russians. 'God knows,' he said, 'what will come of it, and what my poor mother will say when she learns!'

The Baden officer, who could speak French, tried to comfort him by saying that he would get him a horse for his sledge, as his own was dead. He promised soup and meat to us, but during the night he left with the rest of the garrison. The poor officer grew worse, and was delirious all night, and as for us, we got neither soup nor meat. We had only a few onions and some nuts the Jew had sold us, dearly enough, but the shelter was well worth the money.

After our rest we set out early on the 7th, as quietly as possible, so that the young officer might not hear us, as we could not possibly do anything for him. There were very few people on the road, and after a time we rested near a ruined barn. After half an hour, the column of the Imperial Guard came in sight; the fragment of our regiment was there, marching in as much order as possible. I joined their ranks. When we halted, they asked me, in an indifferent way, if I had found any food during the four days I had been away. When I told them I had nothing, they turned their backs to me, cursing and banging the butts of their muskets on the ground.

We continued our march, and got to Joupranoüi very late; almost all the houses here were burnt, and the rest deserted, without roofs or doors. We huddled together as best we could, and as there was plenty of horseflesh, I cooked some ready for the next day.

On the 8th it was late when we started, but the cold was so intense that the men set fire to the houses to warm themselves. All the houses contained unfortunate soldiers, many of whom had not the strength to save themselves, and perished in the flames.

In the middle of the day we got to a small town the name of which I have forgotten. They told us that distributions of rations were to be made here, but we soon heard that the shops had been pillaged before our arrival, and that the people who had charge of the distributions had got away, and the commissaries also. We continued our route, therefore, striding over the dead and dying on our way. When we halted near a wood, one of the men of our company caught sight of a horse, and we gathered round to kill him, and each take some of the flesh; but as we had no knives or hatchets to cut it, we killed it for the sake of the blood, which we collected in a saucepan taken from a German *cantinière*. Finding a deserted bivouac fire, we began to cook the blood, putting some powder in it for seasoning, but it was only half done when we caught sight of a legion of Cossacks. We had just time to eat it as it was, and this we had to do from our hands, so that our faces and clothes were covered with blood. We were ghastly objects to look at.

This halt, caused by some difficulty with the artillery, had gathered together more than 30,000 men of all nations, making a spectacle impossible to describe. We started off again, and reached a large village three or four leagues from Wilna. I recognised the village for the same we had stayed at five months before, in going from Wilna to Moscow. Here I had lost a trophy, that is to say, a little box containing rings, hair necklaces, and portraits of the mistresses I had had in all the countries I had visited. I was much grieved at losing my collection. On the 9th we left Wilna, in twenty-eight degrees of frost.* Scarcely 2,000 arrived at Wilna, out of two divisions of more than 10,000. These, both French and Neapolitans, had joined us during the last two days. This enormous number was lost during this terrible journey. The men were well clothed, and wanted for nothing but food. They had left good quarters in Lithuania and Pomerania only a few days before. When they came they were filled with pity for our condition, but in two days they were worse off than we. They were less demoralized, and at first they tried to help each other; but when they saw what deprivation this meant, they grew as selfish as all the others, officers and privates alike.

I had plucked up a little courage in the hope of soon getting to Wilna, where we should have abundant food.

* Many people said thirty or thirty-two degrees.—*Author's Note.*

I should call the efforts we made superhuman. This terrible cold was more than I had ever felt before. I was almost fainting, and we seemed to walk through an atmosphere of ice. How often in the dreadful time did I long for my bearskin cloak, which had saved me so often in cold like this! I could hardly breathe: my nose felt frozen; my lips were glued together; my eyes streamed, dazzled by the snow. I was forced to stop and cover my face with my fur collar to melt the ice. In this style I got to a barn where there was a fire burning, and where one could breathe a little. In all the buildings we passed were unfortunate men not able to get any further, and waiting there to die.

Now we could see the spires and roofs of Wilna. I tried to hurry on to get there amongst the first, but the old Chasseurs of the Guard prevented me. They blocked up the road in such a manner that no one could pass them without marching in order. These veterans, with ice hanging to their beards and moustaches, marched on, controlling their own sufferings to keep order in the ranks; but this order it was impossible to maintain. Once in the outskirts of the town, everything was in confusion. At the door of a house I saw one of my old friends of the Grenadiers lying dead. They had arrived an hour before us. A house was chosen for our battalion, and a distribution of beef was made. We had not the sense to put it all together and make soup. We each fell on our allowance like wild beasts, every man cooking or warming it as he could, and some even devouring it raw. One of my friends named Poton, who was a Breton gentleman, and a sergeant in my company, waited impatiently for his piece, about half a pound. As he was a short distance off, it was thrown to him. He caught it with both hands, like a cat, and began eating it convulsively, in spite of everything we

218

could do to prevent him. He was incapable of seeing any-thing but the meat before him.

Soon afterwards I went into the town to see if I could not buy some bread and a little brandy. But the doors were almost all shut and bolted. The inhabitants, although our friends, had taken fright on seeing fifty or sixty thousand famished men, most of whom looked imbecile or mad. Many of our men had rushed about like lunatics, knocking at all the doors and shops, but had been refused, as the contractors wished to do every-thing in order. This was impossible, as order did not exist.

I soon saw that I could not get what I wanted, and was about to go back to my quarters, when I heard my name called. I turned round, and to my great surprise saw Picart, who threw himself on my neck, crying with joy. He had come across the regiment twice since we passed the Bérézina, but they had assured him that I was dead or taken prisoner. He said he had some flour, which I should share with him; and as for brandy, he would take me to his Jew, who would furnish me with that, and perhaps bread as well. I begged him to take me there while we were waiting for the distribution of rations. This we were sure to have later, as the shops were full.

I shall never forget the curious effect an inhabited house had on me. It seemed to me years since I had seen one. Picart gave me a little brandy, which I had great difficulty in swallowing. I then bought a bottle for twenty francs, which I carefully stowed away in my haversack. As to bread, I must wait for that till evening. For fifty days I had not tasted any, and it seemed that if only I could eat a little I should forget all my miseries. The Jew told me that the men who had arrived first in the morning had devoured everything. He advised us not to leave his house, even to sleep there, and that he would undertake to get us everything we wanted, also to prevent others from coming in. Taking his advice, I settled down to rest on a bench near the stove.

I asked Picart how it happened that he was on such friendly terms with the Jew, as I noticed they treated him as a member of the family. He said that he had passed himself off as the son of a Jewess, and that during the fortnight we had spent in the town in July he had attended their synagogue with them, and in consequence of this he had always got some schnapps to drink and some nuts to crack.

I had not laughed for long enough, but I burst out into a roar at this, until the blood poured down my lips. Picart went on with his funny stories, until suddenly we heard a rattle of artillery, and our host came hurriedly in. He looked dazed, and could not speak. At last he said that he had seen some Bavarian soldiers, followed by Cossacks, enter by the same gate at which we had come in.

The garrison of the town just then sounded the call. When Picart heard it, he seized his arms and came up to where I sat, unwilling to move.

' Come, *mon pays*,' he said, striking me on the shoulder ; ' we belong to the Imperial Guard, and should be the first to go. We must not let these savages eat our bread. If you have strength, follow me, and we'll join with fellows who'll turn out these rascals.'

I followed Picart. A few men ran to join they hardly knew what, but a great number walked off as far as they could get, and the most part, quite indifferent to everything, paid no attention to what was going on.

When we got near the gate leading to the faubourg,

we met a detachment of Grenadiers and Chasseurs of the Guard. Picart left me to take his proper place, and as I saw a few of our men following, and also some officers, I followed also, without knowing who commanded us or where we were going. We went up a mountain without any pretence of order, each one going as he could ; many fell and remained behind. We had climbed, perhaps, two-thirds of the height—and I was astonished at having got so far—when I fell; and although helped up by a Lithuanian peasant, I could hardly rise. I begged the man not to leave me, and to secure his services I gave him about four francs in Russian money and some brandy in the little cup I still kept. The peasant was so delighted that I believe he would have carried me on his back. We went on over ground covered with dead men and horses. There were a great many firearms lying about. My peasant picked up a carbine and some cartridges, saying that he wished to fight the Russians himself. After great difficulty we at last reached the top of the mountain, where the Prussians were already fighting. Two hundred men, three-parts belonging to the Guard, were facing the enemy, consisting of cavalry, many of whom were scouts. As the Bavarians had in retreating left some men behind them, with two pieces of artillery, two discharges of grape-shot were sufficient to disperse them. As the position was untenable on account of the cold, we faced about to return to the town, where the greatest disorder prevailed. The garrison, almost entirely composed of foreigners, was in a state of panic. Some were preparing to leave the town, loading carts, sledges, and horses. On all sides we heard cries of ' Who has seen my horse ?' ' Where has my cart got to ?' ' Stop the man who is off with my sledge.' This disorder was mainly caused by the thieves who had followed us all through the retreat, and of whom I have spoken before. Now, seeing a good opportunity, they took advantage of it by seizing carts, horses, and sledges loaded with provisions, gold, and silver. The arrange ments for departure were made by the commissariat, contractors, and other army employés, who now were making common cause with us. The thieves thus fled along the Kowno road, sure of not being pursued.

On entering the faubourg, I avoided the house where our battalion was quartered. I had two reasons for going into the town: firstly, for the bread I was to share with Picart; secondly, to let him know that I had taken part in the little expedition which had beaten the Russians. I ran to the right to find Picart, but to my surprise I was told that he had taken the first turning to the left, with ten other Grenadiers and Chasseurs, to be on guard for Murat. Murat had just left the town for the faubourg on the Kowno road.

I decided to look for him at Murat's quarters. On the way I passed the house where Marshal Ney was staying. Several Grenadiers of the line were before the door, warm- ing themselves by a large fire, which gave me a terrible longing to be there, too. Seeing how wretched I looked, they made room for me. Many of them were quite strong and well dressed. When I showed my surprise at their appearance, they said they had not been as far as Moscow; they had been wounded at the siege of Smolensk, and left at Wilna, where they had remained ever since. Now they were well again and fit for fighting. I asked them if they could get me some bread. They answered as the Jew had done—that if I would return that evening, or stay with them, they were certain that I should have some. But, as I was obliged to go back to the battalion, I told the Grenadiers that I would return, and that I would give five francs for each loaf. Before leaving them, they told me that just before I arrived a German General had come to the Marshal, and had advised him to leave if he did not wish to be surprised by the Russians; but the Marshal had replied, pointing to a hundred Grenadiers warming themselves in the courtyard, that with those he could afford to laugh at all the Cossacks in Russia, and that he would sleep in the town.

I asked how many there were in the Marshal's body-guard.

'About sixty,' answered a drummer sitting on his drum; 'and another sixty we found here well and fit. I have been with the Marshal ever since the crossing of the Dnieper, and with him at our back we can manage those dogs of Cossacks. *Coquin de Dieu!*' he said, 'if it were not so cold, and if I hadn't frozen hands, I would sound the attack myself all day to-morrow.'

I returned to the faubourg, and found all my comrades asleep on the floor. There was a large fire, and the room was warm, and as I was completely worn out, I lay down with them.

It might be perhaps two o'clock in the morning when I awoke, and as I had now missed the rendezvous I had given the Marshal's Grenadiers, I told my comrades that I was going to the town to get some bread, and that now was a favourable time, as all the soldiers would be asleep; and, besides, I had some Russian bank-notes. Several of them tried to get up and go with me, but could not do so. Only one, Bailly, a sergeant, succeeded in rising, and the others gave us their money, amounting to about fifty francs.

It was a beautiful moonlight night, but when we were in the street it felt so bitterly cold that it would not have taken much to send us back into the house.

We met no one in the faubourg. At the gates of the

town there was no sentry. The Russians could have got in as easily as we did. When we were opposite the first house on the left, I caught sight of a light through the entrance to the cellar, and, stooping down, I saw it was a bakehouse, and that bread was being made. The smell had made us aware of it before. My comrade knocked, and they asked us what we wanted. We answered: 'Open the door! We are Generals!' They opened at once, and we went in. They took us into a large room, where a number of officers were lying on the floor. They did not trouble to ask us if we were really what we pretended to be. For some time past it had been hardly possible to distinguish an officer from a private.

A very fat woman was standing against the cellar door, so we asked her if she had any bread to sell. She said no, it was not baked yet; we might go down to the cellar and see for ourselves. An officer lying on some straw, wrapped in a great cloak, got up and went down with us. Two bakers were there fast asleep, and looking all round, we could see nothing; and we began to think that the woman had spoken the truth, when on stooping down I saw under a kneading-trough a large basket, which I drew out. In it we found seven large loaves of white bread, weighing three or four pounds each, as good as those made in Paris. What luck! What a glorious find for men who had had no bread for fifty days! I began by taking possession of two, which I put under my arm and my cape. My comrade did the same, and the officer took the three others. This officer was Fouché, a Grenadier-Vélite, then an Adjutant-Major in a regiment of the Young Guard, and a Major-General. We came out of the cellar, and found the woman still standing at the door. We said that we would return in the morning when the bread was baked, and she was so anxious to get rid of us that she opened the door, and we found ourselves in the street.*

As soon as ever we were free, we dropped our muskets into the snow, and began to bite into the loaves voraciously; but, as my lips were cracked and bleeding, I could not open my mouth as comfortably as I wished. Just then two men came up to us, asking if we had nothing to sell or exchange, and we saw that they were Jews. I told them that we had Russian bank-notes for a hundred roubles each, and asked how much they would give.

'Fifty,' said the first in German. 'Fifty-five,' said the other. 'Sixty,' went on the first.

He ended by offering us seventy-seven, and I made the condition that they should give us some *café-au-lait*. They consented. The second then came behind me and said, 'Eighty!' But the price was concluded, and, as the man had promised us coffee, we did not wish to bargain over again for twenty francs at most.

The Jew now conducted us to a banker, as he was only an agent. The banker was also a Jew. He asked us at once for our notes, of which we had to give nine; three of them belonged to me. He looked very closely at them, and passed into another room, while we sat down on a bench to wait, furtively handling our bread.

Our longing for the coffee promised us overcame our patience, and we called out for the banker. No one appeared. The idea suddenly came to us that we were going to be robbed. I said as much to my comrade, who thought so too. To compel attention, therefore, he struck their counter as hard as he could with the butt of his

* Since then I have seen General Fouché, and, on my reminding him of this episode at Wilna, he told me that, after going out, he was nearly assassinated by the people of the house, who tried to make him pay for what we had taken.—*Author's Note.*

musket. As no one came to this summons either, he knocked against a wooden partition dividing the two rooms. The Jews came out, looking as if they were plotting something together. After again asking for our money, we were told to wait ; but my comrade loaded his musket before their eyes, and I took one of them by the throat, demanding our notes. When they were convinced that we should make a scene to their disadvantage, they hastily counted out our money, the most part of it in gold. We took hold of the man who had led us to the place, and forced him to leave with us; but as soon as we were in the street he swore that what had occurred was no fault of his. We thought it better to believe him in view of the coffee he had promised us, and he took us to his house.

After our meal, my comrade wished to go back to the faubourg ; but I felt so tired, and even ill, that I decided to stay where I was till the next day, thinking myself safe with two Bavarian cavalrymen. So I lay down on a sofa—perhaps it might be five o'clock in the morning.

I had only been resting about half an hour, when I was seized with the most violent colic, after which I was terribly sick, and continued so ill that I felt sure the Jew had poisoned me. I thought I must die, as I was so weak as to be unable to get to the bottle of brandy in my knapsack. I begged one of the Bavarians to give me some, and after that I felt better ; so I lay down again on the sofa and dozed off. I do not know how long I slept, but when I awoke I discovered that my bread had gone. Only a very small piece was left, which, fortunately, I had put in my haversack, along with the bottle of brandy, and hung at my side. My Rabbi's cap had also disappeared, so, too, had the Bavarians. That, however, was not what distressed me the most, but my own position, which was a dreadful one; besides my colic and sickness, my right foot was frozen, and my wound had reopened. The first joint on the middle finger of my right hand was on the point of dropping off, and the terrible cold of the preceding day had poisoned my foot to such a degree that I could not get my boot on. I was forced to wrap it up in rags, after rubbing it over with the grease the Poles had given me, and a piece of sheepskin over all, which I tied on with string. The same process I repeated with my right hand.

I was about to go out, when the Jew asked me to stay, saying that he had some rice to sell. I bought some, thinking it would stop my complaint. I begged him to get me some sort of pot to cook it in, and he fetched me a little copper pan; I tied this and my boot to the knapsack, and after giving the man ten francs I went out.

As soon as I was in the street, I heard despairing cries, and I saw a woman weeping over a dead body at the door of a house. She stopped me, asking me to help her to get back what had been taken from her.

'I have been staying in this house since yesterday,' she said, 'with these scoundrels of Jews. My husband was very ill. During the night they took everything we had, and this morning I went out to get help. As I saw I should get none anywhere, I came back to nurse my poor husband; but when I arrived, imagine my horror at seeing his corpse at the door! The villains had taken advantage of my absence to assassinate him. Oh, monsieur,' she went on, 'do not leave me! Come with me!'

I said that was impossible, but the best thing she could do now was to join those who were leaving the town. She made a gesture with her hand to say she could not do it; and, as I had heard several musket-shots, I had to leave the unfortunate woman and go in the direction of Kowno. I got into a crowd of 10,000 men, women, and children all hurrying and thrusting past each other to get out first.

As chance would have it, I met a Captain of the Young Guard belonging to my own part of the country.* He had with him his Lieutenant, his servant, and a wretched horse. The Captain had no company left; his regiment had ceased to exist. I told him all my misfortunes, and he gave me a little tea and a piece of sugar, but directly afterwards a vast number of people coming after us separated us.

A drummer was beating the retreat at the head of the first crowd, very likely a detachment of the garrison I had not seen. We marched on for half an hour, and arrived at the end of the faubourg; then we could breathe a little, and each one walk as he would. When I got outside the town, I could not help thinking of the state of our army: five months before it entered the Lithuanian capital, proud and rejoicing; now it went out, fugitive and miserable.

* M. Débonnez, from Condé, killed at Waterloo.—*Author's Note.*

CHAPTER X.

WE were only a quarter of a league from the town, when
we saw the Cossacks to our left upon the heights, and to
our right on the plain; however, they did not dare venture
within reach of us. After having marched for some time,
I found the horse of an officer of artillery stretched on
the ground; it had a schabraque of sheepskin on its back.
This was just what I wanted to cover my poor ears, for it
would have been impossible for me to go any distance
without risking the loss of them. I had in my haversack
the scissors belonging to the surgeon's case found on the
Cossack I had killed on November 23rd. I tried to set to
work to cut some of it away, and make what we called
ear-lappets to replace the Rabbi's cap; but having my
right hand frozen, and the other benumbed, I could not
manage it. I was in despair, when a man belonging to
the garrison of Wilna came up. He was stronger than I,
and succeeded in cutting the band fastening the schabraque
to the horse; then he gave me half of it. Until I could

arrange it better, I put it over my head and continued my way.

I now heard cannon, and then musketry fire; it was the rear-guard leaving the town, with Marshal Ney in command, engaging the Russians. Those who were no longer able to fight ran as fast as they possibly could. I tried to follow them, but my frozen foot and bad boots prevented me; then the colic, which came on repeatedly, and forced me to stop, hindered me, and I found myself always in the rear. I heard a confused sound behind me, and I was hustled by several men of the Rhine Confederation running off as fast as they could. I fell full length in the snow, and immediately several others passed over my body. I raised myself with great difficulty, for I was in great pain; but I was so accustomed to suffering, I said nothing. The rear-guard was not far off—if it passed me I was lost; but the Marshal called a halt, to give the other men still leaving the town time to join us. To hold the enemy in check, the Marshal had with him about 300 men.

In front of me was a man whom I recognised by his cloak as belonging to the regiment. He was walking very much bent, apparently overwhelmed by the weight of a burden he was carrying upon his knapsack and shoulders. Making an effort to get near him, I saw that the burden was a dog, and that the man was an old sergeant named Daubenton.* The dog he carried was the regimental dog, though I did not recognise it. I told him how surprised I was at seeing him carrying the dog, when he had trouble to drag himself along; and, without giving him the time to reply, I asked him if the dog was to eat—if so, I should prefer the horse.

* This Sergeant Daubenton was a veteran who had been through the Italian campaigns.—*Author's Note.*

230

'No,' he answered; 'I would rather eat Cossack. But don't you recognise Mouton? His paws are frozen, and now he can't walk any longer.'

'Now I do,' I said; 'but what can you do with him?'

As we walked, Mouton, whose back I had patted with my bandaged right hand, raised his head to look at me, and seemed to recognise me. Daubenton assured me that from seven in the morning, and even before, the Russians had occupied the first houses of the suburb where we had lodged, that all that remained of the Guard had left it at six, and that it was certain that more than 12,000 men of the army, officers and soldiers who were no longer able to march, had remained in the hands of the enemy. He had just missed submitting to the same fate himself through devotion to his dog. He saw very well that he would be obliged to leave him on the way in the snow. The evening of the day when we had arrived at Wilna—at twenty-eight degrees—the poor dog had had his paws frozen, and this morning, seeing that he could walk no longer, he had made up his mind to leave him; but poor Mouton got an idea that he was to be deserted, for he began to howl in such a way that in the end he decided to let him follow. But hardly had he taken six steps along the street when he saw his unfortunate dog fall upon his nose; so he fastened him across his shoulders over his knapsack, and it was in this fashion that he had rejoined Marshal Ney, who with a handful of men formed the rear-guard.

Whilst still marching, we found ourselves stopped by an overturned waggon barring part of the way; it was open, and contained canvas bags, but all these were empty. This waggon had probably left Wilna the preceding evening or in the morning, and had been pillaged by the way, for it had been laden with biscuits and flour. I proposed to Daubenton to halt a moment, for my colic had come on again; he consented willingly, especially as he wished to rid himself of Mouton in one way or another.

We had hardly stopped, when we saw at the back of a ravine a troop of about thirty young Hessians who had formed part of the garrison of Wilna, and had left there at daybreak. They were waiting for Marshal Ney, about thirty paces away from us, and ahead of us to the right. At the same moment we saw on our left another troop of horsemen, about twenty in number. We recognised them at once for Russians; they were Cuirassiers in black cuirasses over white coats, accompanied by several Cossacks scattered here and there. They moved on so as to cut off the Hessians and ourselves, and a vast number of other unfortunate men who had just caught sight of them, and who turned back to rejoin the rear-guard, crying out, ' Beware of the Cossacks !'

The Hessians, under command of two officers who had probably caught sight of the Russians before we did, put themselves in order of defence.

At this moment we saw a Grenadier of the line pass near to us, running to take rank among the Hessians ; we prepared to do the same, but Daubenton, hampered by Mouton, wished to put him in the waggon. We had not time, however, for the cavalry came at a gallop along-side the Hessians. There they halted, signing to them to lay down their arms. A musket-shot was the reply ; it was that of the French Grenadier, followed by a general discharge from the Hessians.

At this report, we expected to see half the troopers fall, but, to our astonishment, not one did so, and the officer who was in advance, and who ought to have been shot in pieces, seemed to be whole and sound. His horse simply leapt to one side. He turned round again instantly towards his men ; they all thundered upon the Hessians, and in less than two minutes they were sabred. Several took to flight, but the cavalry pursued them.

At the same time Daubenton, wishing to rid himself of Mouton, called out to me to help him, but three of the men in pursuit of the Hessians passed close by him. So as to defend himself better, Daubenton thought of retiring under the waggon, where I had taken refuge, suffering terribly from colic and cold ; but he had not time, for one of the three horsemen was on the point of charging him. Daubenton was fortunate enough to see the man in time, and get ready for him, but not so well as he could wish, for Mouton, barking like a good dog, hampered him in his movements. Meanwhile, although nearly dying of cold, I felt rather better, and had arranged my right hand to make use of my weapon the best way possible, having hardly any strength left, to speak of.

The man wheeled continually round Daubenton, but at a certain distance, fearing a musket-shot. Seeing that neither of us attempted to fire, he no doubt thought that we were without powder, for he advanced upon Daubenton and hit him a blow with his sword, which the latter parried with the barrel of his musket. Instantly the man crossed to the right, and gave him a second blow upon the left shoulder, which struck Mouton on the head. The poor dog howled enough to break one's heart. Although wounded and with frozen paws, he leapt off his master's back to run after the man ; but being fastened to the straps of the knapsack, he pulled Daubenton down, and I thought all was over with him.

I dragged myself on my knees about two steps ahead and took aim, but the priming of my gun did not burn. Then 'the man, shouting savagely, threw himself on me, but I had had time to get under the waggon and present my bayonet at him.

Seeing that he could do nothing to me, he returned to Daubenton, who had not yet been able to rise on account of Mouton, who all the time dragged him sideways, howling and barking after the cavalry. Daubenton was dragged against the shafts of the waggon, so that his enemy on horseback could not get near him. This man faced Daubenton, his sword raised as if to split him in two, appearing all the while to mock at him.

Daubenton, although half dead with cold and hunger, his face thin, pale, and blackened by the bivouac fires, still seemed full of energy; but he looked odd and really comical, as that devil of a dog was barking all the time, and dragging him sideways. His eyes were shining, his mouth foamed with rage at being at the mercy of such an enemy, who in any other circumstances would not have dared stand up one minute before him. To quench his thirst, I saw him fill his hand with snow and carry it to his mouth, and instantly seize his weapon again; now in his turn he threatened his enemy.

By the man's shouts and gestures, one could see that he had no command over himself, and seemed to have drunk a great deal of brandy. We saw the others passing, repassing, and shouting round some men who had not been able to reach the side where the rear-guard would come; we saw them thrown into the snow and trampled under the horses' feet, for almost all who followed were without arms, wounded, or with frozen feet and hands. Others, who were stronger, as well as some Hessians escaped from the first charge, were able to withstand them for a little, but that could not last, either—they must be relieved or captured.

The cavalryman with whom my old comrade was doing business had just passed to the left, when Daubenton shouted out to me: ' Don't be frightened! don't stir! I'll finish him off.' Scarcely had he said these words, when he fired. He was luckier than I. The Cuirassier was struck by a ball which entered under the right arm first, and passed out again on the left side. He uttered a savage cry, moved convulsively, and at the same moment his sword fell with the arm that held it. Then a stream of blood came from his mouth, his body fell forward over his horse's head, and in this position he remained as if dead.

Hardly was Daubenton rid of his enemy and free from Mouton so as to seize the horse, when we heard behind us a great noise, then cries of ' Forward ! Fix bayonets !' I came out of my waggon, looked towards the side from which the cries came, and saw Marshal Ney, musket in hand, running up at the head of a party of the rear-guard. The Russians, on seeing him, took to flight in all directions. Those who rushed to the right on the side of the plain found a large ditch filled with ice and snow, which prevented them crossing. Several flung themselves in it with their horses, others stopped still in the middle of the road, not knowing where to go. The rear-guard seized several horses, and made their riders walk on foot amongst them. Afterwards they were left on the road. What else could one do ? One could barely look after one's self.

I shall never forget the Marshal's commanding air at this moment, his splendid attitude towards the enemy, and the confidence with which he inspired the unhappy sick and wounded round him. In this moment he was like one of the heroes of old time. In these last days of this disastrous retreat he was the saviour of the remnant of the army.

All this took place in less than ten minutes. Daubenton had rid himself of Mouton, so as to get hold of the horse, when a man, emerging from behind a clump of pines, threw the Cuirassier off the horse, seized the animal by the bridle, and made off. Daubenton shouted to him: 'Stop, rascal! That is my horse. I killed the fellow!' But the other escaped with the horse amongst the rabble of men who were hurrying forward. Then Daubenton called out to me: 'Look after Mouton. I am going after the horse; I must have him, or there will be the devil to pay.' The last word was hardly out of his mouth, when more than 4,000 stragglers of all nations came on like a torrent, separating me from him and from Mouton, whom I never saw again.

This seems to be the place for giving a little biography of the regimental dog.

Mouton had been with us since 1808. We found him in Spain, near the Bonaventura, on the banks of a river where the English had cut the bridge. He came with us to Germany. In 1809 he assisted at the Battles of Essling and Wagram; afterwards he returned to Spain in 1810-11. He left with the regiment for Russia; but in Saxony he was lost, or perhaps stolen, for Mouton was a handsome poodle. Ten days after our arrival in Moscow we were immensely surprised at seeing him again. A detachment composed of fifteen men had left Paris some days after our departure to rejoin the regiment, and as they passed through the place where he had disappeared, the dog had recognised the regimental uniform, and followed the detachment.

Whilst marching in the midst of men, women, and even some children, I was constantly looking about for Daubenton, whom I regretted very much; but behind only Marshal Ney and his rear-guard were to be seen, taking up a position on the little eminence where the Hessians had been attacked.

After this adventure I was forced to stop again, as I was

suffering so much from my colic. In front, I could see the Ponari mountain from the foot to the summit. The road about three-fourths up the left slope could be traced by the number of waggons, carrying more than seven millions in gold and silver, as well as other baggage, and carriages drawn by horses whose strength was exhausted, so that they had to be left on the road.

A quarter of an hour after, I arrived at the foot of the mountain, where some had bivouacked during the night. Traces of the fires were still to be seen—several still alight, and around them men warming themselves before attempting the ascent. Here I learnt that the carts which had left Wilna the evening before at midnight, on reaching a defile, had not been able to go further. One of the first waggons had fallen open on turning over, and the money in it had been taken by those standing near. The other carriages, from top to bottom of the mountain, were obliged to halt. Many horses had fallen to rise no more.

While they told me this, we heard the musketry fire of Marshal Ney's rear-guard, and on the left Cossacks were visible, drawn by the sight of booty. They advanced very cautiously, however, waiting till the rear-guard should have passed to reap their harvest safely.

I started off again, but, instead of taking the road of the waggons, rounded the mountain to the right. Here several carts had tried to pass, but all had been over-thrown into the ditch at the side. One waggon had a great many trunks still in it. I should have liked to carry one off, but in my feeble state I did not dare to risk it, fearing I might not be able to climb out of the ditch again if I once got down. Fortunately, a man of the hospital corps from the Wilna garrison, seeing my dilemma, was kind enough to go down, and threw me a box, in which I found four beautiful shirts of fine linen and some cotton trousers.

Since November 5th I had not changed a shirt, and my shreds and tatters were filled with vermin, so I put the whole into my knapsack, delighted.

A little further on I picked up a band-box containing two superb hats. As it was very light, I put it under my arm; I really don't know why—probably to exchange it for something else if I had the opportunity.

The road I was following turned to the left across some brushwood to rejoin the highway. This road had been beaten out by the first men who at daybreak had crossed the mountain. After half an hour of painful walking, I heard a heavy fusillade, accompanied by loud cries, coming from the side of the waggons. Marshal Ney, seeing that the booty could not be saved, was having it distributed among the men, and at the same time kept the Cossacks off by steady firing.

Over on my side, to the right, I saw some Cossacks advancing steadily. There was no one to check them but some men scattered here and there upon the mountain, trying to gain the road. All at once I was forced to stop : my legs gave way under me. I drank a good mouthful of my brandy and struggled on. I reached at last a point on the mountain not far from the road, and as I was searching for the right direction, the snow crumbled under me, and I sank more than five feet up to the eyes, and was nearly suffocated. It was with great trouble that I dragged myself out, completely exhausted with cold.

A little further on I caught sight of a hut, and seeing some people in it, I stopped there. They were about twenty men belonging to the Guard, all with bags containing five-franc pieces. Several of them, on seeing

me, began to call out, ' Who would like 100 francs for
a twenty-franc piece in gold ?' But finding no one to
exchange with them, they concluded by offering some to
those who were without any. Just then I cared more
for life than for money, so I refused, for I had about
800 francs in gold, and more than 100 francs in five-franc
pieces.

I remained in this hut long enough to fasten the sheepskin over my head, so as to keep the cold off my ears, but
I had no time to change my shirt. I left, following some
musicians carrying money, but who were too heavily laden
to go far.

The firing now came nearer, so that we were obliged to
double our pace. Those who were laden with money, and
could not run, lightened their burden by shaking the five-
franc pieces out of their bags, saying that it would have
been better to have left them in the waggons, especially
as there was plenty of gold to take, but that there had not
been time to bury the chests. However, there were many
who had sacks of double napoleons.

A little ahead I saw several still coming from the
direction of the waggons, carrying bags of money. As
they were terribly weak and their fingers frozen, they
called to those who had none, to give them a share ; but
it very often happened that those who had carried some
money part of the way, and who wished to share it with
the others, had no more to give, as, farther in front, men
who had none had forced a share from them. Those poor
devils who had been carrying money for so long saw it
torn from them, and were lucky if in trying to defend
what they had they held their own, for they were always
the weakest.

I had gained the road, and, as I was not very cold, I
stopped to rest. I saw other men come up, still laden

with money, and who now and again stayed to fire on the Cossacks. Higher up the rear-guard had halted to allow some men to pass, as well as several sledges, some bearing the wounded, and loaded with as many barrels of money as it was possible for them to carry. This did not keep some men, drawn by the love of plunder, from still remaining behind, and when at bivouac in the evening, I was assured that many had rifled the waggons along with the Cossacks.

I went on slowly and painfully. Presently I saw an officer of the Young Guard coming towards me, very well dressed, and in good health, whom I recognised at once as Prinier, one of my friends, passed as officer eight months before. Surprised to see him going in the opposite direction, I asked him, calling him by his name, where he was bound for. He demanded in his turn who I was. At this unexpected question from a comrade in the same regiment for five years, I could not refrain from tears. He did not know me because I was so changed and wretched. But an instant afterwards: 'Why, my dear fellow, is it you? To think you should be so unlucky!' Then he offered me a bottle which hung from his side, containing wine, saying, 'Take some;' and, as I had only one hand free, the good fellow supported me with his left hand, and with the other poured the wine into my mouth.

I asked him if he had met the remnant of the army. He said no; that as he had been quartered the preceding night in a mill some distance from the road, it was very probable that the column had passed, but he had seen terrible traces of it in some dead bodies lying upon the road. He had only heard yesterday, and in a very vague way, of the disasters that we had experienced. He was on his way to rejoin the army, according to orders.

' But there is no army left.'

' What is that firing ?'

' That is the rear-guard, commanded by Marshal Ney.'

Then he replied :

' I shall join the rear-guard.'

He embraced me before leaving, but as he did so he saw that I had a band-box under my arm, and asked what it contained. I told him they were hats : he asked me for them, and I gave them to him with much pleasure. It was exactly what he needed, for he still wore his non-commissioned officer's shako.

The wine he had made me drink had warmed me ; I decided on going on to the next bivouac. An hour after leaving Prinier I caught sight of fires belonging to some Chasseurs. I went up in an imploring way. Without looking at me, they said : ' Do as we are doing ; go and look for some wood, and make a fire yourself.'

I was expecting this reply—the usual one. There were six of them ; their fire was a very poor one. They had no further shelter to protect them against the wind and the snow, should any happen to fall.

I remained a long time standing behind them, sometimes leaning forward and stretching out my hands to get a little warmth. Finally, overcome with sleep, I thought of my bottle of brandy. I offered it to the men ; it was accepted, and they made room for me. We emptied the bottle, passing it round, and when we had finished I fell asleep seated on my knapsack, my head in my hands. I slept perhaps two hours, often disturbed by pain and the cold. When I awoke I took advantage of the little fire that was still left to cook some rice in the kettle I had bought of the Jew. I scraped up some snow, and melted it with some rice. I could not manage it with a spoon, as a Chasseur was eating with me, so I turned it out into my shako, and we ate it in this way. Afterwards I resumed my former position, and fell asleep again, the cold this night not being very severe.

December 11th.—When I woke it was still far from daybreak. After tying up my food, I rose to go on; for if I did not wish to die of cold and hunger, like so many others, I must rejoin my comrades. I walked alone till daybreak, stopping sometimes at a fire, where I found dead and dying men. When day came, I met some soldiers of the regiment, who told me they had passed the night with the staff.

A little further on, I saw a man with a sheepskin over his shoulders walking painfully, leaning on his musket. When I got near him, I saw that he was the quartermaster of our company. He uttered a cry of surprise and joy on seeing me, for they had told him I was a prisoner at Wilna. Poor Rossi had both feet frozen, wrapped up in pieces of sheepskin. He told me, that not being able to walk as quickly as the others, he had been separated from the remnant of the regiment, and that our friends were very uneasy about me. Two great tears ran down his cheeks, and he began to weep, saying, 'Poor mother! if you could only see me now! It is all over with me; I shall never see Montauban again' (the place he came from).

I tried to comfort him by pointing out that my situation was still worse than his own. We walked together for part of the day. I was obliged to stop often, owing to my colic.

It might have been noon when I proposed that we should stop at a village that we saw ahead of us. We entered an empty house, and found three unfortunate soldiers, who told us, not being able to go any further, they had resolved to die there. We warned them of the fate that awaited them should they fall into the hands of the Russians. For answer they showed us their feet. Nothing more terrible could be imagined. More than half their toes were missing, and the remainder.ready to fall off. The feet were blue in colour, and seemed to be almost mortified. The men belonged to Marshal Ney's corps. Perhaps, when he passed by some time after, he may have saved them.

We stopped long enough to cook a little rice, and we also roasted a little horseflesh to eat later. Then we left, resolving to keep together; but the great crowd of stragglers came up, dragged us with them, and in spite of all our efforts we were separated, and could not find each other again.

I now arrived at a water-mill. There I saw a soldier who, in trying to cross the ice of the little mill-stream, had fallen through it. Although the water was only up to his waist, he could not get out, owing to the pieces of broken ice. Some artillery officers, who had found some ropes in the mill, threw them to him, but he had not strength to catch them; although still living, he was frozen and motionless.

A little further on I heard that the regiment, if it could be still called by that name, was to sleep at Zismorg, still five leagues off. I made up my mind that if I should have to drag myself there upon my knees, I would go; but what trouble it cost me! I fell from exhaustion on the snow, and thought I should rise no more. Happily, since my separation from Rossi the cold had greatly decreased. After superhuman efforts I got to the village; it was none too soon, for I had done all that man could do to escape death.

The first thing I saw on entering was a great fire to the right, against the gable end of a burnt house. Completely exhausted, I dragged myself there; and great was my surprise on seeing my comrades. When I got up to them I fell almost unconscious.

Grangier recognised me, and hurried with some others of my friends to help me; they laid me on some straw. It was the fourth time Grangier and I had met each other since we left Moscow. M. Césarisse, Lieutenant of the company, who had some brandy, made me take a little; then I was given some horse-broth. It tasted very good, for this time it was salted with salt, while so far we had eaten everything salted with powder.

My colic came on again worse than ever; so I called Grangier, and told him I thought I had been poisoned. On this he melted some snow in the little kettle, and brewed me some of the tea he had brought from Moscow. I drank a great deal, and it did me good.

Poor Rossi arrived in as miserable a state as myself. He was accompanied by Sergeant Bailly, whom he had met a moment after his separation from me. It was Sergeant Bailly with whom I had changed the bank-notes at Wilna, and who had drunk coffee with me at the Jew's. He was as ill as I was. He asked me how I was, and when I told him how ill I had been after taking the coffee, he was sure that they had meant to poison us, or at least make us good for nothing.

I was settling myself as well as I could on the straw near a large fire, when all at once I felt pains in my legs and thighs, so violent that during a part of the night I did nothing but groan. I heard them saying, 'He will not be able to leave to-morrow.' I thought so too, and decided, as many had already done, to make my will. I called my friend Grangier, and told him that I was certain all was over with me. I begged him to undertake the charge of some small articles, to be given to my family if he had the

good fortune to see France again. These articles were a
watch, a cross in gold and silver, a little vase in Chinese
porcelain. I possess the two last still. I also wished to
dispose of all the money that I had, reserving some gold
pieces that I meant to hide in the sheepskin wrapped
about my foot, hoping that the Russians, when they took
me, would not begin searching among my rags.

Grangier, who had listened without interrupting me,
now asked if I were in a fever or dreaming. I said that
I was in a fever, but I was quite clear-headed. He began
to lecture me, reminding me of my courage in worse
situations than this.

'Yes,' I said, 'but then I was stronger.'

He assured me that I had said as much at the passage
of the Bérézina when I had been quite as ill, and since
then I had come eighty leagues. As for the fifteen that
remained before reaching Kowno, they would be done in
a couple of days ; with the help of my friends I should
manage them very well. To-morrow they would only
walk four leagues.

'So,' he said, 'try to rest, and wrap up those things
again. I will only take your kettle, and carry it for you.'

Another said, 'I will take this other case (the surgeon's
case), which must worry you.'

Meanwhile, Rossi, who was lying near, remarked : 'My
friend, you will not be here alone to-morrow morning ; I
shall share your fate, for I am quite as bad as you are.
The journey to-day has done for me, and I shall not be
able to go any further. But when the rear-guard passes
by, we may be able to march with it, for we shall have
had some extra hours' rest. If we have not enough
strength to follow it, we will go to the right. To the
first village or the first house that we find, and put ourselves under the protection of the Baron or master; perhaps

he will have pity on us until we are better, and we can reach Prussia or Poland. Very likely the Russians will not come further than Kowno.'

I told him that I would do as he wished. M. Césarisse, whom Grangier had just told of my intention, came up to comfort me. He said that the pain I suffered only came from the fatigue of yesterday. He made me lie before the fire, and, as there was plenty of wood, they piled on enough to roast me. This fire did me so much good that the pain gradually left me, and I slept for some hours. Poor Rossi did so too.

In 1830 I was appointed an officer of the staff at Brest. On the day of my arrival, sitting at table with my wife and children at the Hôtel de Provence, a man sat opposite to me, very well dressed, who looked at me a great deal. Every other moment he stopped eating, and, his head resting on his hand, he seemed to think deeply, or to be recalling certain memories. Afterwards he spoke to the landlord of the hotel. My wife, who was beside me, pointed it out to me.

'Yes,' I said, 'that man begins to puzzle me, and if it goes on I shall ask him what it means.'

At that very moment he rose, threw down his napkin, and passed into the office where travellers' names were registered. He re-entered the dining-room, exclaiming aloud, 'It is he—I was not mistaken' (calling me by my name). 'It is indeed my friend.'

I recognised him by his voice, and we were in each other's arms. It was Rossi, whom I had not seen since 1813, seventeen years before. He believed me dead, and I thought the same of him, for I had learnt on my return from prison that he had been wounded under the walls of Paris. This recognition interested all who were present, about twenty in number, and we were asked to relate our adventures during the Russian campaign. This we did willingly, and at midnight we were still at table, drinking champagne to Napoleon's memory. It is hardly surprising that at first I did not recognise my comrade, for I left him delicate, and I found him stout and strong, his hair almost gray. He lived at Montauban, and was now a rich merchant.

When the moment of departure came, I thought no more of remaining behind, but it was impossible to walk alone. Grangier and Leboude held me up under the arms, and others did as much for Rossi. At the end of half an hour's walking I was much better; but all the way I needed the help of one arm, often of two. In this manner we arrived in good time at the little village where we were to sleep; there were very few dwellings to be found, and, although we were the first to arrive, we were obliged to sleep in a yard. By chance we were able to find plenty of straw, which we used to cover us; but, with our usual ill-luck, the straw took fire. Everyone saved himself as best he could; many had their coats burnt. A quarter-master of Vélites, named Couchère, was more unfortunate than the others; the fire caught his cartridge-case, and his whole face was burnt. And as for me, without the help of my comrades I should probably have been roasted, as I could not possibly move by myself. I was taken by the legs and shoulders, and dragged up to the hut, where General Roguet and other officers were quartered. They fled on seeing the flames, thinking that the house itself was on fire. After this misfortune came a high north wind, and, as we were without shelter, we entered the General's house, which consisted of two rooms. We took possession of one, in spite of him; more than half of us were obliged to stand up the whole night, but, still, it was better than staying outside exposed to bad weather. That would have killed three-fourths of us.

December 13th.—Kowno was at least ten leagues off, so General Roguet made us start before daybreak.

A shower of hail had fallen, forming ice upon the road. If, as on the preceding evening, I had not had my friends' help, I should very probably, like so many others, have finished my life's journey on that last day in Russia.

It was hardly dawn when we reached the foot of a mountain which was one sheet of ice. What trouble we had climbing it ! We had to squeeze ourselves into groups to obtain mutual support. On this march there was more readiness to help one another than before. Probably it was the hope of arriving at the end of the journey. I remember that, when a man fell, cries were heard, ' Stop ! there is a man fallen !' I noticed a sergeant-major of our battalion shout, ' Stop, there ! I swear that not one of you shall go on until the two left behind have been picked up and brought on.' It was by his firmness they were saved.

At the top of the mountain it was light enough to see, but the slope was so rapid, and the ice so smooth, that no one dared to venture down. General Roguet, some officers, and several sappers who were walking in front, had fallen. Some picked themselves up, and those who were strong enough went down in a sitting position, guiding themselves with their hands; others who were weaker trusted to Providence—that is to say, they rolled over and over like barrels. I was of this latter number, and I should most likely have thrown myself into a ravine, or been lost in the snow, but for Grangier, who went in front of me, moving backwards and stopping, so that I ran into him. He drove his bayonet into the ice to hold on by, and when

I came up he moved further, sliding and repeating the same process, till I reached the bottom, bruised all over, and my left hand bleeding. The General had ordered a halt to assure himself that everybody had come up—the roll-call had been taken the evening before—and happily no one was missing. It was broad daylight, and we could see that the mountain might have been avoided by turning to the right. The other corps who were marching after us came along this side of it without accident. This climbing had tired me so much that I could only walk very slowly, and, as I did not wish to abuse the kindness of my friends, I begged them to follow the column. One of the company, however, stayed with me, a Piedmontese, by name Faloppa. I had not seen him for several days.

Those who were fortunate enough to keep their health, to have unfrozen feet, and to march at the head of the column, missed seeing all the disasters which I, for instance, sick and crippled, witnessed daily. Those in front could not see the men who fell around them, while we in the rear passed over the long train of dead and dying that each corps left behind it. We had also the disadvantage of being harassed by the enemy at our heels.

Faloppa, the man who had stayed with me, was in no better position. We had been walking together for a quarter of an hour, when he turned towards me, saying: ' Well, sergeant, if we had those little pots of dripping here that you made me throw away in Spain, you would be very glad, and we could make fine soup.' It was not the first time he had made that remark. The episode, comical enough, was this :

One day, after we had made a long expedition in the mountains of Asturias, we were quartered at St. Hiliaume, a little town in Castile, on the sea-coast. I was quartered with my subdivision in a large building forming the right wing of the Court House.* This part of it was very large, and inhabited by an old bachelor, absolutely alone. On arriving at his house we asked him whether we could buy some butter or dripping to make soup, and cook some haricots. He replied that even for gold there was none to be had in the entire town. A moment afterwards the muster was called. I left Faloppa to do the cooking, and commissioned another man to search through the town for some butter or fat, but none was to be had. When we came back, the first thing Faloppa said to us was that the old bachelor was a rascal. 'How is that?' He answered us, 'Look!'

He showed me three gallipots containing some beautiful fat that we saw was goose-dripping. Everyone exclaimed, 'There's your Spanish beggar for you. There's a rascal!' Our cook had made some splendid soup, and had prepared some haricots. We sat down to eat under a great chimney-piece, like the entrance to a house, when suddenly the Spaniard returned, wrapped in his brown mantle, and, seeing us eating, hoped we should enjoy our meal. I asked him why he had not wanted to sell us the dripping. 'No, señor,' he answered, 'I had none. If I had had any, I would have given it to you with pleasure, and for nothing!' Then Faloppa, taking up one of the little pots, showed it to him. 'Then this is not fat, is it, rascal of a Spaniard?' Looking at the little pot, he changed colour, and stood as if thunderstruck. Pressed for a reply, he told us that it certainly was dripping, but the *manteca de ladron* (thieves' fat). He was the town executioner, and what we had found and made our soup with was the fat of hanged men, which he sold for ointment.

* This dwelling was a Gothic castle, of which many are to be found in Spain. — *Author's Note.*

Hardly had he finished, when all the spoons flew about his head. He had barely time to escape; and not one of us, although very hungry, wanted to eat any haricots; the soup was almost all gone. Faloppa only went on eating just the same, saying that the Spaniard had lied. 'And even were it so,' said he, 'the soup is good, and the haricots still better.' So saying, he offered me some to taste, which turned me sick. I went across to a brandy merchant's facing our quarters, and asked him with whom we were quartered. He crossed himself, repeating over and over again: '*Ave, Maria, purissima, sin peccado concebida!*' He told me that it was the executioner. For some time I was ill and sick with disgust; but Faloppa, when he left, carried off the remainder of the fat, pretending he would prepare us soup with it again. I was obliged to make him throw it away; and that is why in Russia, when he had nothing to eat, he was always quoting this story.

For half an hour we had not lost sight of the column, showing that we had walked pretty well. I must say that the road happened to be better; but soon afterwards it became rough and as slippery as in the morning. The cold was very keen, and we had already passed some men dying by the way, although clothed in thick furs. Exhaustion, however, was answerable for a good deal. Faloppa fell several times, and if I had not been with him to help him up again, he would have been left behind.

The road now became better; we could see the long train of the column in front of us. We redoubled our efforts to rejoin it, but did not succeed. We came upon a hamlet of five or six houses, of which half were on fire, where we stopped a little while. Several men were gathered round; many seemed quite unable to go on, and several horses had dropped, dying, and were struggling on the snow. Faloppa cut a piece from the thigh of one of them, which we cooked on the points of our swords at the fire of the burning houses.

While we were busy with this job, cannonading was heard in the direction from which we had come. I then saw more than 10,000 stragglers spreading in disorder over the width of the road. Behind them marched the rear-guard. I have thought since that Marshal Ney was firing in order to make all these unfortunate creatures believe the Russians were upon us, and so hurry them on to Kowno that same day. It was part of the wreck of the Grand Army.

Our meat was not half cooked before we thought it wiser to decamp as quickly as possible, and not to be submerged in this fresh torrent.

There were still six leagues to walk before reaching Kowno, and we were quite worn out. It might have been about eleven o'clock, when Faloppa said : 'Sergeant, we shall not get there to-day, the *ruban de queue* is too long.* We shall never be able to leave this devil's country ; it is all over, I shall not see my beautiful Italy again !' Poor fellow ! he spoke the truth.

We had been walking about an hour since our last rest, when we came upon several groups of forty or fifty men, more or less composed of officers, non-commissioned officers, and some men, carrying in the midst of them the regimental eagle. These men, miserable though they were, seemed proud to have been so far able to keep and guard this sacred trust. It was evident that in marching they avoided mingling with the large masses that covered the road, so as to keep together in an orderly way.

* *Ruban de queue :* a soldier's expression to designate a long march. — *Author's Note.*

We walked as long as we were able with these little detachments; we did all we could to follow them, but the artillery and musketry fire began again. The detachment halted at the command of some person; one could never have told by the rags covering him who he might be. Never shall I forget the tone of his command. 'Come, children of France! Another halt! It must never be said that we went faster at the sound of artillery. Right about face!' and instantly the men fell into rank without a word, and turned in the direction of the firing. As for us, having no colours to defend, we continued to drag ourselves along. It was very lucky for us that on this particular day the cold was not so intense, for we fell more than ten times, and if it had been freezing as on the day before, there we should have remained.

After walking a certain time among stragglers like ourselves, we caught sight of a moving line, a column apparently, in very close order, now moving, then halting, again moving on. This seemed as if there must be a defile just there. The road began to narrow to the right on account of a hill through which it had been cut, and on the left was bounded by a large river that I think must have been the Niemen. There the men, while waiting till some waggons passed coming from Wilna, hustled and shoved one another in great confusion. It was a question of who could get over the first. Many climbed down to the ice-covered river, in order to gain the right of the column or the end of the defile. Several who found themselves on the extreme edge were thrown down the banks, which in this place were at least five feet high; some were killed.

When we reached the left of this column, we had to do as those who preceded us—we had to wait. I came upon a sergeant of Vélites named Poumo, belonging to our regiment, who proposed that I should cross the river with him, telling me that on the other side we should find houses where we could pass the night, and that the next day, being thoroughly rested, we could reach Kowno easily; 'for,' said he, 'it is not more than two leagues further.' I consented to his proposal, especially as I had no strength to go on, and then there was the hope of spending a night in a house with a fire! I told Faloppa to follow us. Poumo went down first. I followed him, sliding on my back; but, after taking a few steps across the snow which covered the river in great heaps, I saw the impossibility of going further, so I signed to Faloppa, who had not got down, to stop, for I had just discovered that beneath the snow was nothing but a mass of jagged ice, with holes in between. This was probably the result of a thaw, followed by a hard frost.

In the meantime Poumo, who was walking some steps ahead of me, stopped; but, seeing that I was not following, he still got across himself with three old Grenadiers of the Guard. It was only, however, with great labour that they reached the other bank.

I got nearer to Faloppa, from whom I was separated only by the height of the bank, to tell him to follow the left of the column; that, as I was down on the ice, I was going to follow it up to the end of the defile, and that I would wait for him there. Then I followed the mass of men, slowly advancing, then stopping, shouting and swearing, for those on the bank were afraid of falling to the bottom.

I had already gone three-fourths of the length of the defile when I saw that the river turned abruptly to the left, while the road, widening again, went straight on. I had to return almost to the middle of the pass, to the spot where the bank seemed less steep; but weak as I

254

was, and having only one hand of any use, I tried in vain to climb it.

I mounted on an ice-heap, so that without stooping very much some helping hand could be given me. I supported myself with my left hand on my musket, and held out the other to those who, within reach of me, could have pulled me up by a slight effort. But I asked in vain. No one answered me; they had not even the appearance of paying any attention to what I was saying. At last God had pity on me again. Just when the crowd of men had halted, I saw an old trooper of the Imperial Guard on foot, his moustaches and beard covered with icicles, and wrapped in a great white cloak. I spoke to him still in the same tone :

' Comrade, I beg of you, as, like me, you're in the Imperial Guard, give me a hand, and you will save my life.'

' How do you think I am to give you a hand ?' he said, ' I have none.' At this answer I nearly fell off the ice-heap. ' However,' he continued, ' if you can take hold of my cloak, I will try to pull you up.'

Then he stooped. I grasped the cloak ; I even held it with my teeth, and scrambled on to the road. Happily, at this moment there was no pressing forward, or I might have been trampled under foot without perhaps ever rising again. When I was really safe, the old Grenadier told me to keep a firm hold of him, which I did, but with much difficulty, as the effort which I had just made had greatly weakened me.

Shortly afterwards they began to move forward. We passed by three fallen horses, the waggon having over-turned into the river. This was what had caused the delay in the march. At last we reached a point where the pass widened, and where we could walk more easily.

Just then Faloppa, whom I had left at the entrance of the pass, came up weeping and swearing in Italian, saying that he would never be able to go further. The old trooper asked me who this creature was who cried like a woman. I told him he was a *barbet*, a Piedmontese.

'He will never see the marmots and bears of his native mountains again,' he answered.

I encouraged poor Faloppa to keep on; I gave him my arm, and we continued to follow the column.

It might have been about five o'clock; we had still more than two leagues to go before reaching Kowno. The old Grenadier related how his fingers had frozen before reaching Smolensk. After suffering frightful distress up to the passage of the Bérézina, he had found a house on arriving at Ziembin, where he had spent the night. During that night all his fingers fell off one after the other, but since then he had not suffered nearly so much. His comrade, who had never left him before, had gone off to the mountain near Wilna to *monter à la roue,** and since that day he had not seen him.

After going on for another half-hour, we reached a little village, where we stopped in one of the last houses to rest and warm ourselves a little; but we could not find room, for the house was crammed with men stretched out on the evil-smelling straw, and shrieking and swearing whenever one happened to touch them. Nearly all their hands and feet were frozen. We were obliged to be contented with a stable, where we came upon a trooper of the Guard of the same regiment and squadron as our old Grenadier. He still had his horse, and, hoping to find a hospital at Kowno, undertook the charge of his comrade.

* *Monter à la roue :* an expression used by old soldiers to indicate the taking of money from the waggons abandoned on the mountain of Ponari.—*Author's Note.*

We had still a league and a half to walk, and the cold had considerably increased. Fearing that it would grow still colder, I told Faloppa that he must go ; but the poor devil, who had laid himself down on the manure-heap, could not get up. It was only by begging and swearing, with the help of the trooper, I succeeded in getting him on his legs and pushing him outside the stable. On the road I gave him my arm. When he was rather warm, he walked fairly well, but without speaking, for about a league.

During the time we had been resting in the village the great part of the stragglers after the army had passed us ; there was no one to be seen either in front or behind but miserable creatures like ourselves—in fact, those whose strength was entirely gone. Several were stretched on the snow—a sign of their approaching end.

Faloppa, whom till then I had been continually coaxing on by saying, ' Here we are. Just a little more courage,' sank upon his knees, then on his hands. I thought he was dead, and fell at his side, overwhelmed with fatigue. The cold, which began to go through me, forced me to make an effort to rise again, or, to tell the truth, it was a fit of rage, for I got upon my knees swearing. Then, seizing Faloppa by the hair, I made him sit up ; but he looked at me stupefied. Seeing that he was not dead, I said to him :

' Courage, my friend. We are not far from Kowno, for I can see the convent* on our left. Don't you see it, too ?'

' No, sergeant,' he answered; ' I see nothing but the snow which is turning round me. Where are we ?'

I told him we were near a place where we could sleep and find bread and brandy.

---

* It was the convent that I had visited on June 20th, at the time of the passage of the Niemen.—*Author's Note.*

At this instant chance brought five peasants near us who were crossing the same road. I proposed to two of these men, in consideration of a five-franc piece each, that they should lead Faloppa as far as Kowno; but under pretext that it was late, and that they were cold, they made some difficulties. I guessed that it was the fear of not being paid (for they spoke German). I took two five-franc pieces from my bag and gave them one, promising them the other on our arrival. They were satisfied. I then told three others to go back to where a foot soldier was lying whom we had passed, and I said they would have some money for leading him, and they went off at once.

The two peasants had lifted Faloppa, but the poor devil could not stand. They seemed at a loss what to do. Then I showed them how to carry him on a musket, each supporting him with an arm behind. But we did not get far this way. They decided to take him on their backs in turn, while the other carried his knapsack and gun, and took me under his arm, for I could hardly drag my legs along. During the distance to the town, which was not more than half a league, we were obliged to stop five or six times to rest and change Faloppa from one back to another. If we had had to walk a quarter of an hour longer, we should never have got there.

Meanwhile the bulk of stragglers had passed us, but many others, as well as the rear-guard, were still behind us. We heard at intervals the sound of artillery, which seemed to us like the expiring sigh of our army. At last we reached Kowno by a road our peasants knew of, and that the column had not taken. The first place we saw was a stable. We went in, and the peasants set us down; but before giving them the last five-franc piece, I implored them to find us a little wood and straw. They brought some of both, and even made us a fire, for it was im-

258

possible for me to stir ; and as for Faloppa, I looked upon him as dead. He was seated in the angle of the wall, saying nothing, but every now and then making faces, and lifting his hands to his mouth, as if to eat. The fire burning before him seemed to restore him a little. I at last paid my peasants. Before leaving us they brought us still more wood, and made me understand they would come back. Trusting to their promises, I gave them five francs, begging them to bring me some bread, some brandy, or anything else. They promised to do so, but never returned.

While we were in the stable, terrible things were happening in the town. The remnant of the corps arriving in front of us on the preceding evening, not being able to find lodgings, bivouacked in the street. They pillaged the flour and brandy stores. Many were intoxicated, and fell asleep on the snow, to wake no more. The following day I was told that more than fifteen hundred had died in this way.

After the departure of the peasants, five men, two of whom belonged to our regiment, came to find a place in the stable ; but as they had met soldiers returning from the town who told them that flour and brandy were to be had there, two went off to try and get some. They left their arms and knapsacks, but did not return. To crown my misfortune, I had nothing to cook any rice in, for Grangier had my kettle. Not one of the three men remaining with me had anything we could make use of, and not one would stir to go and look for a pot.

Meanwhile the roar of the distant artillery and the howling of the wind were mingled with the cries of men dying on the snow. Although the cold on this day was not excessive, a large number of men perished from it.

It was the last effort, and of those who had reached this point, not half had seen Moscow; they were the garrisons of Smolensk, of Orcha, of Wilna, as well as the remnant of the main army of Generals Victor and Oudinot, and of General Loison's division, which we had met dying of cold before reaching Wilna.

The men who were with me in the stable lay down around the fire. To keep myself alive, I ate a piece of the half-cooked horseflesh; it was the last before leaving this country of misfortune.

Afterwards I tried to sleep, but I lay awake a long time in great pain. However, sleep overcame me in its turn, and I dozed I do not know for how long. When I awoke I saw that the three soldiers who had arrived after us were preparing to go, and yet it was still far from daybreak. I asked them the reason. They told me they were going to instal themselves in a house they had discovered where there was some straw and a well-heated stove. The house was occupied by a man, two women, and four soldiers of the Kowno garrison.

I immediately set about following them, but I could not leave Faloppa. Looking towards the place where I had left him, I was astonished at not seeing him there. The soldiers told me that for more than an hour he had done nothing but prowl about the stable on all fours, howling like a bear. Our fire was low, and I had some trouble in finding him. At last I did so, and to see him better I lighted a piece of resinous wood.

When I went near him he began to laugh, growling like a bear, running first after one of us, and then the other, and all the time upon his hands and knees. Sometimes he spoke, but in Italian. I knew that he thought he was in his own country in the midst of the mountains, playing with the friends of his childhood; now and again he called for his father and mother; in short, poor Faloppa had gone mad.

As I had to leave him for a time to go and see the new lodging, I took care that during my absence nothing should happen to him. We put out the fire and shut the door. On reaching our new quarters, we found two of the men busily eating soup. They did not seem to have suffered much, and, indeed, since September they had been at Kowno.

Before throwing myself on the straw, I asked the peasant if he would come with me to fetch a sick man, that I would give him five francs, at the same time showing him the piece. The peasant had not yet replied, when the German soldiers proposed that we should give them the preference.

' We will go for nothing,' said one of the other soldiers.

' And give him some soup as well,' said another.

I showed my gratitude by saying that one could easily see that they were Frenchmen. They took a wooden chair on which to carry the sick man, and we set out, but as I could only walk with difficulty, they gave me an arm. I told them of Faloppa's sad plight if he were left to the mercy of the Russians.

' What, Russians?' said one of the soldiers.

' Certainly,' I said; ' Russian Cossacks will be here perhaps in a few hours!'

These poor soldiers thought that it was only cold and wretchedness we had brought with us.

On entering the stable we found the poor devil of a Piedmontese lying his full length behind the door. He was placed upon the chair, and in this way was carried to the new lodging. When he was laid near the stove on some good straw, he began to mutter disconnected words. I went near him to listen; he was no longer recognisable.

His face was all over blood, but it was the blood from his hands that he had bitten or tried to eat ; his mouth, too, was filled with straw and earth.   The two women had pity on him, bathed his face with water and vinegar, and the German soldiers, ashamed to have done nothing, undressed him.   A shirt was found in his knapsack, which we put on him instead of the ragged one he wore ; then they offered him something to drink : he could not swallow, and every now and again clenched his teeth fast together. Afterwards he gathered up the straw with his hands, as if he would put it over him.   One of the women said it was a sign of death.   I was very sorry for it, as we had reached the limit of our suffering.   I had done all I could to save him, just as he would have done for me, for he had been five years in the company, and would have died for me. He proved it on more than one occasion, especially in Spain.   The gentle warmth of the room made me more comfortable than I could have thought possible.   I felt no more pain, and I slept for two or three hours, a thing that had not happened since my departure from Moscow.

I was awakened by one of the soldiers, who said : ' Sergeant, I think that everybody is going, for there is a great noise outside. We shall have to muster in the square, according to the orders we received yesterday.   As for your soldier,' he added, ' you must think of him no more ; he is done for.'

I raised myself to see ; the two women were at his side. The youngest handed me a leather purse containing money, saying that it had fallen from one of the pockets of the overcoat.   There might have been about twenty-five to thirty francs in Prussian pieces, and some other money. I gave it all to the two women, telling them to look after the sick man till his last moment, which could not be far off, for he scarcely breathed. They promised me not to abandon him.

The noise in the street went on increasing. It was already day, but in spite of that we could not see much, for the little squares of glass were dimmed with ice, and the sky, covered with thick clouds, foretold a great deal of snow still to come.

We were ready to go out, when all at once we heard the sound of cannon from the direction of Wilna, and quite close to us. The discharge of musketry mingled with it, and the cries and oaths of men. We heard the falling of individual blows. We at once thought that the Russians were in the town, and that fighting was going on; we seized our arms. The two German soldiers, not used to this sort of music, were at a loss. However, they came and ranged themselves at our side. We had the muskets belonging to the two men who had left the evening before, and who had not returned, and Faloppa's also. They were all loaded; we had plenty of powder. One of the German soldiers had a bottle of brandy, which he had not so far mentioned; but thinking that he might want something of us, he offered it. It did us good. The other German gave me a piece of bread.

One of them said to me, 'Sergeant, suppose we put one of these guns into the hands of that peasant there, who is trembling beside the stove? Do you not think he would be able to bring down his man?'

'No doubt,' I said.

'Come here, peasant,' said the soldier.

The poor devil, not knowing what was wanted of him, allowed himself to be led forward. He was offered a musket. He looked at it, like an imbecile, without taking it. It was placed upon his shoulder; he asked what he was to do with it. I told him it was to kill the Cossacks with. At that word he let his weapon fall. It was picked up by a soldier, who forcibly made him take hold of it, threatening if he did not fire upon the Cossacks to run a bayonet through his body. The peasant made us understand that he would be recognised by the Russians as being a peasant, and that they would kill him. During this colloquy, other cries were heard from the other extremity of the room ; it was the two women weeping. Faloppa had just breathed his last.

The soldiers took the coat of the dead man, and forced the peasant to wrap himself in it. In less than two minutes he was completely equipped, for a sword and a cartridge-case were hung on him, and a cap put on his head, with the result that he could not have recognised himself.

This scene took place while the two women were making lamentations over the dead (probably on account of the money I had given them). They were therefore not aware of the transformation of their man.

The noise we had been hearing for the last few moments increased tremendously. I thought I could distinguish the voice of General Roguet ; he indeed it was who was swearing and dealing blows to everyone indiscriminately, officers and non-commissioned officers as well as privates, to make them set out. He entered the houses, and made the officers search them to be sure no men were left in them. He did right, and it is perhaps the first good service I ever saw him render a soldier. Certainly this distribution of blows came easier to him than the distribution of bread and wine which he had made in Spain.

I caught sight of a foot soldier who had propped himself against a window, and was fixing his bayonet to the end of his musket. I asked him if the Russians were in the town.

'No, no; not at all. . . . Don't you see it is that brute of a General Roguet striking at everybody with his baton? But just let him come here; I'm waiting for him. . . .'

We had not yet left the house, when I saw Adjutant-Major Roustan come to a halt in front of the door. Recognising me, he said: 'Well, what are you doing there? Out with you! No one is to remain within a house, no matter of what regiment, for I have orders to strike down any and everybody.'

We came out, but the peasant, whom we had forgotten, naturally remained in his own house, and closed the door. The Adjutant-Major, who saw the movement, and thought it was a soldier wanting to hide himself, opened it again in his turn, entered the house, and ordered the new soldier to get out, or he would be knocked down. The peasant looked at him without replying. The Adjutant-Major seized the man by the belt, and thrust him into the midst of us. The poor devil now tried to struggle, and to explain in his own language. He was not listened to; the Adjutant-Major, simply thinking it was because he had not given him the time to bring away his knapsack and gun, re-entered the house, took them both, and brought them to him. In the house he saw the dead man and two women weeping; so, coming out, he said aloud: 'This rascal here is not so stupid as he looks; he wanted to stay in the house in order to console the widow. He looks like a German. Of what company is he? I don't remember having seen him.'

No one paid much attention to what the Adjutant was saying; each one had enough to do to look after himself. The wife, who had heard her husband's voice, had run to the door where we were still standing. The man, on seeing her, began to speak, but could not make her recognise him. There he was amongst us, not able to stir;

she never imagined that a Lithuanian, the Emperor of Russia's subject, had the honour of being a French soldier of the Imperial Guard, marching off, not to glory, but to misery. The whole affair took less than ten minutes. I have thought since that the poor devil must have felt pretty miserable, penned up there in the midst of us.

We set off, but very slowly. We were in an alley, where were several men who had died in the night from drinking brandy, and being afterwards seized by the cold; the greater number, however, were to be found in the town, which I did not enter.

Meanwhile we reached the place where there are two ways leading to the bridge over the Niemen. We now walked more easily, and in a few minutes we were on the banks of the stream. There we saw that several thousand men were already in front of us, squeezing and pushing to get across. As the bridge was narrow, a large number climbed down on to the ice-covered river, which was not strong enough to bear. It consisted merely of pieces of ice that had been thawed and frozen over again. At the risk of being drowned or hurt, everyone tried to get across as quickly as possible, thinking that once on the further side we would be safe. We found out later how greatly we were deceived.

While waiting till we could pass, Colonel Bodelin, who commanded our regiment, ordered the officers to prevent anyone crossing the bridge by himself. We were now about sixty men, or thereabouts, the remnant of 2,000, all grouped around the Colonel. He looked sadly on the remains of his fine regiment, probably drawing a contrast in his own mind. Five months before we had passed over this same bridge with the whole great and brilliant army, and now it was almost annihilated! To encourage us he made us a speech; I am afraid very few listened.

'Come, my men! I will not tell you to be brave—I know how much courage you have. During the three years I have been with you you have given proofs of it under all circumstances, and particularly during this terrible campaign, in battles and all the privations you have had to undergo. But, remember, the more distress and danger, the more glory and honour, and the greater the reward for those who have had the endurance to go through with it.'

Then he asked how many were present. I seized this opportunity to tell M. Césarisse that Faloppa had died that morning. He asked me if I was certain of it, and I answered that I had seen him die, and that Adjutant-Major Roustan himself had seen him.

'Who?—I?' responded the Adjutant-Major. 'Where?'

'In the house you told me to come out of, and which you entered to bring out another person.'

'True,' said he, 'I saw a dead man upon the straw, but it was the master of the house, for the woman was crying over him.'

I told him that the one he had turned into the street was the real husband, and the man on the straw was Faloppa. We looked for the peasant in our ranks, but he had disappeared.

While we were resting on the banks of the Niemen, those who were in front of us had crossed over the bridge, or over the ice. Now we advanced, but when we had got across we could not mount the bank by the road, which was blocked by waggons. Order was now at an end. Everyone went as he pleased. Several of my friends got me to follow them, and we went to the left. When we were about thirty paces from the bridge we began to climb up on to the road. I walked behind Grangier, whom I had fortunately found again, and who looked after me much better than after himself. He beat out a passage through the snow in front of me, shouting out in his Auvergne dialect, ' Come along, *petiot* ' (little 'un), ' follow me.' But the *petiot* could not drag one leg after another.

Grangier was already three-quarters up the side when I had only done a third of the way. Stopping, and resting on his musket, he made signs that he would wait there for me. But I was so weak I could not pull my leg out of the snow. At last, unable to do more, I fell on my side, and rolled as far as the Niemen, landing on the ice.

As there was a great deal of snow, I did not hurt myself much, but I felt a pain in my shoulders, and my face was bleeding from the branches of some bushes I had rolled over. I picked myself up without a word, as if it was something perfectly natural, for I was so inured to suffering that nothing surprised me.

After having picked up my musket, I tried to climb up again at the same place, but the thing was impossible. I now thought I would see whether I could not manage to get under the waggons at the outlet of the bridge. There I dragged myself with difficulty. As I got near the first, I saw several Grenadiers and foot soldiers of the Guards mounted on the wheels, taking out handfuls of the money that was packed in the waggons. I was not tempted to do the same—I only tried to get through. But just then I heard a shouting : ' The Cossacks ! To arms ! to arms !' This cry was followed by several musket-shots, then by a great movement, which spread from the bottom to the top of the slope.

Not one among the Grenadiers and Chasseurs took any notice : their heads were in the waggon. I pulled one by the leg ; he looked round, asking me if I had any money. I said, ' No ; but the Cossacks are up there.' ' Is that all ?' he replied. ' We are not going to disturb ourselves for those beasts, and leave them our money. Who wants some ? I'll give it him.' And he threw two large bags of five-franc pieces on to the ground. All this was only to occupy those who were coming up, for I understood that they had just found some gold—I had heard the words 'jaunets' and 'forty-franc pieces.'

I took possession of the musket of one of the Grenadiers busy taking gold, left my own, which was filled with snow, and returned to the outlet of the bridge to go over the same ground again.

I had hardly reached the bridge, when I met Captain Debonnez of the Tirailleurs of the Guard, whom I have mentioned several times. He was with his Lieutenant and a private soldier—his whole company ! The remainder, as he expressed it, had melted. He had a Cossack horse, which he could not get through the crowd. I told him my miserable condition. For sole answer he gave me a large piece of white sugar soaked in brandy. Then we separated, he to climb down upon the Niemen with his horse, I, biting at my sugar, to begin my climb upwards for the third time. Hardly had I begun, when I heard someone calling me. It was Grangier, who had climbed down the bank and was looking for me. He asked why I had not followed him, and I told him the reason. On that he walked in front of me, dragging me by his musket, I holding on to the end of the barrel. It was with immense difficulty, with the help of Grangier and biting at my lump of brandied sugar, that at last, completely exhausted, I reached the top.

Several of our friends were waiting for us—Leboude, sergeant-major ; Oudicte, sergeant-major ; Pierson, *idem* ; Poton, sergeant. The others had scattered, walking like us in groups. The certainty that on entering Prussia the conditions would be better for us influenced us all, and began to make us indifferent to one another. From the spot where we were we could make out the Wilna road, some Russians marching upon Kowno, and others nearer ; but the presence of Marshal Ney with a handful of men prevented their advancing. A man came towards us, walking with difficulty, leaning on a pine staff. On coming up to us he exclaimed : ' Ah, *per Dio santo!* I am not mistaken : these are friends !'

We looked at him, and recognised him by his voice and accent as Pellicetti, a Milanese, former Vélite-Grenadier. Three years before, he had left the Imperial Guard to enter that of the King of Italy as officer. Poor Pellicetti ! It was only by the remains of his cap that we could guess to what corps he belonged. He told us that three or four houses had been enough to accommodate the only corps remaining of Prince Eugène's army. He was waiting for one of his friends, who had a Cossack horse carrying the bit of baggage left to them. They had been separated on leaving Kowno.

It was December 14th—it might have been about nine o'clock in the morning—the sky was gloomy, the cold bearable, and no snow was falling. We walked on without knowing where we were going, but on reaching the highroad we saw a great post with directions, informing the soldiers of the different corps of the road they must follow.

We took the one inscribed for the Imperial Guard, but many marched straight in front of them without taking any notice. A few steps further on we saw five or six unfortunate soldiers looking like spectres, their faces emaciated and bedaubed with blood off their hands, with which they had been scratching in the snow for crumbs of biscuit fallen from a waggon which had just been pillaged.

We went on till about three in the afternoon. We had only walked three short leagues on account of Sergeant Poton, who seemed to be suffering a great deal.

We had caught sight of a village to our right, about a quarter of a league from the road, and we decided to spend the night there. On reaching it we found two soldiers of the line, who had just killed a cow at the entrance to a stable. This was a good sign, and so we turned in. The peasant to whom the cow belonged came himself to cut some for us, in order to save as much of the meat as possible. He made a fire, and then brought two pots of water for soup. We had some clean straw and a good fire; it was a very long time since we had been so happy. Shortly afterwards we ate our soup; then we went to sleep.

I was lying near Poton, who did nothing but groan. I asked him what was the matter. He said: 'My dear fellow, I am certain I shall not be able to go further!'

Without knowing the reason why he talked like this (a serious accident, unknown to us all), I comforted him, telling him that after he had rested he would be much better; but soon after fever came on, and throughout the night he did nothing but cry and wander in his mind. Several times during the night I found him writing in a memorandum-book, and tearing out the leaves.

Once, when I was sleeping peacefully, I felt myself pulled by the arm. It was poor Poton, who said:

'Dear friend, I am utterly unable to leave here—even to take a step—so you must do me a great service. I count on you, if you have the happiness to see France again; if you do not, you must ask Grangier, on whom I count, as I do on you, to carry out my wishes. Here,' he continued, 'is a little packet of papers that you must send to my mother, to the address given, accompanied by a letter, in which you must describe the situation in which you left me, without, however, letting her lose all hope of seeing me again some day. Here is a silver spoon that I beg you will accept; it is far better that you should have it than the Cossacks.'

Then he handed me his little packet of papers, saying again that he counted on me. I promised him to do all he had just told me, but I little thought we should be obliged to leave him.

On December 15th, when we prepared to depart, I repeated to our friends what Poton had told me. They thought he had lost heart, or that he had gone mad, so that each began to chaff him in his own way.

But for sole answer the unhappy Poton showed us two hernias that he had had for a long time, a consequence of the repeated efforts he had made in climbing the bank at Kowno. We saw indeed that it was impossible for him to stir. Sergeant-Major Leboude thought it would be a good thing to leave him with the peasant who owned the house; but before fetching him, as Poton had a good deal of money—above all, gold—we made haste to sew up his gold in the waist-band of his trousers. Then we called the peasant, and, as he spoke German, it was easy to make him understand us. We offered him five five-franc pieces, telling him he should have four times as much, and perhaps more, if he would take care of the sick man. He promised, swearing in the name of God, and that he would even go and fetch a doctor. Then, as time pressed, we took farewell of our comrade.

Before leaving, he made me promise not to forget; we embraced him and left him. I do not know if the peasant kept his word, but never again did I hear Poton spoken of. According to all accounts, he was an excellent fellow, a true comrade, having received a good education, a rare thing at that period. He was a Breton gentleman, belonging to one of the best families of the country.

I religiously fulfilled my mission, for on my arrival at Paris, in the month of May, I sent all the papers to the address given. They contained his will, and the affecting farewell he had written during his fever. I took a copy of one, which I reproduce :

> ' Adieu, bonne mère,
>   Mon amie ;
>   Adieu, ma chère,
>   Ma bonne Sophie !
> Adieu, Nantes, où j'ai reçu la vie ;
> Adieu, belle France, ma patrie ;
>   Adieu, mère chérie :
>   Je vais quitter la vie—
>   Adieu !'

For several years I gave up writing my Journal of the Russian Campaign—that is to say, I gave up putting those memoirs in order which I had written while a prisoner in 1813. A singular mania had come upon me; I doubted whether all that I had seen and endured with so much courage and patience in this terrible campaign was not the effect of my imagination.

Nevertheless, when the snow is falling, and I find myself sitting with my friends—former soldiers of the Empire— of whom some are of the Imperial Guard, and who, like myself, have gone through that memorable campaign, it is always there that our memories take us ; and I have noticed that with them, as with me, indelible impressions are left. We speak of our glorious campaigns with pride.

To-day my mother has just brought me some letters that I wrote to her during this campaign, and of which I was regretting the loss, so I am taking courage again. I must add to that the advice of friends who are making me promise to finish it. For my own part, it makes me live my life over again. One day, perhaps—who knows?—my memoirs, although badly written, will interest those who read them. The great genius is no more, but his name will live for ever. Thus, taking my courage in both hands, I am going on; so that, after me, my grandchildren, reading their grandfather's memoirs, will say, 'Grandfather was in the great battles with the Emperor Napoleon!' They will see how, in Spain, he 'dressed down' the Prussians, the Austrians, the Russians, the English in Spain, and many others; they will see, too, that grandfather did not always lie upon a bed of roses; and although he may not have been one of the best Catholics in France, they will see that he often fasted, and more than once he fasted on a feast-day!

At seven o'clock on the morning of December 15th, we left the stable where we had spent the night, and walked in the direction of the road until we reached the spot where we had branched off the preceding evening; there we halted.

Grangier still had with him my little copper kettle. He carried it in front of him, fastened with a strap to his belt, for fear someone should make off with it, for a pan in which snow could be melted and something cooked was a precious article. Grangier returned it to me, for he foresaw that I might again be left behind, and might want it. He fastened it firmly to my knapsack.

The sky was clear, but the cold bearable. We saw only a very few men upon the road; from this we concluded that the evening before the greater number had gone on further, and in different directions.

We caught sight of a column of men upon the road in the direction of Kowno, but we could not make out if they were French or Russians; so in this uncertainty we resumed our march.

For an hour I walked fairly well, but at the end of this time a severe colic seized me, and I was forced to stop; it was still the result of my Wilna poisoning. I set down this relapse to the broth that I had taken overnight, and before setting out in the morning.

In this way I progressed till about three o'clock in the afternoon. I was now not very far from a forest that I had caught sight of some time before, and which I wanted to reach in order to pass the night there.

I was no further away from it than a musket could carry, when, to the right of the road, I caught sight of a house where, around a large fire, several soldiers of the different army corps were gathered, the greater part of them being of the Imperial Guard. As I was tired, I stopped to warm and rest myself a little. Some of the men proposed that I should remain with them; I accepted gladly.

The cold had been bearable throughout the day, and was so still, and we thought one might feel easy about the enemy; but some men coming up on the right of the road told us they had just caught sight of cavalry, and that they were sure it was Russian. 'And if it was the devil,' replied an old Chasseur of the Guard, 'it would not prevent me establishing my headquarters here! Friends, do as I am doing—load your weapons and fix bayonets.' We all quietly did as he said. 'And then,' he added, 'we can retreat to the wood. Upon my soul, it's a famous position!'

On this, he went up to a horse that had been killed a little distance from the fire, cut a piece off it, and returned calmly to seat himself upon his knapsack near the fire, and roast his meat at the end of his sword. More than twenty soldiers were also roasting horseflesh, some sitting on their knapsacks, others going on their knees.

Opposite to the Chasseur of whom I have just spoken was a woman, sitting on a soldier's knapsack. Her head was in her hands, her elbows resting on her knees ; a soldier's gray overcoat over an old silk dress in tatters was all her clothing. On her head was a sheepskin cap, held in its place by a torn silk handkerchief tied under the chin. The Chasseur spoke to her :

' Look here, Mother Madeleine !'

She did not answer. Another man near her pushed her, saying :

' They're speaking to you, mother.'

' To me ?' she said. ' My name is Marie. What do you want ?'

' A drink of *rogomme*, as at drill-time.'

' *Rogomme* ! You know very well I have none.' And she returned to her former position.

Another woman who was near the fire wore on her head a schabraque, bordered with red cloth, cut into festoons and drawn around the neck with the cord of a Grenadier's bearskin, the tassels of which fell under her chin. She had also over her dress a Guard's blue overcoat. This woman, hearing the Chasseur's voice, looked up, asking who wanted spirits.

' Ah ! is that you, Mother Gâteau ?' answered the soldier. ' It is I who am asking for spirits. I, Michaut. I dare say you are surprised to see me. Well, if anyone is more amazed than I am at meeting you, particularly *schabraquée* as you are, may the devil take him ! Even before the passage of the Bérézina, thinking of you sometimes, dear Mother Gâteau, I imagined that the crows must long since have made a *fristouille à la neige* of your old carcase !'

' Wretch !' replied Mother Gâteau ; ' they will eat you before they do me, you old drunkard ! Ah,' she continued, in a jeering tone, 'you must be wanting spirits indeed! You've had to go without for three months; but very likely at Wilna, and yesterday at Kowno, you've taken a good dose : that's why you have so much tongue now. One thing astonishes me : that you're not dead of drink, like so many of the others we saw in the street. So many brave fellows left down yonder, and this good-for-nothing, this bad soldier, still lives!'

'Stop there, Mother Gâteau!' replied the old soldier; 'slang me as much as you like, but stop short of *bad soldier! Halte-là!*'

Then, jeering all the time, he continued to eat the piece of horseflesh he was holding in his hand, and which he had ceased to bite at while answering the old *cantinière*.

Directly afterwards she began again : 'For two years now he's had a spite against me, ever since I wouldn't give him credit at the Military School. Ah! if my poor husband were not dead—if a rascally ball had not cut him in two at Krasnoë! . . .'

And then she stopped.

'It wasn't your husband! You weren't married!'

'Not married! not married! Haven't I been with him nearly five years, ever since the Battle of Eylau, and I'm not married? What do you say to that, Marie?'—turning to the other *cantinière*.

But Marie, whose marriage was of the same kind as Mother Gâteau's, said nothing.

The soldier asked Mother Gâteau if she had *monté à la roue* on the mountains at Wilna.

'Ah!' she said, 'if I'd been strong enough, I shouldn't have missed the chance. I picked up some in the snow, but it hasn't done me much good. When you find yourself with rascals who respect nothing, we women can never feel safe. The evening after crossing the mountain, when

I reached our men's bivouac, I had still a little of the brandy I had brought from Wilna, so I gave it them for a place at the fire, and lay down to sleep on the snow near two soldiers of our regiment—or, rather, two thieves, for they cribbed half of my money.. By good chance I was lying on a pocket they could not get to. Trust a comrade after that ! Happily, I still have enough to take me as far as Elbing. Once there, we shall find some way of beginning the campaign afresh. I want no more carts ; I will have two *cognias*, with baskets on their backs. We shall be luckier, perhaps. What do you say, Marie ?'

Marie did not reply.

' Marie,' said the old soldier, ' has had a second husband in a year, and if she likes I will marry her for a third.'

' You, you old scamp !' answered Mother Gâteau. ' She'd be hard up to take you !'

The Chasseur went up to Marie and offered her a piece of horseflesh. Marie took it, saying, ' Thank you, *mon vieux.*'

' So that's settled,' he went on. ' On reaching Paris I will marry you ; I will make you happy.'

For sole answer, Marie sighed, saying, ' How can you chaff an unhappy woman like me ?'

' What I have just said,' the old Chasseur replied, ' is no joke, and to prove it I will offer Mother Gâteau, without any malice, what I have just offered you—a little piece of " gee-gee " on my thumb.'

As he spoke, he moved forward to offer it ; but Mother Gâteau, seeing him coming, looked at him angrily, and said, ' Go to the devil ! I don't want anything of yours.'

At this speech of Mother Gâteau's, Marie, who was sitting in front of me, lifted her head, saying that this was no time to quarrel. Then she stared at me from head to foot.

'I am not mistaken,' she said, addressing me by name
—'*mon pays*, is it you?'

'It is, Marie, really.'

I had just recognised her, too, by her voice, not by her
face, for poor Marie's freshness had disappeared; cold,
hardship, fire, and the smoke of the bivouac had made
her unrecognisable. It was Marie, our former *cantinière*,
whom I thought dead, and whose deserted cart with two
wounded I had come upon on the night of November 22nd.
This is her history :

Marie came from Namur; that is why she called me
her *pays*. Her husband belonged to Liége, a fencing-
master, and rather a bad lot. Marie was a good sort,
thinking nothing of herself, retailing her goods to the
soldiers—to those who had no money as well as to those
who had.

In every one of our battles she had shown herself most
devoted in helping the wounded. One day she herself was
wounded ; it did not prevent her from going on with her
help, careless of the risks she was running, for the bullets
and grape-shot were falling all round her. Besides all
these good qualities, Marie was pretty ; she had a number
of friends, too, and her husband was not jealous.

In 1811, while encamped before Almeida (Portugal),
some months before leaving for the Russian campaign,
the poor fellow must go plundering in a village. He
entered a country-house, carried off a clock not worth
twenty francs, was foolish enough to bring it into camp,
and was arrested. There were very severe orders against
marauders, and General Roguet, our Commandant, court-
martialed him. He was condemned to be shot within
twenty-four hours. Marie therefore became a widow. In
a regiment, particularly during a campaign, if a woman is
pretty, she is not long without a husband ; so at the end

of two months' mourning Marie was consoled and married again, as they marry in the army.

Some months after, her new husband was transferred as non-commissioned officer to a regiment of the Young Guard, so she left us to follow him; she had been with us for four years.

In Russia she met with the fate of all the *cantinières* in the army: she lost horses, carts, money, furs, and also her protector. As for herself, she had the luck to get back. Four months and a half later, at the Battle of Lutzen, May 2nd, 1813, chance brought us together; she had just been wounded in the right hand, while giving drink to a sick man.

I learned afterwards that she returned to France, and reappeared in the Hundred Days. She was taken prisoner at the Battle of Waterloo, but, being a Belgian subject, she was released.*

I asked Marie where her husband was.

'Why, you know very well,' she answered, 'that he was killed at Krasnoë.' (I had not heard this before.) 'He was a good fellow; I miss him very much.'

Then she frowned and bent her head. A moment afterwards she raised it again, and, my eyes being still fixed upon her, she looked at me smiling, but it was a sad smile. I asked her what she was thinking about.

'About eating, as you can guess. I used to have a friend who got me food; now I eat whenever I have anything given me, or when I find something, and that doesn't happen often. There is only drink to be had.'

And as she spoke she took a pinch of snow, and carried it to her mouth. I saw her rise with great difficulty to

* I have learnt that Marie is still living, and is a member of the Legion of Honour, and decorated with the St. Helena medal. She resides at Namur.—*Author's Note*. Bourgogne died in 1867.

set off on the march ; she gave me her hand, and said
' Farewell.' I noticed that she was worn out with fatigue
and privation ; that she walked with difficulty, leaning on
a stick. Mother Gâteau followed her, sheepskin on head,
swearing and mumbling between her teeth. I concluded
that it was still about the old Chasseur.

Just then there might have been about forty of us, and
our number was continually increasing. I caught sight
of Humblot, one of our sergeants. Seeing me, he asked
what I was doing there. I answered that I was resting,
and considering whether I should not do well to pass the
night where I was, and start the first thing in the morning.

Humblot, a good fellow who liked me, observed, first,
that the weather was bearable ; then what advantage it
would be to me to have crossed the forest : for, he said,
on the other side we should find houses where we could
spend the night. The next day early we could reach
Wilbalen, a small town, from three to four leagues distant.
There we should find our comrades, and be able to buy
the necessaries of life. In fact, he said so much that I
took up musket and knapsack and set off with Sergeant
Humblot. While walking, Humblot told me that, although
we were in Pomeranian Prussia, it was not wise to walk
alone or lag behind, for several thousand Cossacks had
crossed the Niemen on the ice.

Then he told me that he had left Kowno the day before
with many others who had not troubled about anything,
for Marshal Ney was still there to keep the Russians off
the town, with a rear-guard composed of Germans and
some French. The Germans, he told me, had formed part
of the garrison of Kowno, and were in excellent condition,
having wanted for nothing ; but they were poor soldiers,
and but for the few French among them, they would have
thrown down their arms and fled.

'I am going to tell you,' he went on, 'what happened to me yesterday, and you will see if I am not right in persuading you to get out of this cursed country as soon as possible.

'After having crossed the Niemen and come within a quarter of a league of the town, we saw, some distance off, more than 2,000 mounted Cossacks and others. We halted to decide what was to be done, and also to wait for those who were behind. Shortly afterwards we found ourselves about 400 men strong, of all equipments. We formed into a column, so as, if need be, to re-form into a square. Some officers who were among us took the command. Twenty-two Poles afterwards joined us. About fifty of the strongest men, who possessed good weapons, took up a position as sharp-shooters, in front and on our flanks.

'We marched resolutely upon the cavalry, who at the approach of the sharp-shooters drew off to right and left of the way. On reaching the level of the Russians, the column halted to wait for some men still in the rear. Only a few would be able to rejoin us, it seemed, for a party of Cossacks detached themselves to cut off those farthest off.

'A man of the name of Boucsin,* who played the big drum in our band, was in the rear, and was doing his utmost to join the column with (marvellous to relate!) his drum still on his back, and in his hands a bag of five-franc pieces. This load hindered him from getting along quickly; he was attacked by the Cossacks at fifty paces to the rear and to the left of the column. He received a lance-thrust between the shoulders, and fell full length into the snow, the drum being thrown over his head. Two Cossacks

---

* Boucsin is the slang for noise (*tapage*) In this case the drummer's nickname was his real one.

instantly dismounted to strip him, but a Polish officer and three men ran upon them, took one prisoner with his horse, and freed the drummer of his instrument, which he left in the field. He got off with a lance-thrust and half of his money, which he distributed among those who had saved his life.

'After this the column set off again to the shouts of " Long live the Emperor!" with the Cossack and his horse in the middle of them.'

Humblot had barely finished his story before I was forced to stop, in the same trouble again. Meantime he walked slowly, so that I could catch up with him. When I resumed my march, I found a great crowd preventing me from getting along. I regained the road, but had hardly done so, when I heard repeated shouts : ' Look out for the Cossacks !' I imagined it was a false alarm, when I caught sight of several officers, armed with muskets, who halted and bravely stationed themselves in the road, facing the noise, and crying out : 'Never mind ! Let the dogs come on !'* I looked behind me ; they were so close that one of the horses touched me—three were ahead, others followed.

I had only just time to fling myself into the wood, where I thought I should be in safety ; but the three Cossacks entered it almost at the same moment, and, unhappily, just at this spot the wood was very open. I tried to get further in, but by a bad stroke of luck one of my attacks came on. Imagine my position ! I wanted to stop, but it was impossible, two of the three Cossacks being only a few steps away. Happily, a few steps further on the trees were closer together. The Cossacks were delayed by them, while I went on at the same pace ; but, stopped short by some branches embedded in the snow, I fell full

* Colonel Richard, ex-commanding officer at Condé, was one among them. He and I have often spoken of the incident.—*Author's Note.*

length, my head remaining buried. I tried to rise, but I felt myself held by one leg. I feared one of my Cossacks was gripping me, but it was only briars and thorns. Making a last effort, I rose and looked behind me. The Cossacks had halted; two were looking for a spot wide enough to get their horses through. Meanwhile, I dragged myself on with extreme difficulty.

A little further on I was stopped by a fallen tree, but I was so weak that I found it impossible to lift my legs over it, and I was obliged to sit down.

I had not been there five minutes, when I saw the Cossacks dismount and fasten their horses to a bush. I thought they were at last coming to take me, and I had already tried to make an effort to save myself, when I saw that the two were busying themselves with a third, who had received a furious sword-stroke on the face. The wounded man lifted up a piece of his cheek that was hanging down on to his shoulder, while the others got ready a handkerchief, which they passed under his chin and tied on the top of his head.

All this took place about ten paces away from me, the Cossacks looking at me while they talked.

When they had finished pasting their comrade's face, they bore down directly on me. But now, thinking myself lost, I made a last effort, mounted the tree-trunk, took up my loaded musket, and determined to fire on the first who came near. I had only the two men to deal with, as the third, after being bandaged, seemed to suffer like one of the damned, walking up and down, and banging the hind-quarters of his horse with his fists.

Seeing my fighting position, the two Cossacks stopped, and made signs that I was to go to them. I understood that they meant no ill towards me, but I remained as I was, all the same.

I heard on my left, in the direction of the road, shouts and oaths, accompanied by musket-shots, which made my enemies uneasy, for I saw them looking frequently in the direction of the sound. I hoped they would leave me, for the sake of their own safety; but a fourth savage now came up, as if making his escape. Seeing some of his comrades, he then caught sight of me, and, on account of the underwood, dismounted, fastened his horse up beside the others, and, pistol in hand, advanced towards me, under cover of the trees; the two others followed in the same fashion. It hardly needed all that ceremony for vanquishing me, but, as luck would have it, at that moment the shouts on the right grew louder, accompanied by shots; the horses, terrified, and not being very securely fastened, escaped in the direction of the road, and the Cossacks set off to pursue them.

Considering my deplorable condition, I felt it would be impossible to walk further without changing my clothes. It may be remembered that in a portmanteau found on the mountain of Ponari I had some shirts and white cotton breeches—clothes belonging to an army commissary.

Having opened my knapsack, I drew out a shirt, and hung it on my musket; then the breeches, which I placed beside me on the tree. I took off my jacket and overcoat, and my waistcoat with the quilted yellow silk sleeves that I had made out of a Russian lady's skirt at Moscow. I untied the shawl which was wrapped round my body, and my trousers fell about my heels. As for my shirt, I had not the trouble of taking it off, for it had neither back nor front; I pulled it off in shreds. And there I was, naked, except for a pair of wretched boots, in the midst of a wild forest, at four o'clock in the afternoon, with eighteen to twenty degrees of cold, for the north wind had begun to blow hard again.

On looking at my emaciated body, dirty, and consumed with vermin, I could not restrain my tears. At last, summoning the little strength that remained, I set about my toilet. With snow and the rags of my old shirt I washed myself to the best of my power. Then I drew on my new shirt of fine longcloth, embroidered down the front. I got into the little calico breeches as quickly as I could, but I found them so short that even my knees were not covered, and my boots only reaching half-way up my leg, all this part was bare. Finally, I put on my yellow silk waistcoat, my riding-jacket, my overcoat, over this my belts and collar; and there I was, completely attired, except for my legs. After this I got down from my tree-trunk, and going a hundred steps or so, I caught sight of two people, a man and a woman, and I recognised that they were Germans. They seemed to be frightened. I asked them if they would like to come with me, but in a trembling voice the man answered ' No,' and, pointing in the direction of the road, he uttered the single word ' Cossack!'

They were a canteen man and his wife, belonging to the Rhine Confederation, probably one of the Kowno garrison, who were following up the retreat, and being, like myself, surprised in the forest by the noise, had taken to flight. The woman advised her husband to join me, but the man would not consent, and, in spite of all I could say to him, I was obliged, to my regret, to go on alone.

After having wandered haphazard for about half an hour, I stopped to take my bearings, for night was coming on. In this part of the forest there was a great deal of snow—neither track nor beaten road, nor even a trace of one. Sometimes I sat down to rest upon trees lying uprooted by the great winds. I had to grasp at the twigs of the bushes in fear of falling, I was so weak. My legs were buried in the snow above my boots, so that they got filled. However, I was not cold—on the contrary, drops of sweat fell down my face; but my legs refused to carry me. In consequence of the efforts I was making to drag myself out of the snow, in which I sank often up to my knees, I felt an extraordinary lassitude in my thighs. I will not attempt to describe what I suffered. For more than an hour I was walking in the dark, lighted only by the stars. Not succeeding in getting out of the forest at that point nearest to the road, and able to do no more, exhausted, breathless, I resolved to rest. I propped myself up against the trunk of a tree and remained motionless. A moment afterwards I heard a dog barking. I looked in the direction of the sound, and saw a light shining. Sighing hopefully, and summoning all the strength I had, I turned towards this new quarter. But thirty paces further on were four horses, and, seated around a fire, four Cossacks. Three peasants were there too. Amongst them were the canteen man and his wife whom I had met, taken, no doubt, by those Cossacks who had wanted to make off with me. I easily recognised the one with the sabre-cut across the face, for I was not twenty steps away.

I watched them for some time, wondering if it would not be better to go and give myself up rather than die like a brute in the midst of the wood. The light of the fire tempted me; but for some unknown reason I did the exact opposite, and drew back. Still I watched them, and noticed that several earthen pots were around the fire. They had straw to lie on, and the horses had hay to eat.

The number of trees made it impossible for me to follow the exact direction I wished to take. I was obliged to bear to the left, fortunately for me, for, after taking a few steps, I found the forest clearer, but the snow in greater quantities, so that I fell several times. One last time I rose and reproached God for my misfortunes, who was yet watching over me. I now found myself at the end of the forest and on the high road. There I fell upon my knees and thanked Him against whom I had just rebelled.

I walked straight on. The road was good, and no doubt the right one; but the wind, which I had not felt in the forest, was too keen for my bare legs. My coat, being long, kept off a little of the cold.

Oddly enough, I was not hungry. I do not know whether the excitement I had been through since the Cossacks' attack were the cause, or if it were the effect of my sickness, but since leaving the stable where I had had some soup and meat I had no desire to eat. However, fancying that there ought to be a piece of meat still left in my bag, I searched for it, and was lucky enough to find it, and, although hardened by the frost, I ate it as I went along. My meal over, I raised my head, and saw two men on horseback on my left, apparently advancing with caution, and further on, along the road, was a man who seemed to be getting along better than I was. I doubled my pace to join him, but all at once he disappeared.

Looking to the left, I caught sight of a little hut, and went in. But hardly was I inside, when I heard the click of a musket, and a deep voice said:

'Who goes there?'

'A friend,' I answered, and added: 'A soldier of the Imperial Guard!'

'Ah, ah!' came the answer. 'Where the devil do you come from, comrade, that I haven't met you while I've been walking all alone?'

I related to him a part of what had happened to me since the Cossacks' attack, of which he knew nothing.

We resumed our march. I saw that my new comrade was an old Chasseur of the Guard, and that he carried on his knapsack and around his neck a pair of cloth trousers that apparently were of no use to him, but could be of the greatest benefit to me. I begged him to let me buy them of him, and showed him the naked state of my legs.

'My poor comrade!' he said, 'I would willingly oblige you if I could, but I must tell you that the trousers are burnt in several places, and are full of great holes.'

'Never mind that; let me have them. They may perhaps save my life.'

He pulled them off his knapsack, saying: 'Take them.'

Then I took two five-franc pieces from my bag, asking him if it was enough.

'Quite,' he answered. 'Make haste and let us be off, for I see two men on horseback coming down this way. They may be Cossack scouts.'

While he was speaking I had put on the trousers—I kept them in place as I had the former ones, with the shawl wrapped round my body—and we set off. We hadn't taken a hundred steps before my companion, who walked faster than I did, was already twenty yards in front of me. I saw him stoop and pick something up. At first I couldn't distinguish what it was, but coming to the spot, I saw a dead man, and recognised him as a Grenadier of the Royal Dutch Guard that, from the beginning of the campaign, had formed part of the Imperial Guard. He had neither knapsack nor bearskin, but he still had his musket, cartridge-pouch, sabre, and great black gaiters on his legs, reaching above the knee. I took the gaiters and put them over my trousers to cover the holes. Then I set off walking again, rather faster than usual, as if the dead man were running after me.

Meanwhile the Chasseur had gone on, and I could not see him. Soon afterwards I came to a great building, and recognising it as a posting-house, I made up my mind to pass the night there. An infantry soldier, the sentinel, called out : ' Who goes there ?'

' A friend,' I answered, and entered.

The first thing I saw was about thirty men, some of them sleeping, others cooking horseflesh and rice, round several fires. To the right were three men, sitting round a bowl of rice. I sank down beside them. After a moment I tried to speak to one of them, pulling him by his coat. He looked at me without a word. Then, in a piteous tone, I said in a low voice, that the others might not hear : ' Comrade, I entreat you, let me eat some spoonfuls of rice. I will pay you. You will do me a great service ; you will save my life.'

At the same time I offered him two pieces of five francs, which he took, saying, ' Eat.'

He handed me his spoon and an earthenware plate, and also gave up his place near the fire. For my ten francs there were about fifteen spoonfuls of rice still left.

I looked about me when I had eaten to see if the old Chasseur were there. I discovered him near a hayrack, busy cutting up a bearskin to make ear-lappets of. This bearskin belonged to the Dutch Grenadier ; he had picked it up when I saw him stoop. I went over to him to rest, but hardly was I stretched on the straw when the sentinel exclaimed, ' Look out !' saying that he had caught sight of Cossacks.

Immediately everybody jumped up and seized their arms. A shout was heard, ' A friend—Frenchman !'

Two cavalrymen entered the barn, and, dismounting, showed themselves. But several began questioning them, in particular the old Chasseur, who said :

'How is it you are on horseback, and dressed like a Cossack? Probably to rob and pillage our sick and wounded.'

'Nothing of the sort,' replied one of the two troopers; 'when you see us you will believe it. We can prove it, and when we are settled we will tell you all about it.'

The speaker, after having tied up the two horses and given them some straw, of which there was plenty in the barn, returned to his companion, who seemed to walk with difficulty, and, taking him by the arm, led him up to a place beside me. After eating some bread and drinking brandy, and having also given a pull to the old soldier and myself, the man who had spoken before began:

'Yesterday evening I saved my brother from the Cossacks, who had wounded and taken him prisoner. I must tell you about it, as it is a most wonderful story.

'The evening before the arrival at Kowno, dying of cold and hunger, and spent with fatigue, I wandered from the road with two officers of the 71st, armed, like myself, with muskets, to find some village in which we could spend the night. But after having walked about half a league, we were able to go no further without running the risk of perishing in the snow, so we decided to pass the night in a deserted, tumble-down house, where, most luckily, we found both wood and straw, and, as I still had some flour left from Wilna, we made a good fire and had some broth.

'The next day, early in the morning, we set about finding our way back to the high road; but just as we were about to leave the house we were surrounded by about fifteen Cossacks. We stopped in front of the door to reconnoitre them; they made signs to us to approach, but we did the opposite. We re-entered the house, closed the door, and, opening the two little windows, began a fire which made the Cossacks fly. At long musket-shot they stopped, but we had reloaded our weapons and left the house, firing a second volley, at which a horse and rider fell. The latter freed himself of the horse and left it. We set off at our quickest pace, but had hardly taken fifty steps before we saw them bearing down upon us.

' Directly afterwards they went to the right to pick up a portmanteau off the horse we had shot. Soon they were lost to sight, and we gained the road to Kowno, which we were to reach that same day. We were now in the midst of over 6,000 stragglers, and, as it always happened amid this rabble, I was separated from my comrades.

' I walked all day, and it was hardly dark when I found myself near the Niemen, and about a league from Kowno. As there were houses to be seen on the other side, I decided to cross the river on the ice, so as to find a shelter, as I did the night before.

' On gaining the bank, I saw two or three houses about half a league to the right, where I was received fairly well by the peasants, and passed a quiet night. The next morning at daylight I took to the road, to rejoin the column on the other side of Kowno; but hardly had I gone a couple of hundred steps, when I was suddenly surrounded by a dozen Cossacks, who, without doing me any harm, or even thinking of disarming me, made me march in front of them in exactly the direction I had wanted to take. I was a prisoner, though I could not realize it.

' After an hour's walking, we came to a village. There I was relieved of my arms and of my money, but I was lucky enough to save some pieces of gold hidden in the lining of my waistcoat. I took off my shako and covered my head with a cap of black sheepskin I had found. I noticed that the Cossacks were laden with gold and silver, and that they did not pay much attention to me, so I decided to take the first opportunity of escaping.

'It might have been about ten o'clock when we left the village. We met another detachment of Cossacks escorting prisoners, some of whom were men belonging to the Imperial Guard, taken in the sortie from Kowno. I was placed among these.

'We marched, with frequent stoppages, till about three o'clock. I noticed that the leader was uncertain of the way, not knowing the country. Before nightfall we had reached a little village, and were put into a barn, where we all went through a very minute inspection. I trembled for my gold, but I trembled for nothing.

'The search was barely over when I heard my name called by a prisoner unknown to me. "Here," I answered. Another prisoner at the far end answered too. Then, moving in the direction whence the voice had come, I asked who answered to the name of Dassonville. "I!" replied my brother, whom you see here. Think of our surprise on finding each other! We embraced, weeping. He told me that he had been wounded in the leg on November 28th, near the Bérézina bridge. I told him my plan was to make our escape before they forced us to recross the Niemen; for being now in Pomerania, a country belonging to Prussia, we must take the opportunity that offered.

'The peasants brought us potatoes and water, a piece of good luck we were far from expecting. They were distributed among us—four for each of us. We threw ourselves upon them ravenously, and almost all declared that just then it was better to be a prisoner eating potatoes than to be free, but dying of hunger and cold on the high road. But I said that, all the same, it would be better to get out of their clutches. "Who knows," I said, "that they will not take us to Siberia!" I showed them a possibility of escape, for, close to where I was lying beside my brother, I had found out a place where, by taking down two boards, we could get out easily. They agreed with me; but an hour afterwards, as ill-luck would have it, we were told we must leave. Night had come on; many of the men, worn out with fatigue, had fallen asleep. The Cossacks, seeing their orders were not obeyed quickly, struck those still lying down with the knout. They would have struck my brother, who could not rise quickly enough because of his wound, but I placed myself before him and warded off the blows, meanwhile helping him to rise, and, instead of leaving the barn like the others, we hid ourselves behind the door, and were lucky enough not to be seen.

'The Cossacks and all the prisoners were gone; we did not dare to breathe. Three Cossacks on horseback crossed the barn at a gallop, looking to right and left to see if there was anyone left. When they had gone, I dragged myself along to peep outside; I saw a peasant coming, and crept back to my place. He entered the barn on the side opposite to us; we had just time to cover ourselves with straw. Very luckily for us, he did not see us, and shut the two doors. We were now alone.

'It might have been six o'clock. We rested for another hour, and then I rose to open the door; but I couldn't manage it, so I had to return to my first project, that of getting out by removing the two boards. This I did. I told my brother to wait for me, and got out.

'I went as far as the entrance to the village. At the first house I saw a light coming through a window, and, peeping in, there were three great Cossack rascals counting money at a table, a peasant holding a light for them.

'I was just going back to rejoin my brother in the barn,

when I saw one of them make a movement towards the
door, open it, and come out. Luckily for me, a sledge
laden with wood was near, so I lay flat on my stomach in
the snow behind it.

'The Cossack then re-entered the house and closed the
door. Instantly I rose to fly, but, afraid of being seen,
instead of crossing in front of the window, I took a turn
to the right. I hadn't gone ten steps, when a door opened,
and to escape notice I crept into a stable, and hid myself
under the trough from which the horses were eating. I
had hardly done so, when a peasant entered with a lantern,
followed by a Cossack. I thought it was all over with me.

'The Cossack was carrying a portmanteau; he fastened
it upon his horse and went out, closing the door.

'I was just going myself, when I thought of taking a
horse with me. As quickly as possible, I seized the one
with the portmanteau, but, in turning his head round to
get him out of the stable, something fell on my shoulder;
it was the Cossack's lance, propped up against his horse.
I took it away with me for defence, and went out. I
reached the barn, helped my brother to mount, and, taking
the bridle in my hand, proceeded in the direction of the
road.

'When we had gone a couple of hundred steps, I looked
round to see if anything was coming. I handed my brother
the Cossack's lance, and covered him with the great
camel's-hair cape that I found on the horse. After half
an hour's walking, we reached the road; then, turning in
the direction of Gumbinnen, we saw some peasants busy
removing the wheels of a deserted waggon. To avoid
passing near them, we took a road to our left, leading to the
entrance of a village. We wished we could have avoided
the village, so fearful were we of falling again into the
enemy's clutches. God only knows what would have

happened to us, for, seeing us with a horse and weapon belonging to one of their people, they would have made sure we had killed the owner.

'We had stopped to consult, when we heard a noise behind us ; we thought at once of flight, but there was no chance, for the masses of snow on each side of the road prevented our getting into the ditches. Our situation became critical, and I did not dare tell my fears to my brother on account of his wound.

'We were starting again straight on, when we saw in front of us the cause of our fright—some men only a few steps away from us. They came to a stop, calling to us in German : " Good-evening, friend Cossacks !"

'" Listen," I said to my brother : "you are a Cossack, and I am your prisoner. You can speak a little German, so only keep cool."

'As he had only a dilapidated sergeant's cap upon his head, I exchanged it for mine, which was like a Cossack's. We recognised these people for the peasants we had seen a while before busy round the wheel on the road. There were four of them, dragging two of the wheels behind them with ropes. My brother inquired if there were any fellow-Cossacks in the village. They said, " No."

'" Then," said he, " take me to the burgomaster, for I am cold and hungry, besides being wounded and obliged to look after this French prisoner."

'One of them then told us that they had been waiting for the Cossacks since morning, and that they would have done well to come, for more than thirty Frenchmen had lodged with them the previous night, and they had almost all of them been disarmed as they were leaving.

'On hearing this we wished ourselves at the devil ; but just then some more peasants came up, who, seeing me being led by a Cossack, threatened and insulted me. They were reproved by an old man, who, I learned afterwards, was a Protestant minister, the curé of the place.

'We were led before the burgomaster, who made my brother exceedingly welcome, telling him that he should be quartered with him, and his horse taken care of; but as for the Frenchman, he would have him sent to the prison.

' "That is to say," he said, "if you do not want to keep him about you as a servant."

' "I would like that," answered my brother, "especially as I am wounded, and this Frenchman is a Surgeon-Major. He will dress my leg."

' "Surgeon-Major!" replied the burgomaster; "that is lucky, for we have here a good fellow in the village who had his arm broken this morning by a Frenchman. The Surgeon-Major will set his arm for him."

'We were taken into a very warm room, where there was a bed intended for the Cossack; but he refused it, and asked for some straw for himself, and some for me, which he had put to one side so as not to awaken suspicion. For brother Cossack they brought bread, lard, sauer-kraut, beer, and gin; potatoes and water for me. The burgomaster showed my brother a quantity of weapons in a corner of the room; they had belonged to the Frenchmen whom the peasants had disarmed that morning. There were pistols, carbines, five or six muskets, as well as cavalry swords and several packets of cartridges.

'While we were at our meal, a peasant with his arm in a sling entered the room, accompanied by a woman; it was the man with the broken arm. He came and sat down near me, so I decided to go in for bravado. I asked for linen bandages, and a little splint of pine-wood. The arm was broken clean between the wrist and the elbow. During the last five years, I had seen so many operations that I did not hesitate to set to work. There was no wound to be seen. I signed to a peasant to hold the sick man by the shoulders, and to the wife to hold his hand. Then I set, and pretty well, too, I think, the broken bone, just as I should have set a piece of wood. To begin with, I felt my way a little, while the devil of a fellow shouted and made villainous faces. Then I applied compresses, sprinkled with schnapps; afterwards four splints that I bound up with linen bandages. The man felt better, and told me I was a good fellow. His wife and the burgomaster complimented me, and I was able to breathe. They gave me a large glass of gin to reward me.

'But this was not all. The burgomaster gave me to understand I must go and see a woman who for the last few days had been suffering horribly; it was a case of a young woman in labour. They had been to Kowno for an accoucheur, but all was in such disorder because of the Russians and French that one could not be found.

' " As a general thing," he said, " it is a service the old women render, but it seems this is a complicated case."

'I tried to make the burgomaster understand that, having lost my surgical instruments, I could undertake no operation; that, moreover, I was no accoucheur—I understood nothing about it. But I couldn't make myself understood; they thought it was simply ill-will on my part. I was obliged to go. Conducted by two peasants and three women, I was led to the end of the village. I do not know if it was my having left such a warm room, but I was as cold as death. Finally we reached the place.

'I was taken into a room where I found three old women, just like the three Fates; they were round a young woman lying on a bed, who was shrieking every now and again a great deal louder than the man with the broken arm. One of the old women took me up to the sick woman, and a second lifted the coverlet. Imagine my embarrassment! Saying nothing, I looked at the three old crones, to gather from their looks what they wanted me to do. But they were waiting likewise, looking at me to see what I intended. The sick woman, too, had her eyes fixed upon me. Finally, I understood one of the old women to say I must find out whether the child still lived. I made up my mind, and placed my great paw, as cold as ice, on the patient. The touch made her leap up and utter a scream enough to make the house shake. This cry was followed by a second; the three old cronies seized her, and in less than five minutes all was over—a Prussian subject was born.

'Then, proud of my fresh cure, I rubbed my hands; and as I knew what was usual in my village under similar circumstances, the infant being bathed in warm water and wine, I ordered some to be brought in a basin. Afterwards I asked for some schnapps. They gave me a bottleful of it. I tasted it several times; then, taking a piece of linen which I wetted in the warm water, I sprinkled the schnapps upon it, and applied the compress to the patient, who was feeling extremely comfortable, and who thanked me, pressing my hand.

'I left, escorted by the two men who had brought me, and by two of the old duennas. I was reconducted before the burgomaster, and praised up to the skies. My Cossack brother had been in a fearful fright, but was delighted to see me again.

'I had still one wounded man to patch up, and that was himself. I bathed the wound with warm water, and dressed it with a little more knowledge of what I was about. We were left alone. When I was certain that everyone was asleep, I picked out two pairs of pistols, as well as a beautiful infantry sword, and two lots of cartridges of the right size for our pistols. We took the precaution to load these at once. Mine were hidden while awaiting the time of our departure, and then we rested.

'In the morning they brought us something to eat. This time I was treated to the same food as the Cossack. While we were breakfasting, the burgomaster complimented me on my skill, asked me if I would like to remain with them, and said that he would give me one of his daughters in marriage. I told him that that could not be, as I was already married and had children. Then, turning to the Cossack, he asked him in what direction he was going. " I am going to rejoin my brother and my comrades, who are following the road to the town; I do not remember its name, but it is the first I should come to along the road." " I know," said the burgomaster, "you mean Wilbalen. Well, we will go together. I will guide you to a place about a league from here, where you will find more than 200 Cossacks; for I have just received orders to send there everything in the way of hay and flour, and to follow afterwards myself. We will set out in half an hour. I will get your horse ready with my own."

'Hardly had he gone from the room, when I thrust my pistols into my belt, and about thirty cartridges into my pockets. My Cossack brother fastened on the sword I had chosen for him, and also put a pair of pistols in his belt. A moment afterwards they came to tell us that all was ready for our departure. I took the Cossack's portmanteau, and we went out.

'We found the burgomaster at the posting-station in travelling dress. He wore a long coat lined with fine sheepskin, a fur cap, and boots of the same. His servant wore a sheepskin coat. I helped my brother the Cossack to mount; and, as I was fastening on the portmanteau, I said softly, so as not to be heard, that, should the opportunity offer, he must seize the burgomaster's horse and coat, and that of his servant as well, so that by means of these disguises we might escape ; and that, in our present position, we must act promptly, as it meant life or death.

' We set off on our march, the servant in front as guide, I next and between the two on horseback, as a prisoner would. A little before the end of the village we took a road to the left, and after a quarter of an hour's walking we reached a little pine-wood. While crossing it, I thought of putting my project into execution. After we had crossed the wood, I looked in front of me and to right and left, looking out for anything likely to harm us. Seeing nothing, I strode to the burgomaster's side, and seizing the horse's bridle with one hand, and presenting a pistol with the other, I ordered him to dismount. As you may imagine, he was terribly taken aback ; he looked at the Cossack as if to tell him to run me through the body. Meanwhile the servant, with a great stick, rushed to knock me down ; but, without letting go of the horse's bridle, I struck him such a violent blow across the chest with the butt-end of the pistol that I sent him sprawling yards off, and threatened to kill him if he made the slightest movement towards getting up.

' While this was happening, my brother told the burgomaster that he had better dismount; but he was so stupefied that the order had to be repeated several times. Finally he dismounted, and I gave his animal to my brother to hold.

' Immediately I took off the servant's boots, coat, and cap. Then, taking off my own cloak and coat and my cap, I threw them down on him, forcing him to put on the coat, so that in his turn he looked like the prisoner.

' Imagine the burgomaster's face at seeing his servant

dressed up in such a fashion! But that was not all. Telling my brother, who had dismounted, to keep an eye on the servant, I effected a change of costume in his master, who, at my invitation and without much trouble, gave me his overcoat, boots, and cap. I gave him in exchange my coat and his servant's cap. Then I made my brother put on the servant's coat and boots, and when he was completely attired and remounted, and in a position to mount guard over our two prisoners, I dressed myself in my turn in the burgomaster's clothes. Mounting his horse, I took possession of his sword, and we set off at a gallop, leaving our two Prussians thunderstruck, and probably not knowing whether my brother was really a Cossack or not. We did not feel comfortable, either, for, although disguised, we were afraid of falling into the clutches of the Cossacks of whom the burgomaster had spoken before our setting out.

'After advancing at a gallop for about ten minutes we reached a little village, where the inhabitants, on seeing us, began shouting out: "Hurrah! hurrah! Our friends the Cossacks! Hurrah!"

'They told us that our comrades had slept at a large village a quarter of a league away, and that they had left to cut off the French in their retreat before they should have reached the wood which intersected the route. They wanted to make us dismount and drink, but as we were not easy in our minds, we were satisfied with some glasses of schnapps without dismounting. Then my brother shouted "Hurrah!" and we decamped, carrying off the bottle of schnapps, and accompanied by the hurrahs of the whole population.

'It might have been about three o'clock when we saw the wood in front of us and heard firing. A fight was going on between the French and the Russian cavalry near a house on the borders of the road. So the peasants had not lied to us : the Cossacks had really intended to cut off the retreat of the column of stragglers before they could reach the wood.

'On seeing this we set our horses to a gallop, and, without thinking of our resemblance to the Cossacks, we stationed ourselves along the road, in order to try and gain the entrance of the wood towards which the stragglers were rushing. They took us for Cossacks, and ran faster. The Cossacks, on their side, taking us for some of themselves, and thinking we were pursuing the French, came a dozen strong to support us and follow us into the wood. I had a Cossack to my right, my brother to my left; behind me, the remaining Cossacks. Anyone would have thought I was their chief.

'The road was hardly wide enough to allow three horses to go abreast. After having trotted forward about fifty yards, we saw several of our officers barring the way with crossed bayonets, and shouting to those in flight, "Don't mind these dogs ! let them come on !"

'I seized the opportunity, and, slackening my horse's pace, I slashed at the face of the Cossack to my right with my sword.'* He took another step and stopped, turning his head in my direction ; but, seeing that I was preparing to go on, he turned and escaped, bellowing. Those who were following did the same, and our horses imitated the movement, so that there we were, going in our turn after the Cossacks, who ran as if all the devils were after them.

'I caught sight of a road to the right, with a Cossack in front of us. Seeing us, he slackened speed, stopped,

---

* This Cossack, whose face the sergeant cut with his sabre, was the one I saw in the wood, and whose face his comrades bandaged.— *Author's Note.*

and spoke to us in a language we did not understand. I hit him a violent blow on the head with my sabre, which I believe would have severed it had it not been for the bearskin cap he wore. Astonished at this manner of reply, he made his escape, and being the better horseman, was soon out of sight. A quarter of an hour later we had reached the other side of the wood. There was the Cossack again, who, seeing us, set off at a gallop, and we had no desire to follow him. We skirted the wood to its extremity. Afterwards we manœuvred about till evening to find the right road, and we got here with much difficulty.

'Now,' concluded the sergeant, 'we must rest a little, and set off, for at daybreak we may have to be off again.'

On this we each of us settled down to take a little rest, while six men of the Kowno garrison, soldiers in good condition, voluntarily offered to take a turn at watching at the door of the barn.

We had not been resting an hour, when we heard a shout, 'Who goes there?' Directly afterwards a man came in and fell down full length. Some of the men rose to help him. He was a gunner in the Imperial Guard, who had been found at the bivouac I had missed. He had more than twenty wounds on his body, lance-thrusts and sword-cuts. They asked for linen to bandage him with. I hastened to give one of my best shirts. The sergeant, one of the two brothers, made him swallow some drops of gin; the old Chasseur gave some lint that he drew out of the depths of his bearskin. The wounded man was made more comfortable, and settled as well as could be. Happily, his wounds were mainly on the back and head; a few on the right arm, but his legs were sound.

I went up to ask him how he was. Almost before looking at me, he exclaimed : ' It is you, sergeant ! You were wise not to stay at the house by the wood where you had made up your mind to pass the night, for a quarter of an hour after your departure more than 400 Cossacks came up.* We took up arms to defend ourselves, being then about 400 men. Seeing that we were ready to give them a reception, they halted ; a detachment was formed, with an officer at their head, who advanced, telling us in good French to surrender.

' But a Chasseur of the Guard, named Michaut—the old *cantinière's* friend—left the ranks, and advancing so as to be heard by the Russian officer : " Tell me, you *lapin*, how long have Frenchmen surrendered with arms in their hands ? Come on, we are waiting for you !" The officer instantly retired. They prepared to charge ; we waited for them, and when they were about five-and-twenty yards off half our men fired. Some of them fell. Then, thinking that we all had discharged our weapons, and that we should not be able to reload, they advanced again, shouting and hurrahing. But they were met by another volley, that put the greater number of their men *hors de combat*. At this they took to flight, and we thought we were rid of them ; but five minutes later they returned in greater numbers, and just at the moment when we were retreating to the wood, not having had again time to reload, we were overcome by the blows of lance and sword. Almost all were killed or wounded.

' I remained on the ground, wounded, and pretending to be dead ; and, finding myself on the edge of a ditch bordering the road, I rolled into it. The peasants came

---

* The gunner was mistaken as to the number of Cossacks, for I learned from one of my friends who was there that they were not more than 250, probably those whom the burgomaster spoke of to the two brothers.— *Author's Note.*

up, and set to work to despoil the dead and wounded, accompanied by some Cossacks whose horses had been killed. I was lucky enough to escape notice, and when they had withdrawn, raising myself with difficulty, I gained the wood and crossed it. And, finally, my friends, I am so lucky as to have met you. But what is to become of me ?'

' We will lead you,' replied the soldiers of the garrison. ' And I,' said the sergeant brother, 'will lend you my horse.'

In spite of the sleep which overwhelmed me, I began to think of setting off, for, not being strong, I took a great deal of time to go a very little way. A young soldier offered to accompany me, if I wanted to set out at once ; I accepted his offer, especially as this young man, who had suffered nothing, was strong and would be able to help me. And so we took our departure.

We entered a wood, through which the road lay. Here the soldier, who was unarmed, wished to carry my gun ; I gave it up to him, as, in my feeble condition, he was better able to make use of it than I. After walking I do not know how long, supported by my young companion's arm (for I often dozed while marching), we reached the extremity of the wood ; it might have been about four o'clock in the morning, December 16th.

We walked on, haphazard, for about another half-hour ; very luckily, the moon rose. But with it came a high wind and so fine a snow that it cut our faces and prevented our seeing before us.

I suffered greatly from the longing to sleep, and without the help of the little soldier, who held me all the time by the arm, I should certainly have fallen down sleeping. My companion pointed out to me a large group of buildings some way in front. I saw it was a posting-station, and concluded from that that we had gone about three leagues. In a quarter of an hour's time we had reached the doors. Entering, I threw myself down near a fire. There were several left by the soldiers, almost all of the Imperial Guard, who had marched on to Wilbalen. Some gunners, also of the Guard, were still there, but getting ready to leave.

I had slept peacefully for about ten minutes, when I felt myself shaken by the arm. I tried to resist, but someone raised me by my shoulders; I awoke at last and heard a shout coming from an old gunner: 'The Cossacks! Get up, my boy! Courage a little longer!'

Eleven Cossacks had come to a standstill, and were probably only awaiting our departure to come and take our places. 'Come,' said the gunner, 'we must give up the position and beat a retreat on Wilbalen. We have only another league; so come, let us be off!'

We had to take to the road again; there were six of us —four gunners, the little soldier and myself. We left the barn. It was December 16th, the fifty-ninth day's march since leaving Moscow. The wind was high and the cold terrible. All at once, in spite of all that my comrade could do to hold me, I sank down, overcome with sleep and fatigue. The efforts of my companion and two gunners were necessary to get me on my feet, although when there I was still asleep. I awoke, however, when a gunner rubbed my face with snow. Then he made me swallow a little brandy; that pulled me together a little.

They each took an arm, and so made me walk much faster than I could have done alone. It was in this way that I reached Wilbalen. On entering the town, we learned that King Murat was in it with all the remnant of the Imperial Guard.

In spite of the great cold there was plenty of bustle

going on in the town on the part of the soldiers, who were in hopes of buying bread and brandy from the numerous Jews in the place. At the door of each house, too, there was a sentinel, and whenever anyone presented himself for admission he was answered that some General lodged there, or some Colonel, or that there was no more room. We were told by others to go and 'look for our own regiment.' The gunners found some comrades of their own, and went off with them. I was beginning to be in despair, when I was told by a peasant that in the first street to the left there were only a few people. We went there, but always found a sentinel at every door, and everywhere the same response. I saw for myself that inside the houses the men were heaped up on one another. However, we could not remain very long in the street without dying of cold.

It would be difficult to express how much I suffered on this day from cold, but still more from disappointment at seeing myself repulsed everywhere, and that, too, by comrades.

At last I spoke to a Grenadier, who told me there were people everywhere, but ill-will and selfishness as well, and that no attention must be paid to the houses being sentinelled; that one must go in, 'For I see,' he continued, 'that you are in a bad way.'

Making a sign to my comrade to follow me, I turned to enter the first house I came to. An old fellow barred the way with his musket, saying that it was the Colonel's quarters, and that there was no more room. I answered that, even were it the Emperor's lodging, there would have to be room for two, and that I should go in. Just then I caught sight of another Grenadier busy fastening a pair of officer's epaulettes on to the shoulders of his overcoat. To my great surprise I recognised Picart, my old companion, whom I had not seen since leaving Wilna, on December 6th. Instantly I said :

' Tell Colonel Picart that Sergeant Bourgogne is asking him for room.'

' You are mistaken,' he answered.

But without listening to him, I forced my way past the sentry; the other followed me, and we entered.

No sooner did Picart recognise me, than he threw his big epaulettes on to the straw, exclaiming :

' *Jour de Dieu!* it is *mon pays*, my sergeant ! How is it that you are alone ? Have you been in the rear-guard ?'

Without replying, I let myself fall upon the straw, exhausted with fatigue, want of sleep, and hunger, and suffocated as well with the heat of a great stove. Picart ran to his knapsack, brought out a bottle of brandy, and made me swallow a few drops, which brought me round a little. Then I begged him to let me rest. It might have been about eight o'clock in the morning : it was two in the afternoon when I awoke.

Picart placed between my knees a little earthen plate of soup with rice, which I ate with pleasure, looking meanwhile all round me, trying to collect my thoughts. Finally everything became clear to me, so that I could remember all that had happened during the last twenty-four hours.

Picart broke into my reflections to tell me all that had happened to him since we were separated at Wilna :

' After having driven away the Russians who showed themselves on the heights of Wilna, we were brought back to the square ; from there we were led to the suburb on the Kowno road, to act as guard to King Murat, who had just left the town. There I looked round for you, thinking you had followed, and was astonished not to see you.

At midnight we had to set out for Kowno, to accompany Murat and Prince Eugène, who also was lodged in the suburb. But on reaching the foot of the mountain we found it impossible to cross it on account of the quantity of snow and the number of carriages and waggons along the road.

'When the day had broken, the King and Prince, by making a sweep around the mountain, succeeded in continuing on their way; but I and many others, having no horses, began to climb the road again. Lucky for us, for we had the opportunity to *monter à la roue* and make a few five-franc pieces . . . at your service, you hear, *mon pays.*'

Picart gave me the details of his journey up to the moment when chance had brought about our meeting. I then told him that every time I met him it gave me the same pleasure, but that this time I was especially pleased at finding him a Colonel. He began to laugh, telling me it was a *ruse de guerre*, which he had played to get a good lodging. He had appointed himself Colonel the day before, and was recognised as such by those about him, who showed him all respect.

Picart told me that at three o'clock a review was to be held by Murat, when orders would be given, telling the remnants of the different corps the places at which they were to meet. I decided to go, so as to meet my comrades there. Picart shaved me with a blunt razor that we had found in the kit of the Cossack killed on November 23rd. It was my first shave since leaving Moscow, and although he ground the razor on his scabbard, and then passed it over his hand to give it an edge, he none the less rasped my face.

At the appointed hour we left our lodging to repair to the rendezvous. The muster was to take place in a large

street. Soldiers of all ranks and regiments came. Several
of the veterans of the Guard, to draw attention to themselves, had dressed themselves as if for grand parade: to
see them one would have thought they had come from
Paris, rather than from Moscow. At the rendezvous I had
the luck to meet all those with whom I had been on the
preceding day, as well as a good many others whom I
had not seen since leaving Wilna; but our numbers had
diminished. Grangier said to me:

'I hope you will not leave us again; you must come to
our quarters, and as we are allowed to make use of sledges
or carts to travel in, we will try to find one.'

We stopped in the street a long time waiting for King
Murat. Meanwhile there were many surprises at meeting
friends, in finding those living whom one had long
thought dead. I had the pleasure of meeting Sergeant
Humblot, with whom I had been travelling the evening
before, and from whom I had been separated in the wood
at the time of the Cossack attack. I learned also that the
cantinières, Marie and Mother Gâteau, had got into good
quarters.

As Murat did not come, the names of those men unable
to walk were taken, these to be despatched the next day
at six o'clock in the morning on sledges furnished by
the authorities. We could not find one for ourselves,
however, and had to comfort ourselves by preparing to
pass a good night, so as to be fit to march the following
day.

Picart had said that he wanted to speak to me before
we separated. Hardly was the order for departure given,
when I felt a smart tap on my shoulder. I turned and
saw Picart. He made a sign to me, and Grangier also,
to follow him, and when we had moved away a little, he
said:

'You are going to do me the kindness of accepting a good pull of white wine—Rhine wine.'

'Is it possible?' I exclaimed.

For only answer he said: 'Follow me.'

He then told us that the evening before he had made the acquaintance of a Jew with the idea of selling him things he wanted to dispose of—his Colonel's epaulettes, for instance—and as he had been often taken for a Jew, he passed himself off as one, saying that his mother was the daughter of the Rabbi at Strasbourg, and that he was called Salomon. The Jew was delighted at the hope of making a good bargain, and had pointed out to him his house, assuring him that he would find some good Rhine wine there.

We went to the back of the synagogue. To one side was a little house, where Picart stopped. He looked all round to see if anyone was there; then, pinching his nose, he called out in a nasal voice, 'Jacob! Jacob!'

At a barred opening we saw a figure appear in a long fur cap and adorned with a dirty beard. Recognising Picart, he said to him in German: 'Ah, my dear Salomon, it is you. I will open the door.'

We entered a very warm room, stinking and disgusting. As soon as we were seated on a bench around the stove, we saw three other Jews, who, Jacob said, constituted his family.

Picart, who knew how to go to work with his pretended co-religionists, began by opening his knapsack and drawing out, to begin with, a pair of epaulettes—not a Colonel's, but a Field-Marshal's—and a parcel of lace stripes, the whole of it new, picked up on the Wilna mountain out of the deserted waggons.

There were also some silver covers that had come from Moscow. The Jews opened their eyes wide. Picart now asked for wine and bread. Some excellent Rhine wine was brought. The bread was not exactly of the same quality, but just then it was better than one could have hoped for.

While we were drinking, the Jews were inspecting the articles spread out upon the bench. Jacob asked Picart how much he wanted for all that.

'Name it yourself,' answered Picart.

The Jew mentioned a price very far from what Picart wanted.

He said : 'No.'

Jacob went a little higher.

This time Picart, on whom the wine was beginning to take effect, looked at the Jew sneeringly, and answered him by laying a finger on the side of his nose, and humming the Rabbi's chant in the synagogue on the Sabbath.

The four Jews began to rock like Chinamen, and chant verses. Grangier looked at Picart, thinking he was tipsy, and I, in spite of my sufferings, was almost dying of laughter. At last Picart stopped singing to pour us out some drink. Meanwhile the Jews talked together about the price of the articles. Jacob offered a still higher price ; but it was not yet as much as Picart wanted, so he recommenced his chant, till finally a bargain was concluded, on condition that he received gold. Jacob paid Picart in Prussian gold pieces. He was probably satisfied with his bargain, for he gave us nuts and onions. The wine had gone to our heads, for when Picart received his money we began to 'perform the Sabbath' like him.

This charivari would have gone on a long time if there hadn't been a knocking at the door made by the butt-ends of muskets. Jacob looked through the grating and saw several soldiers, who told him they were billeted on him, and that if he didn't open at once the door would be beaten in. He opened directly. We made up our mind to retire, and I said good-bye to Picart, with a promise to meet again at Elbing, the place to which we were under orders to march.

On reaching our lodging we had some rice bouillon; then I attended to my feet and shoes and stockings, and, as we were in a warm room and on fresh straw, I soon fell asleep.

The next day—the 17th—by five o'clock in the morning the town looked deserted. Men who had not been under a roof for two months, and who now slept warmly, were in no hurry to leave their quarters. Two or three drummers, still remaining among those belonging to the Guard, beat the *grenadière* for us, and the *carabinière* for the infantry. When in the street, we noticed that it was less cold than on the preceding evening. A sledge drove up, drawn by two horses, and stopped. It was driven by two Jews, and laden with groceries. I proposed that they should drive us—for payment, of course—as far as Darkehmen, our day's destination, or that we should seize the sledge if they refused.

At first, under one pretext or another, they made a good many difficulties. We offered half the price down, the other half on our arrival. The Jews then agreed. The price was fixed at forty francs, we paying them the half at once; but as they reckoned the five-franc pieces at the value of only a thaler each (worth no more than four), that cost us an additional ten francs. We made no difficulty, however, and to win their confidence we foolishly let them see we had a great deal of money. A sergeant-major named Pierson showed them several pieces of silver plate he had. On this they began to speak in Hebrew, so that we could not understand what they were saying.

There were five of us—Leboude, Grangier, Pierson, Oudict, and myself. The sledge was unloaded, the horses rested, and we prepared to start. We placed our muskets in the bottom of the sledge, our knapsacks upon them, and off we went. It was past six o'clock; the entire remnant of the army was already in motion, but without order or organization, so that we could hardly get out of the town. Those who had not the strength to walk tried to seize the sledges.

Our drivers made us understand that they were going to take us round a road to the left, where there was not a soul to be seen, and that in less than an hour we should have rejoined the highway and overtaken the head of the column. We ought to have inquired why other sledge-drivers, who ought to have known of the road, did not take it, as it was such a good one; but this we did not think of. After we had been travelling at a fast trot a good quarter of an hour, I saw that the way we were following was turning imperceptibly towards the left, separating us from the road the army was following, and that the ground over which we were gliding, and which they made us believe was a road, was nothing but an embankment between a canal on our right and a ditch on our left. I wanted to point this out to my comrades, so I shouted as loud as I could several times, ' Halt ! Stop !'

Grangier asked me what I wanted.

I redoubled my cries : ' They are tricking us ! We are with rascals !'

Then Pierson, who was on the front seat, carrying a silver urn that he had brought from Moscow, and which he continually made use of for brewing tea, began to shout ' Halt !' in his turn.

The rascal Jews jumped down from the bundle of hay on which they were seated, and, still going on, but not so rapidly, they took the horses by the bridle, turned the sledge, and upset us from the top to the bottom of the bank into the ditch. Happily for me, I was sitting at the back, with my legs hanging over the side of the sledge, so I had been able to see their intention, and letting myself slip down, I avoided the fall; but my comrades rolled to the bottom, more than twenty-five feet, and came down, bruised all over, on the ice. As their feet and hands were frozen, they shouted loudly. These cries changed into cries of rage against the Jews, who, keeping their hold upon the horses' bridles, had prevented the sleigh, although overturned, from rolling to the bottom, and had by now already dragged it to the edge of the bank. They were preparing to escape with our baggage; but I drew my sword, and gave one of the Jews a cut on his head. He had to thank his fur cap that his head wasn't split in two. I struck him a second blow, which he parried with his left hand covered with sheepskin. They would have escaped us, but Pierson came up to help me, while the others, still at the bottom of the embankment—which they had not the strength to climb—were swearing and shouting to us to kill the Jews. The one whom I had struck escaped by crossing the canal; the other, who was holding the horses, asked for mercy, saying it was his comrade's fault. Pierson, however, gave him a few blows with the flat of his sword, while he entreated pardon, calling us 'General' and 'Colonel.'

Pierson, taking the horse's bridle, ordered the Jew to go down and help our comrades to climb out. He hastened to obey, and was rewarded by blows of the fist very forcibly applied. When they were all up again, Leboude announced that we had acquired a right to the sledge and horses, as these two rascals had attempted to kill us in order to make off with our possessions.

We ordered the Jew to drive us at a gallop, and by the shortest way, to where we might rejoin the army, but we had to go back the whole way we had come.

When we got near the town, the Jew wanted to go there under pretext of fetching something from his house; no doubt it was to give us up to the Cossacks, who were now filling the town. We gave him a taste of sword-point in his back, and threatened to kill him if he took another step in the direction of the town. Accordingly, he hastened to turn to the right, the road the army had taken; we caught sight of the last stragglers a long distance ahead. We got up with them a quarter of an hour later, and then, rapidly descending a hill, left them behind.

I was at the back of the sledge; the pole of one of the sledges, descending, caught me on the right side, and threw me six feet out on the snow. I lay unconscious. A quarter-master belonging to the Mamelukes, who knew me, hurried to lift me up and seat me upon the snow.* My comrades came running up, too; they imagined the pole had wounded me, but my clothes, fortunately, had deadened the blow. Also, as luck would have it, the edge of the pole was covered with sheepskin.

I was lifted up and placed again upon the sledge, and, except for some sickness, I was no worse for the accident.

It might have been about nine o'clock when we arrived at a large village; a great many men were already there. We turned into a house to warm ourselves; we left our sledge at the door, after having taken the precaution to unload our baggage and make the Jew come in with us, for fear that he might make off with our conveyance.

---

* This Mameluke was named Angelis, and we knew each other in Spain. He was one of the Mamelukes whom the Emperor had brought from Egypt; only a few of this fine body escaped the fatalities of this campaign.—*Author's Note.*

The soldiers who were warming themselves told us that herrings and gin were on sale in the village. As the others had been very kind to me, and as they all, except myself, had frozen feet, I undertook to go for them, and on leaving I recommended them to keep their eyes upon the sledge.

'Don't bother about that,' said Pierson; 'I'll answer for it.'

I went off with our Jew as guide and interpreter. He led me to the house of one of his friends, where I found some herrings, some gin, and some poor rye-cakes. While I was warming myself over a glass of gin, I noticed my guide had disappeared with another Jew, with whom he had been talking a moment before. Seeing that he did not come back, I returned to rejoin my friends with the provisions; but on nearing the house I saw that the sledge was gone. My comrades, calmly warming themselves, asked me for the provisions. I asked them for the sledge. They looked into the street; the sledge was gone! Without saying a word, I threw the provisions down, and, feeling miserable, lay on the straw beside the stove. Half an hour afterwards there was a call to arms, and we were told that two short leagues away there were sledges for everybody, so that Gumbinnen should be reached the same day.

On reaching the place, we found a great number of sledges, and directly afterwards they made us set off. During the journey I felt ill; the movement of the sledge made me sea-sick. I chose at last to march for a while on foot, but I nearly perished with the cold, which had now become almost unbearable. My comrades happily saw my wretched condition, had the sledge stopped, and came to fetch me. I couldn't go a step further. We reached Gumbinnen none too soon. We all five of us received a billet, and had a very warm room and some straw.

The first thing we did after we were installed was to inquire if anything to eat and drink was to be had for money. The villager, who looked like a good fellow, said he would do his best to get us what we wanted; an hour later he brought us soup, roast goose and potatoes, beer and gin. We devoured it with our eyes, but, unhappily, the goose was so tough that we could eat only very little of it, and that little nearly choked us; we were reduced to potatoes.

With Sergeant-Major Oudict, I went into the town to see if we could find anything to buy. Chance led us to a house where Oudict met a Surgeon-Major, a fellow-countryman. He was quartered with the remnant of the regiment, two officers, and three soldiers. They were in a pitiable condition; they had almost all lost their toes and hands. While we were here a man offered to sell us a horse and sledge, which we eagerly purchased for the sum of eighty francs.

The next day, the 18th, after having made an attempt to eat our goose, which was no more tender than the day before, we mounted our sledge and set out for Wehlau, where we were to sleep; but we were hardly outside the town before Pierson, who drove the sledge, and understood nothing about it, turned a somersault with it, broke the shaft, and threw us out upon the snow. We were near a house, which we entered to get the sledge mended; while the peasant was busy at the job, we warmed ourselves, but when we came to set out again our weapons were gone. The Prussians had taken our muskets, piled up against the door. We shouted, we swore: ' We will have our arms, or we will set fire to the house !' But the peasant swore in his turn that he had seen nothing of them. We had to make up our minds to leave without them. Happily, after about an hour's progress, we met a waggon which had left Gumbinnen that morning with a consignment of muskets for the Imperial Guard, so we were able to get others. Finally, at three o'clock we reached Wehlau.

We saw more than 2,000 soldiers gathered together near the Hôtel de Ville, waiting for their billets. A big Prussian rascal came up to us, and told us, if we cared about it, we could lodge with him for a small sum; he had a well-warmed room, straw for us to sleep on, and a stable for our horse. We accepted eagerly. On reaching his house, he put the horse in the stable, and made us mount to the second floor, and there showed us a room only passably clean; it was the same with the straw, but it was warm—that was the essential.

A woman appeared, nearly six feet high, with a veritable Cossack face. She told us that she was the mistress of the house, and that if we needed anything we had only to give her some money, and she would go and fetch it. This was just what we wanted, for we had none of us any inclination to go out. I gave her five francs to bring us some bread, meat, and beer. She brought us all three shortly afterwards. Soup was made, and after having eaten, and seen that the horse was cared for, we slept till the following morning.

Before leaving, we gave our hostess a five-franc piece for the night, but she told us that was not enough. We gave her a second; but still this did not meet her reckoning. She required five francs a head for each man, and one more for the horse.

At that I told her that she was a cheat, and that she should have no more. She passed her hand over my face, and answered: ' Poor little Frenchman ! Six months ago that was all very well—you were the stronger; but to-day things are different. You are going to give me what I ask, or I will keep my husband from putting the horse into the sledge, and have you taken by the Cossacks!' For reply, I told her that I snapped my fingers at the Cossacks and at the Prussians. 'Oh yes,' she answered; 'but you wouldn't say so if you knew they were close at hand.' On this, seeing the whole wickedness of the woman, I caught her by the neck to strangle her, but she was the stronger; she threw me down upon the straw, and tried, in her turn, to strangle me. Luckily, a kick behind from one of my comrades made her get up. Just then the husband came in; but he received a great blow from his dear wife's fist. She was like a fury, telling him he was no more than a great coward, and that if he did not instantly go and fetch the neighbours and the Cossacks she would tear his eyes out. As we were five against two, we prevented them leaving the house, and forced them to harness the horse to the sledge. But we had to give what this female scoundrel demanded; there was no time for bargaining, the Cossacks being close by. Before leaving, I told this she-devil that, should I come back, I would make her return the money we had given her, with interest. She replied to this by spitting in my face. I wanted to strike her with the butt-end of my musket, but my comrades kept me back.

We mounted the sledge to get away as quickly as possible.

This day, December 19th, we were to sleep at Insterbourg, where we arrived by nightfall. We were quartered with some worthy people.

The next day, the 20th, fell on a Sunday. We left at daylight, in order to sleep at Eylau. There we repaired at once to the town-hall, and without any difficulty obtained our billets. We were with good people again;

we found a fire in the room, and each of us was offered a glass of gin. Afterwards our hostess went in search of our rations, taking our billet with her, for the inhabitants had just received orders to supply us with provisions.

When we were warmed and had rested a little, we made up our minds, while waiting for our soup, to pay a visit to the field of battle. We walked over most of it, and saw several simple wooden crosses. We noticed one in particular, with this inscription:

'Here rest twenty-nine officers of the brave 14th (line regiment), who died on the field of honour.'*

After making some notes on the placing of the troops the day of this terrible battle, we entered the town, which appeared to us deserted.

It was Sunday, and on account of the season the inhabitants were shut up in their houses, and we were the only Frenchmen about, the others having taken another direction.

Returning to our lodging, we stretched ourselves out on the straw while waiting for our meal.

Hardly were we settled down, when a Prussian veteran entered to warn us that Cossacks had been seen on a hill about a quarter of a league from the town, and that he advised us to be off as quickly as possible. As it was only too true, we made hasty preparations for departure. Our meat, barely half cooked, we packed up in straw.

Our peasant set off with us to put us in the right road. On reaching it, he pointed the Cossacks out to us, upon a hill. There were more than thirty. The weather was foggy; the snow had not ceased to fall since our departure. We had not gone half a league before night overtook us.

* Besides 590 non-commissioned officers and soldiers.—*Author's Note.*

322

We met two peasants and asked them if there was still far to go before we got to a village. They told us a large wood would have to be crossed first; but that we should find to the right, about twenty-five paces from the road, an inn, owned by a forest-keeper, and that we might be able to lodge there. After about half an hour's progress, we reached the house indicated. It was nine o'clock; we had gone four leagues.

Before the door was opened we were asked who we were and what we wanted. We answered that we were Frenchmen, soldiers of the Imperial Guard, and that we wanted, for payment, lodging, food, and drink. The door was instantly opened, and we were made welcome. We first put up our horses in the stable. Then we were shown into a large room, where we saw three Chasseurs of the Guard laid on the straw. They had arrived during the day, but in worse plight than ours, for they had lost their horses, and, although their feet were frozen, they were thus forced to go on foot. Something was brought us to eat, and then we lay down and slept like the blessed.

On waking, we were surprised not to see the Chasseurs, but we learned from the master of the house that about an hour previously a Jew, travelling with a sledge, had offered to drive them three leagues for two francs, and that they had eagerly accepted. We heard this news with delight. After paying five francs—all that was asked—for our horse and ourselves, we set out, our host advising us to follow the track of the sledge in front of us.

We had a nine leagues' journey that day, and reached Heilsberg, where we were to sleep, by nightfall.

We first repaired to the burgomaster for our billets; we were lucky enough to find ourselves all told off to the same house, where we were fairly well received. Six

Chasseurs of the Guard were there already. They gave us soup, meat, a quantity of good potatoes, and beer; we asked for wine, which of course we paid for. They procured us some at a thaler (four francs) a bottle, which was good and not dear. Before lying down to sleep on some good straw, we asked our hostess to have something ready for us by five o'clock in the morning, for we had a long stretch between us and our next halting-place.

The next day, December 22nd, we rose very early. A servant appeared, bringing us a candle; we ordered him to see to the horse, promising him a *pourboire* when he was ready harnessed to the sledge. Soup was brought us—in fact, everything we asked for. So each of us flattered our hostess, calling her 'Good woman! beautiful creature!' and giving her little slaps on the back and arms. When our meal was over, we prepared to set off; the sledge was ready, and we were bidding good-bye to the woman, when she suddenly said:

'This is all very well, gentlemen, but before leaving don't forget to pay me.'

'What! pay you! We are billeted on you! You have to feed us!'

'Yes,' she answered, 'that holds good for yesterday, but for what you have had to-day I must have two thalers (ten francs).'

I declared I would not pay; but when the woman saw that we were getting ready to leave without giving her any money, she ordered the door to be shut, and a dozen great Prussian rascals entered, armed with big sticks the thickness of my arm. It was not a case for discussion; we paid and went away. *Autre temps, autre mœurs.* Now we were the weaker.

The Chasseurs had left while we were breakfasting. We had still two days' journey to Elbing, twelve leagues;

and, as we did not wish to tire our horse, we made up our minds to put up at three leagues from the town.

After going about a league, we saw several sledges coming on our left, also going towards Elbing. This made us think we could not have followed the road taken by the remnant of the army, and that, instead of going to Eylau, we ought to have taken the direction of Friedland.

A large-sized sledge, drawn by two powerful horses, passed close by us. It was going so swiftly that we could not distinguish to what regiment the men in it belonged. In about half an hour's time we caught sight of a good house. It turned out to be a posting-station, and an inn also. There were several soldiers of the Guard at the door, setting out on sledges that had been procured for them.

We dismounted and entered, asking for wine, as we had been just told that there was plenty of it and very good. The men who told us seemed to have themselves partaken copiously; they were both in a state of wild gaiety. This happened to almost all those who, like ourselves, had endured so much misery and privation. The least amount of drink went to our heads. One of them asked us if we had met the regiment of Dutch Grenadiers who had formed a part of the Imperial Guard.

We said, ' No.'

' It passed you,' said the Vélite, ' and yet you didn't see it? That big sledge that overtook you contained the entire Dutch regiment! There were seven of them!'

The posting-master told the two soldiers that there was a sledge at their disposal, and that he would drive them the three leagues to Elbing for fifteen francs. As they had a driver, we decided to go with them, and five minutes later we were on the way.

Grangier and I were unwell and dreadfully sick. This was the result of our being unaccustomed to nourishing food ; we ought to have taken it quietly, by degrees. We resolved to do this in future. On reaching a village, we each took a glass of Dantzig gin, and went on again till we reached the village where we were to put up. It was night ; we presented ourselves at the burgomaster's to get our billet, but were brutally refused, and told that the only place for us to sleep in was the street. We had something to say about this, but the door was shut in our faces. We went to several inns where we asked for a lodging, offering payment, but everywhere we met with the same reception.

We decided, and the Chasseurs also, that we would keep together, that they should make use of our sledge, and that, as it was not big enough to hold us all, two should each go on foot in turn.

In this way we meant to try and reach some village where we might find the inhabitants more hospitable. At about a gunshot off, we caught sight of a house a little way back from the road. We made up our mind to force a lodging, if they would not take us in with a good will. However, the peasant told us that he would lodge us with pleasure ; but that if it was known to the villagers, he would suffer for having given us shelter. If no one had seen us enter, he would risk putting us up. We assured him that no one had seen us, that he could take us without any fear, and that before we left we would give him two thalers. He seemed very pleased, and his wife still more so, and we established ourselves round the stove.

While the man was out, putting our horse up in the stable, the woman came up to us and told us in a low voice, and all the time looking to see if her husband was coming, that the peasants were ill-disposed towards the French, for this reason: When the army passed through in May, some Chasseurs of the Guard had been quartered for a fortnight in the village; and one of them, who stayed at the burgomaster's, was so young and handsome that all the women and girls flocked to their doors to see him. He was quartermaster. It happened one day that the burgomaster caught him kissing and embracing his wife, with the result that the lady got a thrashing. The quartermaster, in his turn, beat the burgomaster. The lady is now in a certain condition, and the fault is put down to the quartermaster. We all listened, and smiled at the way in which the woman related the story.

'That is not all,' she continued; 'there are three other women in the village in the same condition as the burgomaster's wife, and that is why they mean mischief towards the French, such handsome fellows as they are.' She had scarcely uttered the words before the old soldier had risen, caught her round the neck, and kissed her.

'Take care! here is my husband!' she cried.

And in he came, telling us that he had fed the horse, and would give him something to drink presently; but that, if we wanted to oblige him, we would set off before daybreak, so that no one might know that he had taken us in.

'I have a sledge,' he said, 'and for a small consideration I will drive those of you who have none.'

The Chasseurs accepted.

They now served us with milk, soup, and potatoes; afterwards we lay down to sleep fully dressed, with our arms loaded.

The next day, the 23rd, the peasant came to awaken us before four in the morning, saying that it was time we set out. We paid the woman, kissed her, and took our leave.

At a second village the inhabitants mobbed us, throwing stones and snowballs. We reached one of the suburbs of Elbing, and stopped at an inn to warm ourselves, for the cold had increased. We had some coffee there, and at nine o'clock we entered the town with the rest of the army who had arrived, like ourselves, but by other roads.

CHAPTER XI.

WITHOUT losing time, we went to the town-hall for our
billet ; it was crowded with soldiers.

We noticed several cavalry officers far more wretched
than we were, for nearly all had lost fingers and toes,
and others even their noses : it was distressing to see them.
The magistrates of the town did all they possibly could do
for their comfort, giving them good lodging, and ordering
that every care should be taken of them.

After half an hour's waiting, we were given a billet for
the five of us, and for our horse ; we hurried off to the
place at once.

It was a large tavern, or, rather, a low smoking den. We
were very ill-received ; they showed us a large corridor
without fire for our rooms, and some bad straw in it.
We expostulated, and were told that it was good enough
for Frenchmen, and that, if that didn't suit us, we could
go into the street. Indignant at such a reception, we left
the house, expressing all our contempt to the brute who
had received us in such a way, and threatening to make
him give an account of his behaviour to the town magistrates.

We decided that we must try to get our billet changed, and I was charged with the mission, my comrades waiting for me at an inn.

On reaching the town-hall, I found there were not many people there. I addressed myself to the Mayor, who spoke French, and told him how brutally we had been received. I showed him my right foot, wrapped up in a piece of sheepskin, and my right hand, from which the first joint of the middle finger was nearly coming off. He spoke to the man in charge of the billeting, who then said that we could not all be quartered together. 'Here,' he said, ' is a billet for four and a horse, and here is another which I advise you to keep for yourself. It is at a Frenchman's who has married a woman in the town.' After thanking him, I returned in search of my companions.

On reaching the suburb, we went to the quarters for four men and a horse. It was a fisherman's house on the border of a canal, in the direction of the port ; we were received well enough. When we were settled, I offered the billet for one to anyone who would have it, but as no one wanted it, I inquired if it was far from the place where we were, and found there was only a bridge to cross.

I thought the house looked very imposing. The first person whom I met, as I went in, was the servant, a stout German with florid cheeks. I showed her my billet. She said there were four soldiers quartered in the house already, but at the same time she went in search of the lady of the house, who told me the same thing, pointing to their room. They were men of our regiment, who, like ourselves, had just arrived, but separately. I determined to return to the first quarters and rejoin my comrades. But the lady, having just read upon the billet that I was a non-commissioned officer of the Imperial Guard, said :

330

' Listen, my dear sir : you seem to be in such suffering that I do not want to turn you out. Follow me ; I will give you a room to yourself, and you shall have a good bed, for I see that you have need of rest.'

I answered that it was very kind of her to take pity on me, but that all I asked was some fire and straw.

' You shall have all that,' she answered.

While speaking, she showed me a small room, warm and clean, with a bed in it covered with an eider-down. But I begged as a favour that she would give me some straw, with some sheets and some warm water to wash myself in.

All I asked for was brought me, besides a great wooden tub to bathe my feet in. I was in want of it, and more besides. My head, my face, and my beard had not been attended to since December 16th. I begged the servant, whose name was Christian, to fetch a barber. He shaved me, or, rather, flayed my face, saying that my skin was hardened by the continued cold, but his razors felt like saws.

This operation over, I had my hair cut. After well paying the barber, I asked him if he knew of some dealer in old clothes, for I wanted some trousers. When he had gone, a Jew arrived with some trousers in a bag. They were there in all colours—gray and blue—but all either too small, too big, or not clean. The son of Israel, seeing he had nothing to fit me, told me that he would go and come back with something that would please me. He soon returned with some trousers *à la Cosaque*, dark red in colour, and of fine cloth. They were a trooper's trousers, probably belonging to an aide-de-camp of King Murat. I tried them on, and, foreseeing they would be very warm, I kept them. The mark was still there of a wide stripe down each side, which the Jew had taken the

precaution of removing. In exchange I gave him the
doctor's little case mounted in silver that I had taken
from the Cossack on November 23rd. He demanded five
francs besides, which I paid.

Three fine shirts belonging to the Commissary were
still left, so I made up my mind to change my linen ; but,
looking myself over, I saw to do it properly I ought to
have a bath, for there were traces of vermin still all over
my body. I inquired of the servant if there were any
baths near, but, not able to understand me, she went in
search of her mistress, who came immediately. It was
then I noticed that my hostess was a young and beautiful
woman. For the moment, however, my observations
went no further, for in my present position I was too
much occupied with myself. She asked me what I
wanted, and I said that I wanted a bath, and begged her
to be so good as to tell me where I could get one. She
answered that there were public baths, but that they were
too far away; that, if I liked, one could be got ready for
me in the house. She had hot water and a large tub; if
I could content myself with that, it should be prepared
for me. As may be well imagined, I accepted with joy,
and shortly after the servant made signs to me to follow
her. So, taking my knapsack and my red trousers, I
went into a sort of wash-house, where I found everything
necessary, even soap.

I cannot express the comfort I felt in that bath. I
stayed in it so long that the servant came to see if anything had happened to me. As she came in she saw that
I was at a loss in washing my back. Without asking my
permission, she went out and brought a large piece of red
flannel, and coming up to the tub, she put her left hand
on my neck, and with the other she rubbed me on the
back and arms and chest. As may be imagined, I

allowed her to do it. She asked me if it was doing me good, so I said yes. On that she redoubled her zeal, until I was tired. Finally, after having thoroughly curry-combed, scrubbed, and dried me, she ran off laughing, without giving me time to thank her.

I put on one of the War Commissary's shirts, then afterwards the trousers *à la* Cossack, and, bare-footed, went back to the bedroom and dropped on the bed. It was not too soon, for I felt very weak and lost con-sciousness. I do not know how long I remained in this condition, but when I opened my eyes I saw beside me the lady of the house, and also the servant and two of the soldiers who were billeted there, and who heard that something serious was amiss with me ; but it was only weakness caused by the bath, and also by the privations and fatigue I had undergone.

Madame Gentil—this was the lady's name — fed me with some broth, supporting my head on her left arm. I made no resistance, as it was so long since I had been petted. Madame Gentil was remarkably beautiful : her figure was slender and supple, her eyes were black, and her pink and white colouring was that of a beautiful Northern woman. She was four-and-twenty. I remembered having been told that she was married to a Frenchman, and she said it was so.

'In 1807 a convoy of wounded Frenchmen had arrived at Elbing from the neighbourhood of Dantzig, and as the hospital was filled with the sick, the new-comers were billeted among the inhabitants. A Hussar, wounded by a musket-ball in the breast, was sent to us. He also had a sword-cut in the left arm. My mother and I nursed him, and he soon got well.'

'And so,' I said, 'he married you in gratitude for your care.'

Laughing, she answered that it was the case. I told her that I should certainly have done the same, as she was the most beautiful woman I had ever seen. Madame Gentil began to laugh, to blush, and to talk, and she was talking still when I fell asleep, and did not awake till nine o'clock the next morning.

For some little time I could not remember where I was. The servant entered, accompanied by Madame Gentil, who was bringing me coffee, tea and rolls. It was a long time indeed since I had had such a feast! I forgot the past; I thought only of the present and Madame Gentil. I even forgot my comrades.

Madame Gentil looked at me attentively; then, passing her hand over my face, asked me what was the matter. I replied there was nothing wrong.

'But there is,' she said; 'your face is swollen.'

Then she told me that a non-commissioned officer of the Imperial Guard had come the preceding afternoon to inquire if she had not a non-commissioned officer lodging with her. She had said yes, there was one, and had shown him my room; but he had gone away again, saying I was not the man he was looking for.

While Madame Gentil was relating this, my friend Grangier came in, but was going out again, saying:

'I beg your pardon, but ever since yesterday I have been looking for one of my comrades, and can't find him. And yet this is certainly the street and the number of the house marked upon his billet.'

I said: 'It's I you are looking for, isn't it?'

Grangier then burst out laughing. He hadn't recognised me. This was not surprising. I had no *queue*, my face was swollen, I was as white as a swan, in consequence of my bath, or, rather, of the way the servant had curry-combed me; I was wearing fine white linen, my head well brushed, my hair curled. He told me that he had called the day before, but seeing a pair of red trousers over a chair, he had gone away convinced he had made some mistake. He had just been informed, he said, that there was to be a muster of the remnánt of the Guards at three o'clock, and that everyone must do his utmost to appear. He would come back for me.

At two o'clock he came to fetch me, as he had promised, accompanied by my other comrades, who on seeing me began to laugh so much that their poor lips bled, cracked as they were with frost.

I had a pleasant surprise ready for them, in the shape of some old Rhine wine, and some little cakes Madame Gentil had had the kindness to get for me. She was most thoughtful, and anticipated everything that could give me pleasure. I inquired about her husband, adding that, as he was a Frenchman, it would give me great pleasure to meet him and drink some wine with him. She said he had been away for some days. He had gone with her father to the Baltic, where they both did business in fruit, which they exported to St. Petersburg.*

It was December 24th. A little before three o'clock we repaired to the great square facing the palace in which Murat was lodged. I caught sight of Adjutant-Major Roustan, who came to me and asked who I was. I began to laugh.

'Hello!' he said; 'it isn't you, Bourgogne? Devil take me! No one would ever say you had come from Moscow, for you are looking big and fat and fresh. And where's your *queue*?'

I told him it had come off.

* This fruit was despatched from Tournai in Belgium.—*Author's Note.*

'Well,' he replied, 'if it has come off, I shall put you under arrest when we get to Paris, till it has grown again.'

There were very few present at this first muster, but we were pleased to meet again, for since December 17th, at Wilbalen, we had hardly seen each other at all. Everyone had gone his own way, and taken a different route.

The following days passed in the same way—a muster each day. On the fourth after our arrival we heard of the death of one of the superior officers of the Young Guard. He had died of grief at the tragic end of a Russian family of French origin, and dwelling at Moscow, whom he had invited to follow him on the retreat. I have already related their terrible fate.

By December 29th I was really better. The swelling in my face had disappeared ; my frozen foot was going on well, also my hand, and all thanks to the care of Madame Gentil, who nursed me like a child. Her husband returned from his journey, but only remained at home two days, leaving again with goods to rejoin his father-in-law, who would forward the things on sledges into Russia. Communication was opened again with that country since we had left. He told me that he had served three years in the 3rd Hussars, but that after receiving two severe wounds near Dantzig he had obtained his discharge as disabled. But he had preferred remaining in this country and marrying there, where he had made friends, to returning to Champagne - Pouilleuse, his own country, where he had no property.

The next day, December 30th, I went with Grangier to pay a visit to my brave Picart, who had had an accident. A Grenadier who had been quartered with him showed me the place.

On reaching it, a woman dressed in black, and with a melancholy air, showed us to his room, at the end of a

long corridor. We saw that the door was half open.
We stopped to listen to Picart's deep voice singing his
favourite piece to the tune of ' The *Curé de Pomponne* ':

> ' Ah ! tu t'en souviendras, la-ri-ra,
> Du départ de Boulogne !'

Great was our surprise at seeing him with a face as
white as snow, a mask of skin covering his whole face.
He told us about his accident, speaking of himself as a
raw recruit, an old stupid. ' Listen, *mon pays*,' he said.
' It was just like the musket-shot in the wood the night of
November 23rd. I see I am good for nothing. This
miserable campaign has done for me. See,' he continued,
' if something horrible doesn't happen to me.' So saying,
he laid hold of a bottle of gin that was on the table, and
taking three cups from the chimneypiece, filled them, to
drink, as he said, to our safe arrival. ' Look here,' he
said : ' we will spend the day together, and I will invite
you to dinner.'

He at once called the woman, who came in weeping.
I asked Picart what was the matter with her, and he
replied that an uncle of hers had been buried that morning, an old bachelor, a coaster or privateer, very rich, as it
seemed, and that there were great doings in the house.
He had been invited, and for that reason he had invited
us too, as there would be *noisettes à croquer*. But on
second thoughts, he said that it would be much better to
have the dinner brought to his room than to spend our
time with a heap of blubbering creatures who were pretending grief—the usual result of the death of a rich uncle
who had something to leave. He told the woman he
should not be able to dine with her, on account of friends
having come to see him ; and, besides, he was so sensitive
he should do nothing but weep. So saying, he pretended

to wipe away a tear. The woman began to cry again, and at such a comedy we were obliged to cover our faces with our handkerchiefs so as not to burst with laughter. The good woman thought that we were all crying, and called us first-rate fellows, saying we should be served at once. On this she withdrew, and two female servants brought us dinner. There were so many things we couldn't have eaten them in three days.

As may be imagined, our dinner was of the gayest; still, when we remembered our miseries, the fate of those friends whom we had seen perish, and others who had disappeared, we grew sad and thoughtful.

Night was coming on, and we were still smoking and drinking, when the mistress of the house came in to tell us that they were waiting for us to have their coffee. She led the way, and after a good many turnings we reached a large room, Grangier in front, I second ; Picart had stayed behind. On entering, we saw a long table, well lighted by several candles. Around it were fourteen women, more or less old, and all dressed in black. In front of each was a cup, a glass, a long clay pipe and tobacco, for in this country almost all the women smoke, particularly the sailors' wives. The remainder of the table was furnished with bottles of Rhine wine and Dantzig gin.

Picart had not yet come in ; we thought he did not dare put in an appearance because of his face. But suddenly we saw a movement among the women ; they all shrieked, and looked towards the door. It was old Picart, with his mask of white skin muffled in his cloak of the same colour, a cap of black Russian fox on his head, and smoking a meerschaum pipe with a long tube, which he carried gravely in his right hand ; the cap and the pipe belonged to the deceased. Passing down the corridor, he had seen them hanging up in the dead man's

338

room, and had taken them for a joke. Hence the fright of the women, who had taken him for the dead man coming to his own wake. They begged Picart to accept the cap and pipe, as a reward for the tears he had shed that morning, before the mistress of the house.

The conversation grew livelier and livelier, for all the women smoked and drank like troopers. Soon one could not make one's self heard.

Before breaking up a psalm was sung, and a prayer said for the repose of the dead man's soul; it was all sung and said with much unction. and we took part silently.

Afterwards they left us, wishing us good-evening; it was snowing and blowing a furious gale, so we decided to sleep at our old comrade's. There was plenty of straw and a warm room, and more we did not want.

The next morning coffee was brought us by a young servant. She was accompanied by the mistress of the house, who wished us good-day, and asked if there was anything else we wanted. We thanked her. She began to chat with the servant; the latter told her she had just been assured the Russian army was not more than four days' march from the town, and that a Jew, arrived from Tilsit, had met Cossacks near Eylau.

As I spoke enough German to understand part of the conversation, I heard the lady exclaim: ' My God! what will become of all these brave young fellows?' I showed my gratitude to the good German for the interest she took in us by telling her that, now we had had food and drink, we could snap our fingers at all the Russians.

If the men were hostile, the women were always on our side.

I reminded Picart that the next day was New Year's Day, 1813, and that I wished to spend the day at my own lodgings. He looked into a glass to see what his face was like, then decided that he would come too. As he did not know my lodgings, it was arranged that I should meet him at eleven o'clock in front of Murat's palace. We now thought of getting home, but so great a quantity of snow had fallen that we were obliged to hire a sledge. We reached our lodgings, I with a splitting headache and a little fever, the result of the festivities the evening before.

My absence had made Madame Gentil uneasy; her servant had waited up till midnight. I told her how sorry I was, and made the bad weather my excuse. I said that the following day I should have two friends to dinner. She replied that she would do all she could to please me, which meant that it was to be at her expense. She gave me afterwards some grease that she said was very good for chilblains, and wished me to use it at once. I obeyed her. How good Madame Gentil was! But all the German women were good to us.

I spent the rest of the day in the house—in bed almost the whole time—cared for and comforted by my charming hostess.

When evening came, I began to think what I could give her for a present on New Year's Day. I resolved to get up early, and see if I could not find something among the Jews. Thereupon I went to bed, as I wanted a good night's rest, for the party the evening before had tired me.

The next day, January 1st, 1813, the ninth after our arrival at Elbing, I got up at seven o'clock to go out, but first I looked to see how much of my money was left. I found that I had 485 francs left, of which more than 400 francs was in gold, the rest in five-franc pieces. On leaving Wilna I had 800 francs. Could I have spent 315 francs ? The thing was impossible. I must have lost some. That was not surprising, but I was still rich enough to spend twenty or thirty francs on a present for my charming hostess.

At the very moment when I was opening the door, I met the fat servant Christian, who had scrubbed me so thoroughly in the bath. She wished me a 'Happy New Year,' and as she was the first person I had seen, I kissed her and gave her five francs. She went off, saying that she would not tell Madame I had kissed her.

I turned in the direction of the palace square. I had not reached it, when I saw two soldiers belonging to the regiment walking slowly and painfully, bowed down under the weight of their accoutrements, nearly spent with fatigue.

Seeing me, they came up, and to my great surprise I recognised two men of my company, whom I had not seen since the passage of the Bérézina. They were in such a wretched state that I made them follow me to an inn, where I ordered hot coffee to warm them.

They related that on the morning of November 29th, a little before the departure of the regiment from the banks of the Bérézina, they had been ordered on fatigue-duty to bury several men belonging to the regiment, who had been killed the preceding evening, or who had died of exposure. When they had finished they started off, thinking they were following the route the regiment had taken ; but, unfortunately, they obeyed the direction of some Poles, who guided them towards their own country. They did not find it out till the following day.

' The end of it was,' they told me, 'that for a whole month we were walking about in an unknown, deserted country, always under deep snow. We were unable to make ourselves understood, not knowing where we were, nor where we were going. Our money was of no use to us, and we could only procure such things as milk or dripping at the cost of our clothes, by parting with our "eagle" buttons, or some handkerchiefs that we had kept by chance. We were not alone in this ; there were many others of different regiments going the same way, and like ourselves, not knowing where they were going, for the Poles we had been following had disappeared, and it is only by chance, sergeant, that we have got here, and have had the good luck to meet you.'

I told them how glad I was to see them again ; they had been in my company four years. Suddenly one of them exclaimed :

'Why, sergeant, I have something to hand over to you ! You remember that when we were leaving Moscow you entrusted me with a parcel ? Here it is just as you gave it me ; it has never been taken out of my knapsack.'

The parcel consisted of a military overcoat of fine dark-gray cloth that I had had made for me during our stay in Moscow by the Russian tailors whose lives I had saved, and of another article—an inkstand—that I had taken from a table in the Rostopchin Palace, thinking it was of silver (that it was not, however).

The year was beginning well for me. I hoped that it would prove the same for this man. I gave him twenty francs, and then I made haste to get into my new overcoat.

I now had a second delightful surprise. Putting my hands into the pockets of the new coat, I drew out an Indian silk handkerchief, and in one of its corners, tightly knotted, I found a little cardboard box, containing five rings, set with beautiful stones. I thought I had lost this box with my knapsack, and now here it was all ready for a present for Madame Gentil. The finest one was to be for her.

Telling my two soldiers to wait till roll-call to be re-
entered in the company and receive a billet, I returned to
my own lodging.

On the way I bought a large sugar-cake, which I presented to my hostess, with the ring, begging her to keep
it as a souvenir from Moscow. She asked me how I had
bought it. I told her that I had paid for it very dearly,
and that not for a million would I go on a similar search.
for another.

At eleven o'clock I returned to the square in front of
the palace. There were already a good many men there ;
in three days our numbers were almost doubled. One
would have said all those one believed dead had come to
life again to wish each other a 'Happy New Year.' But it
was a melancholy sight, for a great number were without
nose or fingers or toes ; some had suffered all three misfortunes combined.

The rumour that the Russians were advancing was confirmed. The order was given that we should hold ourselves
in readiness, as if on the eve of a battle, and to sleep with
one eye open, to avoid a surprise ; to keep our arms
primed and ready, to supply ourselves with new cartridges,
and to attend the roll-call with all our weapons and
accoutrements.

The muster was not yet over, when I felt a tap upon my
shoulder and a loud laugh in my ears. It was Picart, in
fine array and without his mask, who threw himself on my
neck, embraced me, and wished me a 'Happy New Year.'
On the other side there was Grangier doing the same, and
putting thirty francs into my hand. My travelling companions had just sold our sledge and the horse for 150
francs. This was my share. After a great many questions
about my new overcoat, we set out to dine at my place,
as had been arranged. On our arrival we found two other

ladies, so there was one for each. Shortly afterwards we sat down informally to table.

It was late enough when our dinner ended, as it had begun, very joyously.

I heard one of the ladies on leaving say to Madame Gentil : ' *Tarteifle des Franzosen !*' She added : ' They are always gay and amusing.'

The next day, at the muster, Picart came to look for me and tell me that on returning to his lodging he had found the whole family of his hostess gathered together and swearing at the defunct uncle. The mistress told him that during the day a woman had arrived from Riga, accompanied by a little boy of nine or ten, whom she said she had had by M. Kennmann, the deceased, and that he had acknowledged him as his heir. Everything was to be sealed up, and Picart had asked if they were going to seal up the cellar. They told him to bring up some bottles for his own consuming as a precaution. He answered that he would get as many as possible, and thereupon had set to work on the job, and had already fetched more than forty, which he had hidden under the bundle of straw he used as a bolster, and that after the muster he was going to empty his knapsack to fill it with bottles. As a matter of fact, he arrived an hour later, knapsack on back. He told me we must make haste to drink up the wine, as everyone in the town was talking of the speedy arrival of the Russians.

During the short time we remained in the town he brought me some wine every day. He must have ended by emptying the cellar, as he said. But one day— January 11th—he came to my place early in the morning in marching order, and told me that he did not think that he should return to sleep at his lodging ; he was holding himself in readiness to hear the alarm sounded, and he advised me to do the same, and to begin saying farewell to Madame Gentil.

Grangier came in, also in marching order. He arrived just in time to breakfast with me, as there was plenty of wine.

It was perhaps eight o'clock in the morning when we sat down to table ; at half-past eleven we were still there, when Picart, who was just emptying his glass, stopped short, and said : ' Listen ! I fancy I hear artillery !'

The noise indeed grew louder, the alarm sounded, the men ran to take up their arms. Madame Gentil rushed into the room exclaiming :

' Gentlemen, the Cossacks !'

' We are just going to make them dance,' said Picart.

Hurriedly I arranged my things, and directly afterwards I was embracing Madame Gentil, while Picart and Grangier, like proper soldiers, were emptying the last bottle. I tossed off a final glass, then rushed into the street behind my friends.

We had not taken thirty steps, when I heard someone calling me. I turned, and saw the fat Christian, who was making signs to me to stop, saying I had forgotten something. Madame Gentil was standing in the passage. As soon as she caught sight of me, she cried out :

' You have forgotten your little kettle.'

My poor little kettle that I had carried from Wilna, that I had bought from the Jew who tried to poison me— I had really not given it a thought. I went in to embrace this dear woman once more, who had nursed me and cared for me as if I had been her brother or her child. I told her to keep my kettle as a remembrance of me.

' You can use it to boil water in for tea, and every time you do so you will think of the young sergeant-vélite of the Guard. Farewell !'

345

I heard the roar of artillery still louder; again I rushed out into the street, this time not to return.

I caught sight of Grangier waiting impatiently for me on a little bridge. We took the shortest road along the quay to the place of muster. We had not been walking five minutes, when we saw Picart in the middle of the street, swearing in a rage, holding a Prussian down with his foot, and in front of him four Prussian soldiers commanded by a corporal under the orders of a police superintendent. The reason was this: several people had thrown snowballs at Picart in front of a café. He stopped, threatening to enter the house and have them arrested, but they took no notice; one of them, coming down into the street and advancing behind Picart, rested a billiard-cue on his shoulder, and began to cry: ' Hourra! Cossack!' Picart, turning rapidly, gripped hold of him and flung him flat on his face in the snow. Then, placing his right foot on his back, he fixed his bayonet, and, turning in the direction of the café, defied all those within.

The guard was fetched; Picart had in the meantime made his man understand that if he made the least movement he would be bayoneted. He said the same to those who were in the café; no one stirred, and then the guard came up with the superintendent of police.

The guard did not frighten Picart. He was just then like a lion holding his prey in his claws, and looking proudly at his hunters. He did not see us; the superintendent was trembling with fear. The women said, ' He is right; he was going quietly on his way, and they insulted him.'

Finally a Protestant minister, who had seen everything, and who spoke French, came forward and explained to the superintendent how the whole thing had happened. On this they told Picart that he might let the man go,

that justice would be dealt him. Picart said, ' Get up !'
He did not require to be told a second time.

When he had risen, Picart gave him a sound kick behind,
saying, ' This is justice on my own account.' The man
made off amid the hootings of all the women present,
holding his hand to the place where he had been kicked.

Meanwhile the superintendent was exacting a fine of
twenty-five francs from all those persons who had insulted
Picart, as well as from the one who had had the kick. He
pocketed half of it ' for the King,' he said, ' and to defray
the expenses of justice.' The other half he presented to
Picart, who at first refused, but on second thoughts offered
half of it to the policemen, the other half to the Protestant
minister, saying, ' If you should ever meet the wife of an
old soldier, give her that from me.' We had to explain
to them what Picart meant, for they could not understand
so much disinterestedness on the part of a soldier. They
would have liked to say flattering things to him ; even the
superintendent of police began jabbering compliments.
We pursued our way in the direction of the palace,
Grangier making remarks upon the Prussian character,
Picart singing his refrain :

> ' Ah ! tu t'en souviendras, la-ri-ra,
> Du départ de Boulogne !'

We reached the square, and we saw a regiment of
negroes opposite the palace where Murat was staying.
It was really comical to see the contrast of their faces
against the snow-covered square. The officers commanding them were black also. I could not find out what route
this corps took in the retreat, but I think they crossed the
Vistula at Marienwerder.

The artillery had almost ceased firing ; the Russians had
been driven from the neighbourhood of the town by a

body of fresh troops, who had not been on the Russian campaign. A little grape-shot scattered among their cavalry had been quite enough for them.

We were stopped by the service waggons of the different corps leaving the town. We were now near Picart's quarters, so he exclaimed, 'Halt, friends! I must say adieu to my landlady, and get my white cloak and the pipe and cap belonging to the deceased uncle, and there are still some bottles of wine under my straw bolster that we must empty.'

We went into the house and straight to his room without meeting anyone. Picart then got out five bottles, two of wine and three of Dantzig gin. He told us to each put one in our knapsacks, an order we obeyed at once. Then he called the landlady.

'Allow me to embrace you,' said Picart, 'and say adieu, for we are going.'

'So I suppose,' she said; 'and you will be hardly out of the town before the dirty Russians will come to take your place. What a pity! But before leaving us you must take something. You must not go away like this.'

And she went in search of two bottles of wine, some ham and bread, and we sat down to table.

Presently the noise of artillery was heard quite near. The woman cried, '*Jésus! Maria!*' and we ran out.

I was a little in front of my two comrades. A few steps before me I saw a man I fancied I recognised, who had stopped. I went up and found I was not mistaken; it was the oldest man in the regiment, who had sword, musket, and cross of honour, and who had disappeared since December 24th—Père Elliot, who had been through the Egyptian campaign. He was in a pitiable condition: both his feet were frozen and wrapped in bits of sheepskin;

his ears, also frozen, were covered with the same; his beard and moustache were bristling with icicles. I looked at him, so much surprised I was unable to speak.

At last I said, 'Well, Père Elliot, and here you are! And where the devil have you come from? And how you are dressed! You seem to be in terrible suffering.'

'Ah, my good friend,' said he, 'I have been a soldier now for twenty years, and I have never wept; but I am shedding tears to-day more from rage than misfortune, for I shall be taken by these brutes of Cossacks without being able to strike a blow. For nearly four weeks I have been going about alone, ever since the passage of the Niemen, all across the snow in a savage country, and unable to get any news about the army. I had two companions; one died a week ago, and the second is very likely dead, too. Four days ago I had to leave them in the house of some poor Poles, where we had been sleeping. I have travelled more than 400 leagues in the snow since leaving Moscow, unable to rest, my feet and my hands frozen, and even my nose.'

I saw great tears flowing from the old soldier's eyes.

Picart and Grangier just then rejoined me. Grangier recognised Père Elliot instantly; they belonged to the same company; but Picart, although he had known him for seventeen years,* could not remember him.

We entered the nearest house, and were made very welcome; it belonged to an old sailor, and these people are generally kind.

Picart made his old comrade in arms take a seat beside the fire; then, drawing one of the two bottles of wine from the pocket of his overcoat, he filled a big bumper.

'Come, my old comrade of the 23rd Brigade, swallow

* Since the Italian campaigns.—*Author's Note.*

this! Good! And now this! Very good! And now a morsel of bread, and you will feel better.'

Since leaving Moscow he had not tasted wine, nor eaten such good bread, and he seemed to forget his miseries at once. The sailor's wife bathed his face with a linen cloth soaked in warm water; this melted the icicles on his beard and moustache.

'And now,' said Picart, 'we'll have a little chat. Do you remember when we embarked at Toulon on our way to Egypt? . . .'

Grangier, meanwhile, had been out to see if the march had begun again, and now came in to tell us that a conveyance, laden with heavy baggage belonging to Murat, had stopped before the door. A fine chance for Père Elliot. He must get into it at once. 'Forward!' cried Picart; and with the help of the sailor we soon had the old sergeant perched on the vehicle.

Picart put the other bottle of wine between his knees, and the white mantle over his back to keep him from the cold. Shortly afterwards we began to march, and half an hour later we were outside Elbing.

The same day we crossed the Vistula on the ice, and marched on, without accident, till four o'clock, when we halted at a large town where Marshal Mortier, who was in command, decided we should spend the night.

I have not written my memoirs either out of vanity or from a desire to talk about myself. I have merely wished to recall the memory of this gigantic campaign, so fatal to us and those fellow-soldiers who went through it with me. Their ranks, alas! are thinning day by day. The facts I have related appear incredible, sometimes impossible; but no one must imagine I have added anything which is not true, or have tried to make my narrative interesting

350

by embellishing it. On the contrary, I must ask my readers to believe I have not told all, for I scarcely can believe it myself. I made a note of everything while I was prisoner in 1813, and in 1814 on my return from captivity, while the impressions of such disasters were still fresh in my mind.

Those who went through this lamentable but glorious campaign proved, as the Emperor said, that they must have been made of iron to bear so many privations and so much misery; this was surely the very greatest test to which men were ever exposed.

If I have omitted anything, such as a date or the name of a place, which I think unlikely, I owe it to myself to say I have added nothing.

Several witnesses to what I have written, who were in the same regiment with me, and some in the same company, are still living. I will quote some in particular:

M. CÉSARISSE, Grenadier-Vélite, now Field-Marshal in the service of the King of Holland, a native of St. Nicolas in Brabant. He was Lieutenant in the same company in which I was then sergeant.

ROSSI, Quartermaster in the same company, a native of Montauban, and whom I had the pleasure of meeting again at Brest in 1830. We had not seen each other for sixteen years.

VACHAIN,* then a Lieutenant in the same battalion, now living at Auzin (Nord). I met him again after an interval of twenty years.

LEBOUDE, then Sergeant-Major, now Lieutenant-General in Belgium, belonged also to the same battalion.

GRANGIER, Sergeant, who came from Puy-de-Dôme in Auvergne. He was my intimate friend. On more than one occasion he saved my life. His constitution was

* Died at Valenciennes in 1856.—*Author's Note.*

weak, his courage equal to any trial. He died of cholera in 1832.

PIERSON, also Sergeant-Vélite, now Captain on the staff at Angers.* He was very ugly, but a good fellow, as were all the Vélites. There never was a face like his; he was so different from everyone else. One need only set eyes on him once to remember him. In this connection I will relate a fact that bears me out in what I have been saying.

At the beginning of this campaign, when we were at Wilna, the capital of Lithuania, Pierson was one day mounting guard at the works. It was July 4th, and big ovens were being constructed for the baking of bread for the army. The Emperor came to see how the work was getting on. Pierson thought he would take advantage of the occasion to beg for a decoration, and, going up to His Majesty, he made his request. 'Very good,' answered the Emperor, 'after the first battle!' After that came the siege of Smolensk, the great battle of the Moskowa, as well as several others during the retreat. But during the disastrous retreat no opportunity arrived of reminding the Emperor of his promise. It was not till March 16th, 1813, some days after our return to Paris, at Malmaison, where a review was being held—the same day I was made Lieutenant—that Pierson was able to remind the Emperor of the promise he had made him. Seeing him approaching, the Emperor asked him what he wanted. 'Sire,' he replied, 'I want the cross your Majesty promised me.' 'True,' answered the Emperor, smiling, 'at the works at Wilna!' It was ten months since the promise had been given. The man had certainly an unforgettable face, but what a memory the Emperor had!

* That is to say, in 1835, the date when I was arranging my Memoirs.—*Author's Note.*

I will quote some further witnesses :

M. PÉNIAUX, of Valenciennes, superintendent of the Emperor's relays and stages, who saw me almost dying, laid upon the snow, on the banks of the Bérézina.

M. MELLÉ, a Dragoon of the Guards, whom I often met during the retreat, leading his horse by the bridle, and making holes in the ice of the lakes to give him drink. He was from Condé, the place I came from. He might be called, with truth, one of the best soldiers in the army. Before entering the Guard, M. Mellé had already gone through the Italian campaign. With the same weapons and the same horse he went through the campaigns of 1806 and 1807 in Prussia and Poland, 1808 in Spain, 1809 in Germany, 1810 and 1811 in Spain, 1812 in Russia, 1813 in Saxony, and 1814 in France.

After the departure of the Emperor for the Isle of Elba, he remained in the Royal Guard, awaiting his pension, and always keeping his horse with him. On the return of the Emperor from Elba, he reappeared again in the same corps as one of the Imperial Guards at Waterloo. He was wounded, and his horse killed—the horse which had gone through so many campaigns with his master, and had taken part in more than fifteen great battles commanded by the Emperor.

Had the Emperor remained in France this brave soldier would have been worthily rewarded. Although Chevalier of the Legion of Honour, he is now in great want. During the retreat from Russia he sometimes penetrated alone at night into the enemy's camp to get hay or straw for Cadet, the name of his horse. He never returned without killing one or two Russians, or bringing back what he called a witness, viz., a prisoner.

MONFORT, trooper, now a retired officer of Cuirassiers at Valenciennes. Although from the same country, and also belonging to the Imperial Guard, I only knew him in the army by reputation, by the manner in which he distinguished himself in the different combats we had in Spain. In Russia, he crossed the Bérézina on horseback over the blocks of ice. But he left his horse behind. At Waterloo, on Mount St. Jean, during a charge against the Queen of England's Dragoons,* he killed the Colonel with a thrust in the chest, sending him to sup with Pluto.

PAVART, retired Captain at Valenciennes, belonging during the Russian campaign to the infantry of the Imperial Guard. All that he relates of their campaign, of what happened to him, and of what he saw, is very interesting.

During the retreat, at Krasnoë, we were fighting for three days, November 15th, 16th, and 17th, against the Russian army of 100,000 men. On the night of the 16th, the eve of the battle of the 17th, Pavart, then a corporal, was in command of a patrol of six men. Making his rounds, he caught sight of another patrol of five men upon his right. Imagining—indeed, almost certain—that they belonged to us, he said to his men, ' Wait for me. I am going to speak with the one in command, so that we may both move in the same direction, and avoid the Russian outposts. The men halted instantly, and he went up to the second patrol, who, seeing a man coming alone, no doubt believed he was one of them. But Pavart now saw they were Russians. It was too late to draw back. He advanced resolutely, and, without giving the Russians time to reflect, he fell upon them and put three of them *hors de combat* with the bayonet. The others took to flight. After this bold stroke he turned to rejoin his men, but found them close at hand, running to help him.

* Queen's Own.

354

WILKÉS, non-commissioned officer in a line regiment a native of Valenciennes ; taken prisoner on the banks of the Bérézina ; led in captivity 1,400 leagues from Paris, where he was kept three years.

CAPTAIN VACHAIN, of whom I have spoken above, had a very lively discussion while we were in Spain with my sergeant-major, which ended in a duel and a sword-cut which divided my sergeant-major's face in two from the top of his forehead to the bottom of his chin. He did as much on various occasions for Austrians, Prussians, Spaniards, Russians, and English, against all of whom he was fighting for ten years without stopping, for during this time he took part in more than twenty great battles commanded by the Emperor Napoleon.

At the Battle of Esslingen, May 22nd, 1809, Vachain was carrying a skin filled with wine, hung at his side. One of his friends, a non-commissioned officer like himself, signed to him that he would very much like a drink. Vachain called to him to come near, and, stooping to one side, he offered him some wine. This took place during the action, when bullets and grape were flying on all sides. The man had hardly swallowed it, when a brute of an Austrian ball carried away his head as well as the gourd of wine.

Two days before they had dined together at Vienna, and there they had made each other gifts of what they possessed in the way of watch, belt, etc., in case of the death of one or the other. But Vachain had no desire to put his promise into execution. He drew back and fell into rank, thinking himself lucky not to have been struck by the same ball, but reflecting that at any moment as much might still happen to him, for it was warm work just there. I was wounded that same day.

Besides the old soldiers whom I knew individually, I

can quote others who made a glorious and terrible fight with Russia :

MM. Buoy, retired Captain at Valenciennes, and a native of that place, Chevalier of the Legion of Honour.

Hourez, retired Captain at Valenciennes, and a native, Chevalier of the Legion of Honour.

Piète, Sub-Lieutenant, Valenciennes.

Legrand, ex-gunner of Grenadiers of the Imperial Guard, Chevalier of the Legion of Honour.

Foucart, Barrack-Master, wounded and taken prisoner, Chevalier of the Legion of Honour.

Izambert, former non-commissioned officer of the Museum Guard, Chevalier of the Legion of Honour.

Petit, Sub-Lieutenant of the Young Guard.

Maujard, of the Engineers, retired at Condé (Nord), Chevalier of the Legion of Honour.

Boquet, of Condé.

Bourgogne,
Ex-Grenadier-Vélite of the Imperial Guard,
Chevalier of the Legion of Honour.

THE END.